THE JUDICIAL FUNCTION IN
FEDERAL ADMINISTRATIVE AGENCIES

The Judicial Function in Federal Administrative Agencies

JOSEPH P. CHAMBERLAIN

NOEL T. DOWLING

PAUL R. HAYS

BOOKS FOR LIBRARIES PRESS
FREEPORT, NEW YORK

INTERNATIONAL STANDARD BOOK NUMBER:

0-8369-5495-5

LIBRARY OF CONGRESS CATALOG CARD NUMBER:

79-128875

PRINTED IN THE UNITED STATES OF AMERICA

FOREWORD

THE Legal Research Committee of the Commonwealth Fund undertook some years ago a series of studies in administrative law. Under its auspices a general survey of the subject appeared in 1928, in a book by Ernst Freund entitled *Administrative Powers over Persons and Property,* revealing the extent to which administrative control had been in fact conferred. As a logical complement of this work, there followed a comprehensive study by the same author of the ways and means of written law, entitled *Legislative Regulation,* published in 1932.

The actual exercise of administrative powers has been set forth in various special studies of administrative organs to which such powers have been delegated. These studies have resulted in the publication, in the years indicated, of *The Federal Trade Commission* by Gerard C. Henderson, in 1924, *The Administrative Control of Aliens* by William C. van Vleck, in 1932, *The Interstate Commerce Commission* by I. L. Sharfman, in five volumes which appeared during the years 1931–1937, and *Administration of Workmen's Compensation* by Walter F. Dodd, in 1936.

The present volume focuses attention upon the judicial function as exercised by several administrative agencies of the federal government. As in the case of the other studies conducted under the auspices of the Legal Research Committee of the Commonwealth Fund, the authors have been allowed entire freedom and the responsibility for the statements of fact and the opinions expressed is solely their own.

TABLE OF CONTENTS

PREFACE

THIS study is concerned with the judicial function of federal administrative agencies. It is based principally on procedures and practices of the Federal Communications Commission, Federal Trade Commission, Interstate Commerce Commission, National Labor Relations Board, Securities and Exchange Commission, Department of Agriculture in the administration of the Packers and Stockyards Act and Perishable Agricultural Commodities Act, Post Office Department in the administration of fraud orders, Food and Drug Administration, General Land Office, Immigration and Naturalization Service, and on the administration of the Longshoremen's and Harbor Workers' Compensation Act.

The judicial function is only one of the many devices resulting from the increasing use of administrative action to fill the gap in the regulation of society which lies between Congress and the courts and to supply governmental machinery to supplement, not to supplant, both Congress and the courts in the administration of the law. Instead of depending on individuals to defend what they consider their rights in the courts or on the action of Congress to assure through legislation the fair and orderly functioning of the social and economic system, these agencies have been created by the National Government to protect both private parties and the public interest by a direct control over business management and social relations. This extension of governmental controls has led Congress to create new agencies or establish new powers in existing agencies to administer the new legislation which the movement toward closer regulation has brought about. The powers with which these administrative agencies have been vested by their legislative creators are frequently very broad. Within statutory limits they lay down the law for the future by regulation, they decide cases involving private parties, they carry on extensive investigations; they have wide powers of discretion in controlling the operation of an

industry and of industry as a whole in respect to certain of its practices, and in regulating specified social relationships./
[The judicial function includes the manner in which the agencies
deal judicially with the rights and duties of private persons and the
position of their decisions when contested in the courts. It includes
proceedings brought by the government against private persons, the
settlement of differences between private persons, and matters in
which both government and private persons are concerned as parties
but in which the government does not bring the action./A study of
the judicial function, however, must go further to include the commencement of the proceeding and the settlement of cases by informal
methods before the use of the judicial process, and must continue
through action in the courts. It is necessary to an understanding of
the agencies and their operation to study the methods by which they
enforce their policies and orders, without reference to the courts and
even without formal proceedings in the agencies themselves. It is in
this way that the greater part of the enormous volume of business
pressing for settlement is disposed of, with the result that only a small
part ever reaches the courts or even the stage of formal proceedings
within the agency.

In several agencies the judicial function is a minor one, either as the
agency was originally set up or as it has developed in the course of
years, but, as far as possible, this study has been directed toward it and
has dealt with other functions only when essential to the understanding of the judicial. It is not always easy to distinguish between the legislative and the judicial in the work of the agencies in which the development and application of policy plays an important part. In many
instances the judicial method may be used in pricking out and declaring policy, while in others the legislative may be deemed more appropriate.

Procedures in the agencies studied present a striking variety, imposed by statute or the courts or developed by experience. This variety
arises from the diversity of the social or business situations to which
the powers of the different agencies extend and from the necessity to

adjust the forms of administration and even of procedure in the administrative tribunals to these varying situations. This circumstance has been recognized in the statutes and, while following a certain broad pattern in the regulation of the judicial function, Congress has not permitted this pattern to become a Procrustean bed but has allowed each agency freedom to develop its procedure and in many cases has itself laid down special rules to provide for variations in the conditions with which the agency is confronted.

With the increasing importance of administrative action in the social and economic life of the nation, there should be a great increase in the practice of administrative law, and that body of law cannot be properly understood or properly taught unless the student is led far behind the decisions of the courts to the decisions of the agencies themselves and to the process of administration. It is in careful studies of the procedure and practices of separate agencies such as those sponsored by the Commonwealth Fund that the materials can be found for the instruction of lawyers who, as government officers or as counsel for litigants, are to help frame the policy of the agencies to protect private rights and to guide the legislatures in the control of the powers and policies of the existing agencies or of new ones which may be created. It is to be hoped that the scholarly examination of administrative agencies will be continued on the model of the studies already published, and that there will be added critical comparison of the methods used in the various agencies of which this study is a modest beginning.

Perhaps it should be added, though no elaboration is needed, that a study such as this, concerned principally with the work of the administrative agencies themselves, does not result in a law book in the sense of an analysis of court cases and other legal materials. Only limited consideration is given to the courts, and this in turn is concerned mainly with the relationship between them and the administrative agencies and with statutes, as interpreted by court decisions, providing for judicial review of the action of those agencies.

The great storehouse of material on administrative methods which has been collected by the staff of the Attorney General's Committee on Administrative Procedure, directed by Professor Walter Gellhorn, will facilitate critical and comparative studies of the procedures of different agencies and of the adjustment of methods to the situations which they face. The monographs prepared by that staff have made it unnecessary to include here the large amount of detail, in respect to the procedures of the agencies, which was collected and used as a basis for this study. An exception is in the chapter on sanctions: the many examples of the sanctions, it is believed, are not available in any one place and the importance of the subject warrants the fulness of the presentation.

In the prosecution of this study valuable assistance was rendered by Messrs. Richard A. Buddeke, Robert L. Hausser, Solomon Klinger, Seymour Linfield, Charles S. Lyon, Sidney A. Saperstein, and Nelson Seitel, who served from time to time as members of the staff of the Legislative Drafting Research Fund. In the preparation of the manuscript Miss Anna Russell and Mrs. Harriet Percy Souder were indispensable aides, and to Miss Mariana Smith fell the long and exacting responsibility of office supervision of the entire study and of assisting the authors throughout its course. To all of them the authors record their gratitude.

They wish to thank the authors and the publishers who have kindly given permission to quote from previously published materials.

J. P. C.
N. T. D.
P. R. H.

October 1941

CHAPTER I. METHODS

THERE is no novelty in vesting in administrative agencies the power to decide when and in what circumstances to apply the law to private parties, either in checking conduct which in the opinion of the administrative agency transgresses the law or in determining whether or not to grant a privilege, such as a license. Familiar examples are the powers of health officers over persons and over buildings or conditions on property which the officers consider injurious to the health of the community and in respect to which they are vested with authority to act, often summarily, or the powers of officials to destroy animals or plants declared by law to constitute a menace to the community, or the common law right of public officers to abate nuisances. It was through the courts and the legislatures that the policies were worked out on which these simple exercises of administrative power are based and through the courts and the legislatures that the rights of individuals were protected.

As, however, the powers of administrative agencies have been extended to an ever greater degree of control over business and social conditions, involving decisions harder to make, relating to more complicated situations, and requiring supervision over great business and social interests, necessarily involving the exercise of wide discretion on the part of the agency, new forms of administrative organizations have come into being to carry on these newer, more complex, and more delicate duties. Congress and the courts also have been faced with the difficulty of devising methods of control of the agencies which wield this greatly increased power. Mr. Elihu Root, in an address before the American Bar Association in 1916, strikingly called attention to this development:

There is one special field of law development which has manifestly become inevitable. We are entering upon the creation of a body of administrative law quite different in its machinery, its remedies, and its necessary safeguards from the old methods of regulation by specific statutes enforced by the courts. . . . There will be no withdrawal from these experiments. We shall go on; we shall expand them, whether we approve theoretically or not, because such agencies furnish protection to rights and obstacles to wrong doing which under our new social and industrial conditions cannot be practically accomplished by the old and simple procedure of legislatures and courts as in the last generation. Yet the powers that are committed to these regulating agencies, and which they must have to do their work, carry with them great and dangerous opportunities of oppression and wrong. If we are to continue a government of limited powers these agencies of regulation must themselves be regulated. The limits of their power over the citizen must be fixed and determined. The rights of the citizen against them must be made plain.[1]

The present study deals with the judicial function in certain of these experiments. That function consists of finding the facts upon which action shall be based, determining the law which shall govern the action, and deciding the case according to the facts as found and the interpretation of the law. The judicial procedure has been engrafted on the administrative process to enable the agency to perform its duties effectively and to give a degree of security to the rights of the persons under its jurisdiction. Its kernel is a hearing and order based on findings supported by evidence in the record.[2]

TYPES OF CASES

There appear to be four types of cases in which administrative agencies employ judicial procedure in the discharge of their judicial function. Conflicts between private parties are the first type. In these cases one person seeks to enforce rights against another. The legislature is concerned primarily in providing an appropriate means of do-

[1] Root, Public Service by the Bar, *Reports of Amer. Bar Assoc.*, vol. 41, pp. 355, 368–369 (1916).

[2] Professor Ernst Freund has called attention to the requirement of notice and hearing prior to the issuance of an order, referring principally to state agencies. Freund, *Administrative Powers over Persons and Property*, pp. 154–156.

ing justice as between the parties. While these cases might have been tried by courts, the lawmakers were persuaded that they could be more satisfactorily and promptly dealt with by administrative officers acting with less formality than the judges. The best-known cases of this type are claims arising under workmen's compensation laws. The tribunals which adjudicate them might well be termed small claims courts. Nevertheless there is a certain public duty which the agency carries on in connection with compensation claims. It is the duty of making sure that the workmen or their dependents receive their due and that the statute is liberally interpreted. The enormous increase in the load on the courts which would have resulted from their having to handle compensation claims was another practical reason for setting up these special tribunals.

Other examples of this type are cases arising under the Perishable Agricultural Commodities Act, which allows a producer to bring proceedings before an administrative official in the Department of Agriculture against a broker or dealer to recover damages in respect to shipments of certain perishable commodities. The organization of the Department of Agriculture provides for field agents as well as for officers in the great market places, and gives it a convenient means of fixing grades at the point of shipment and of making the proper investigations as to the conditions under which the shipment was made or handled and disposed of.

Still other instances of this type are those adjudicated by the Interstate Commerce Commission under its authority to render reparation awards against carriers. In addition to determining a specific controversy between a shipper and a carrier, these cases have a significant relationship to the rate-fixing powers of the Commission, for they may well bring to the attention of the Commission a weakness in the rate structure as it affects a particular shipper,or an industry or region and result in an order fixing future rates as well as an order for past damages. The Supreme Court, however, has pointed out the essential difference in the two functions, although they may be included in the same proceeding, as follows:

But awarding reparation for the past and fixing rates for the future involve the determination of matters essentially different. One is in its nature private and the other public. One is made by the Commission in its *quasi*-judicial capacity to measure past injuries sustained by a private shipper; the other, in its *quasi*-legislative capacity, to prevent future injury to the public.[3]

The second type of cases, the type with which this study is chiefly concerned, comprises the cases in which the major emphasis of an agency is, more than in cases of other types, upon the effectuation of a broad policy of control of business or social activity. The determination of particular controversies becomes one of the methods of effectuating this control. Two distinct situations may be isolated within this second type. In one the agency acts in a disciplinary capacity to discover whether a particular business is being carried on in such a way as to contravene the provisions of the law committed to its enforcement and, if the contravention is established, to punish the violator or to bring about compliance, either by adjusting certain methods used in that business or by requiring a cessation of the practice complained of. Examples are the activities of the Federal Trade Commission in preventing unfair trade practices, of the National Labor Relations Board in checking certain practices which have been declared by Congress to be unfair to labor, and of the Securities and Exchange Commission in suspending or revoking licenses of brokers whose practices are deemed to be contrary to the standards set down in the Act.

In the other situation, instead of punitive action or negative action requiring an individual to cease and desist from certain practices, the decision of the administrative agencies may be positive, resulting in the authorization of action by a private party, as, for example, the grant by the Federal Communications Commission of a license to operate a radio station, or the consent by the Federal Power Commission to the use of a water power. Licenses are often granted without a hearing, but where the public interest or convenience is involved or

[3] *Baer Bros.* v. *Denver & R. G. R. R. Co.,* 233 U.S. 479, 486 (1914).

other licensees would be seriously affected by the grants, there is reason for giving an opportunity for a hearing before affirmative action is taken. Licenses for brokers or commission merchants under the Perishable Agricultural Commodities Act, for example, may be granted without a hearing, since their primary purpose is for identifying and regulating the persons employed in the particular occupation. However, no license or permit for a radio station under the Communications Act of 1934 should be granted without a hearing. The issuance of such a license by the Federal Communications Commission, while partly for the purposes of identification and regulation, involves in addition a decision which concerns the public welfare and may affect the interests of other licensees or prospective licensees. A new station may interfere with the operation of an existing station or cut down on its earnings so as to render it unable to carry on its service, and the public to be served by the proposed installation may have an opinion as to whether it is needed. If the agency is in doubt the applicant and the interested public should be heard.

Although one agency may, by virtue of the wide powers conferred upon it, be concerned with both of these situations, there is, nevertheless, a significant difference between them. Where an authorization is required for the carrying on of an enterprise, the agency must make an order before any action can be taken by the applicant, and thus the agency may enforce its policy in advance of any activity by a private party. However, where the conduct of the private interest comes under the notice of the agency on information that there has been an infraction of the law or of the policy adopted by the agency, its duty is disciplinary to correct what it considers an infraction and to bring about compliance with the policy of the law. Until the administrative machinery is set in motion, the conduct complained of may be continued. In many cases the objectionable practice can be modified or may be abandoned as a result of informal consultation between the managers of the business and the agency.

In cases of the second type the public interest predominates, although a private party will frequently urge the agency to act and will be interested in the form of the final order because of some private object of his own. An interesting variation occurs under the National Labor Relations Act in that the private complainant in an action against an employer for unfair labor practices has a certain share in the proceedings and, where a labor organization is seeking to be recognized as a bargaining agent or seeking an election, it may withdraw its request and the action will end. The procedure is adjusted to the situation in cases where a privilege is sought and where, generally, the applicant may stop the proceeding by withdrawing his request. Even if the applicant and the agency have agreed on the terms of a grant, another person opposed to the grant may want a hearing to record his objection.

Deportation and exclusion cases under the Immigration and Naturalization Service are also included in this type, though they represent not regulatory control by the government so much as police action for the enforcement of the law. There are definite precepts in the law in respect to the persons who may be admitted into this country and in respect to the causes for deportation, so that in the administration of these statutes there is no such latitude for adjustment in particular cases as there is in the administration of a statute with broad standards like the Federal Trade Commission Act. However, several of the grounds for exclusion or deportation are stated broadly enough to give the agency, in the construction of the statute, a field for using its discretion, for instance, the application of the provision forbidding the entry of a person likely to become a public charge or excludable for certain political opinions.

There is a wide difference in the latitude given in dealing with this second type of cases. In some instances, as in the Federal Trade Commission Act, a broad standard is set up in the mandate given the Commission to prevent "unfair methods of competition in commerce, and unfair or deceptive acts or practices in commerce."[4] The Commission determines what trade practices are unfair so as to bring them

---

[4] 15 U.S.C. §45 (a). The Packers and Stockyards Act, 1921, contains a broad standard making it unlawful for any packer to "engage in or use any unfair, un-

within the ban of the statute. It must find that the practice is unfair, subject to the opinion of the court in interpreting the statute as to what the words "unfair methods of competition" and "unfair or deceptive acts or practices" signify. The businessmen affected by the statute are not given any exact information concerning what they may or may not do, but must depend on the interpretation by the Commission of the words of the statute. However, where Congress has expressly declared certain specific practices to be unfair, as in the Clayton Act,[5] then it is the task of the Commission simply to determine in a particular case whether these practices are being carried on.

The third type involves disputes between the government and private parties, which are referred to specialized tribunals. These tribunals, sometimes called courts, are generally looked upon as courts of limited jurisdiction, and their procedure is like that in ordinary courts. They are not parts of administrative agencies, but are independent tribunals, whose task has less to do with the development of a policy than with the application of the law to the cases which come before them. Examples of these tribunals are the Court of Claims, the Court of Customs and Patent Appeals, and the Board of Tax Appeals. It is a well-known principle of public law that the National Government can be sued in its own courts with its consent, and under the conditions which have been laid down by law. In a few instances Congress has provided for the settlement of claims against the government directly by the courts,[6] but it has confided to these special tribunals a large share in the enforcement of the rights of the individual against the government. This study is not concerned further with them, although they form an important part of our system for controlling judicially the acts of government agencies.

justly discriminatory, or deceptive practice or device in commerce." 7 U.S.C. §192.

[5] 15 U.S.C. §§12–27.

[6] See, e.g., the statutes authorizing admiralty suits against the United States: 46 U.S.C. §§742, 781. For other examples, as well as a treatment of the problem of suing the government, see Borchard, Governmental Responsibility in Tort— A Proposed Statutory Reform, 11 *A.B.A.J.* 495 (1925).

A fourth type presents cases in which property, money, or other benefits may be granted by the government under specified conditions. Typical are cases in the General Land Office where the right of an individual to receive a patent to a piece of public land is determined by the agency. The individual is not without rights, for the statute directs that a patent issue to him if he has fulfilled certain conditions, and the duty of the General Land Office is only to determine whether or not he has fulfilled them. It frequently happens, however, that two claimants present themselves, each alleging that he has fulfilled the conditions and is entitled to a patent. Where such a situation arises, an action is carried on before the administrative officer, who must ascertain which of the claimants has established his right under the law in accordance with the procedure provided for proving a claim.

Other cases of this type arise in the Veterans' Administration, which decides on claims for compensation arising from war services. Here the statute grants certain payments under specified conditions. A claim is made to the administrative authorities and remains always within the administrative channel. The claimant is restricted to an administrative review provided by the statute, with no right to carry his claim into the court even if he considers the decision against him to be contrary to the law or the procedure to be a denial of a fair hearing.

With the growing social and economic importance of benefits awarded by the government through its administrative agencies, it becomes apparent that obtaining a benefit to which an applicant is entitled by a policy of the government expressed in the law becomes a right in much the same sense that an applicant in a court is given a right to recover for a tort or on a contract. At present the courts distinguish between benefit rights, which they hold can be recovered only through an administrative remedy, and rights which can be asserted in a court. But the distinction is actually one of degree rather than one involving the essential character of the rights asserted. On the one hand, the actual determination of substantive rights of both types is with the agencies. On the other hand, where the right is a benefit conferred by the government, there is an indication, as shown by the immigration cases and possibly also land office cases, of a tendency on the part of the courts to recognize that in the determination of rights of this type there is the same necessity for assuring fair play and requiring that the elements of judicial procedure be used by the agency as there is in the determination of rights ordinarily assertible in a court.

Informal Settlement

By far the greater number of matters which come before the agencies are settled informally and never reach the stage of formal procedure.[7] The method of settlement varies from conciliation between private parties, as in compensation cases and those under the Perishable Agricultural Commodities Act, to an arrangement between the government and the person against whom charges are made, as in the Federal Trade Commission. In some agencies, like the Federal Communications Commission and the National Labor Relations Board,

[7] *Final Report of the Attorney General's Committee on Administrative Procedure*, 1941, p. 35.

Formal proceedings are necessary, however, in the exercise of the legislative function, notably of rate making or when grants of licenses are made in which affirmative action must be taken.

The following figures will make clear how few are the cases which are dealt with by orders after formal hearing compared to those disposed of by informal methods:

During the fiscal year ending June 30, 1940, the radio and periodical division of the Federal Trade Commission sent questionnaires to advertisers in 739 cases and to advertising agencies in 109 cases, negotiated 190 stipulations, and recommended the issuance of complaints in only 36 cases, half of which involved violation of the terms of existing stipulations previously accepted and approved. Federal Trade Commission, *Annual Report*, 1940, p. 123.

In the administration of the Walsh-Healey Act (41 U.S.C. §§35–45) about 85 per cent of the cases were settled without holding a formal hearing. Gellhorn and Linfield, Administrative Adjudication of Contract Disputes: The Walsh-Healey Act, 37 *Mich. L. Rev.* 841, 853 (1939).

In the Securities and Exchange Commission, 99 out of 100 problems presented to the Commission do not reach formal proceedings and 9 out of 10 of the

the adjustment between the agency's officers and the principal party may be shared in by other parties affected.

There is no uniformity in the subject matter with which the different agencies are concerned under the legislation which they administer, and there is consequently no uniformity in the administrative methods which they have adopted. The statutes leave to the agency wide freedom in devising ways and means of enforcing the law by administrative process preliminary to formal disposition. Where a new regulatory body is set up, Congress in creating it, and the body

Commission's orders do not reach the courts. Lane, *in* Symposium on Administrative Law, 9 *Am. L. School Rev.* 139, 154, 163 (1939).

William C. O'Brien, attorney in charge of fraud order matters for the Post Office Department, has said, in conversation, that the Department finds that most investigations started preliminary to the issuance of fraud orders do not reach the formal stage. But when they do, 80 fraud orders are issued out of every 100 hearings held.

In the National Labor Relations Board, of 22,987 cases in almost four years, 18,823 were closed either by voluntary adjustment (52 per cent), dismissals by the Board before hearing (16 per cent), or withdrawals without hearing (26 per cent); less than 6 per cent required a formal hearing. National Labor Relations Board, Press Release R-2044, 1939, p. 3. Cf. National Labor Relations Board, *Annual Report,* 1939, pp. 18–19, giving other statistics showing that 84.2 per cent of the cases were settled informally.

Professor Dodd reports that in the fiscal year 1930–1931, 2,601 informal proceedings, as against 118 formal hearings, were held in the New York district under the Longshoremen's and Harbor Workers' Compensation Act. Dodd, *Administration of Workmen's Compensation,* p. 330. The figures are particularly striking in the case of workmen's compensation in the states. Professor Dodd says (pp. 117–118): "The importance of the system by which undisputed compensation claims are adjusted can scarcely be overemphasized, since such a great proportion of all compensation cases falls in this category. Recent statistics from some of the more important industrial jurisdictions serve to illustrate the point. In Illinois, during the fiscal year 1929–1930, there occurred approximately 56,100 industrial injuries which were compensable under the law. Over 53,300 of these involved no contest. In Massachusetts, during a similar period, 37,000 out of 41,000 compensable injuries were uncontested, in Pennsylvania 80,000 out of 85,000, in Wisconsin 19,800 out of 21,700, and in Ohio 57,600 out of 64,000. Although minor injuries constitute the great mass of uncontested cases, there are always some major disabilities and death claims, and the successful administration of a compensation law depends to a much greater extent upon the machinery

itself in organizing its procedure, can gain suggestions from the experience of existing bodies dealing with substantially similar problems, but a new agency will need freedom to build up its administrative organization and methods as a result of its own experience.

The questions with which an agency has to deal are frequently brought to it by a private party through a communication, which is usually informal, but they also come to its attention through the activities of its own investigating staff. The private party may act by presenting a claim against another private party, as under the Perish-

adopted for disposing of the undisputed claim than upon the methods of procedure employed in the litigation of the contested case, important as the latter undoubtedly is."

In the Federal Communications Commission this point comes out notably in the treatment of an application for renewal of a station license when complaints against the programs which the licensee has been carrying or against his operation of the station in other ways are considered. In very few cases do these renewal applications result in a public hearing. Even when there are complaints, the matter is in most cases settled administratively. During 1940, of 106 investigations of licenses which were instituted or pending from the previous year 73 were closed. All but 3 of these were informally adjusted. Federal Communications Commission, *Annual Report,* 1940, p. 57.

In dealing with complaints against railroads by private parties, the Interstate Commerce Commission has usually been able to secure a settlement without formal proceedings. During the fiscal year 1940, the Bureau of Formal Cases received 216 original complaints. However, during the same period, the Bureau of Informal Cases received 687 complaints, and in addition the carriers filed 2,891 special-docket applications for authority to refund amounts collected under published tariffs and admitted by them to be unreasonable. Orders authorizing refunds were entered in 2,663 cases and reparations amounting to $468,030.60 were awarded thereunder. Interstate Commerce Commission, *Annual Report,* 1940, pp. 70, 71.

This informal method of settling cases is not a recent innovation in administrative practices. As early as 1901, the Interstate Commerce Commission stated: "The great mass of complaints are handled and disposed of by the Commission by preliminary investigations and correspondence or conference with carriers and shippers. The matters considered and acted upon in this way range from overcharges upon small shipments to rate relations affecting the interests of entire communities, and are of the same nature as those which find their way to the regular case docket of the Commission." Interstate Commerce Commission, *Annual Report,* 1901, p. 17.

able Agricultural Commodities Act, or in the reparation procedure of the Interstate Commerce Commission, or in workmen's compensation cases. The matter may come before the agency in the first place through an application for a privilege or license, as in the application to the Securities and Exchange Commission for registration of a security issue, or to the Federal Communications Commission for a radio station license. Where the matter is concerned with the exercise of a disciplinary power, a private party may call the attention of the regulatory body to what the complainant believes is a breach of the law which that body administers. The Federal Trade Commission and the Immigration and Naturalization Service, for example, depend largely on such information from private sources for the initiation of action.

Prior to the commencement of formal proceedings the procedure is in the main informal and private. It is aimed both at finding the facts and at securing compliance with the law and with the regulations and policies of the agency. It may result in a conclusion not to take action or in a settlement acceptable to the agency.

In the negotiations leading to settlement a government agency has many advantages. A private party will not want to be in the bad graces of the agency which administers a law affecting his business. There will therefore be a tendency on his part to come to an agreement with the agency rather than to carry the matter into a formal hearing. This tendency is stronger where the time element is important in the particular transaction, as in the case of an application for registration of a security by the Securities and Exchange Commission, or where the holder of a radio station license is seeking a renewal from the Federal Communications Commission. If there is delay in the approval of his license, or if doubt is cast on the likelihood of his getting a license, his operations and the possibility of his making advertising contracts may be seriously affected. Since the Commission issues licenses for only one year[8] and its rules require an ap-

[8] Formerly six months. Rules and Regulations, §3.34 (1939); Monograph of the Attorney General's Committee on Administrative Procedure, Sen. Doc. No. 186, 76th Cong., 3rd Sess. (1940) pt. 3, p. 3.

plication for a renewal, the Commission has a strong hold over the licensee. Even in an original application for a permit for the construction of a station and license to operate, time may be of great importance, and the applicant is therefore likely to accept any reasonable solution of an objection made on behalf of the Commission.

The expense too of an action against the government, particularly if it is to be carried through to the courts after formal proceedings in the agency, is a factor favoring acceptance of a settlement offered by the government. It is possible for the agency's officer, under the liberal and in principle thoroughly justifiable policy of allowing ample opportunity for the introduction of evidence and for the purpose of continuing hearings or of holding them in different parts of the country, to delay the conclusion of formal proceedings. Even with the best intentions on both sides, the proceedings may draw out to great length, and a government officer has not the same inducement to close the hearings promptly and to complete them as would a private party who was paying the expense directly and who was being hampered in his operations by delay and uncertainty.[9]

The informal procedure is necessary not only to enable an agency to get its work done, but it has a further and more important significance. A large part of the success of any agency must lie in its ability to educate private parties and to learn from them as it educates them. It is in informal conferences and personal visits of investigation that the education of both government officers and private persons can best be carried on. It is therefore important that the proper kind of inspectors be employed and that they be instructed to look upon themselves not as police officers but as advisers of the private parties with whom they are concerned. They should try to work out each particular problem within the broad language of the law and the policies of the agency, so that there will be the least possible injury to the private party affected, but nevertheless they should try to make sure that the public interest, the chief end of the regulatory activities of the agencies, will be served.

These informal procedures of settling and adjusting differences are

[9] See Henderson, *The Federal Trade Commission*, pp. 331–332, 338.

13

ppriate in those situations in which the agency is
ative function, as in rate making, or in which ad-
al must necessarily precede action by private per-
a license. Frequently these cases involve a wide
well as public interests, and the rights of each in
relation to the entire problem may be ascertained and protected only
through the procedure of a formal hearing. There may be in such
cases long informal negotiations which may result in agreement on
many points, but the end must be a formal order preceded by formal
hearings.

FORMAL PROCEDURE

General Requirements

The formal procedure points to a hearing at which the evidence on
both sides is produced under rules which will give to each party a
fair opportunity to present and argue his side of the case.

Congress and the courts have laid down certain broad conditions
as necessary for a fair hearing and, since the orders made as a result
of a hearing may be subjected to judicial review, the courts may
insist on observance of the minimum conditions which they have
prescribed. The hearing would not be fair unless the issues were
sufficiently defined so that the defendant knew what he would be
required to meet. There must have been timely notice and an opportunity to prepare for the hearing and to produce evidence. As a matter of policy the hearing as a rule should be public and certainly the
decision of the agency should be published, so that the parties affected
will have the protection of publicity against arbitrary action and the
agency itself will have a safeguard against the charge of using star
chamber methods.

The heads of the agency rarely hear a case themselves and usually
consider it on the record made at a hearing before a trial examiner.
During the consideration by the agency the parties concerned should
have a chance to submit briefs or argue the points which they think
should influence the decision. The agency must itself make suffi-

ciently definite the findings on which its order is based to enable the courts, if their jurisdiction is invoked either by the agency or an aggrieved party, to understand the basis for the agency's order. Findings are necessary to inform the parties of the basis for the agency's action, and the opinions based on such findings also inform the wider public, especially in the industry concerned, where they are carefully watched and serve as a guide in future operations.

The rights of the parties, however, within these broad lines can be most effectively secured if each agency has adequate rules of procedure, not conceived in a narrow sense but covering the important steps to be taken, rules which should not be changed to the detriment of a party during pendency of a particular case.[10] In view of the diversities in the different agencies and the advantage of protecting the flexibility of their procedure, it is wiser to allow each agency to establish its own rules, subject to the control of the court to protect

[10] This point is stressed in an immigration case: "the contention is made that under certain circumstances it is discretionary with the inspector as to whether or not he will disregard the rules of the department, made pursuant to the authority of the statute. We are unable to subscribe to this proposition. . . . If the appellant's position prevails, the administration of this statute will be according to the caprice of men, and not according to the fixed requirement of law. Aliens must be deported according to law, and not according to men. This statute must be administered according to its terms and the rules established by the Commissioner General of Immigration. Those charged with the enforcement are not at liberty in any particular case, and for reasons that may appeal to them at the moment, to set aside any one of the rules on which the rights of aliens depend. Otherwise an alien would never know what he was to meet, nor when nor how to prepare his defense." *Sibray* v. *United States,* 282 Fed. 795, 797–798 (C.C.A. 3d, 1922).

A change in the regulations to cover a particular situation may render a proceeding so unfair as to warrant judicial cancellation of the order of deportation. In *Colyer* v. *Skeffington,* 265 Fed. 17 (D. Mass., 1920), a case involving many procedural irregularities, a regulation with respect to representation by counsel was changed in time to place the aliens involved at a disadvantage. Less than a month later it was returned to its original form. The court chided the government for having failed to give a convincing answer to the charge that the rules had been changed for the purpose of affecting this particular case. The proceeding was held not to be a fair hearing.

the essentials of due process, rather than to set up these rules in a general statute subject only to amendment by Congress.

A shortened procedure which omits the hearing has been worked out in cases involving controversies between private parties. The cases are determined on memoranda and briefs submitted by the parties, but the shortened procedure can be used only with the consent of the parties except where it is prescribed by statute.[11]

Complaint

Formal proceedings are commenced by notification to the defendant that the matter has been set for a hearing and informing him of the charges against him. This information may be either in a pleading called a complaint or in an order to show cause, but it is essential that the issue be stated clearly enough to inform him of the nature of the case which he will have to meet. This requirement appears in the statutes—as, for example, in the Federal Trade Commission Act:

Whenever the Commission shall have reason to believe that any such person, partnership, or corporation has been or is using any unfair method of competition or unfair or deceptive act or practice in commerce, and if it shall appear to the Commission that a proceeding by it in respect thereof

---

[11] This shortened procedure has been long in use in the Interstate Commerce Commission, but only with the consent of the parties. From the inauguration of the procedure in 1923 until November 1, 1936, about one third of the formal complaints were dealt with under it with "substantial savings of both time and expense." Sharfman, *The Interstate Commerce Commission,* pt. IV, p. 226.

A similar procedure, submitting a case on written evidence, is followed under the Perishable Agricultural Commodities Act, 1930, where the statute requires this method for all cases involving claims of less than five hundred dollars. 7 U.S.C. §499f (c). Under the rules of the Secretary of Agriculture claims between five hundred dollars and two thousand dollars may be dealt with by this procedure with the approval of both parties. In practice this method is widely used and is peculiarly valuable in the saving of expense and time to complainants who are seeking to recover small sums and in saving to the government the time and expense which would be involved in conducting a public hearing. Up to June 30, 1937, there had been 906 decisions upon complaints received under the shortened procedure as against 772 rendered after hearings. Unpublished MS of Frederic P. Lee, *Administration of Federal Agricultural Commodity Standards,* p. 395.

would be to the interest of the public, it shall issue and serve upon such person, partnership, or corporation a complaint stating its charges in that respect and containing a notice of a hearing upon a day and at a place therein fixed at least thirty days after the service of said complaint.[12]

The agencies are not technical in their interpretation of such a statutory provision, usually expanded in their procedural regulations; but the principle is so essential to a fair hearing that it is not questioned in the practice of the agencies. The informal proceedings will usually have developed the points at issue sufficiently to inform the parties, and this may be taken into consideration in determining whether a complaint is sufficiently specific.[13]

The Interstate Commerce Commission has expressed its insistence upon the importance of the specificity of the complaint:

The Commission's Rules of Practice do not require strict conformity to the technical rules of pleading. They do require, however, that complaints shall conform to the more elementary requirements of pleading; that they shall be so sufficient, clear, and certain in their averments that the Commission may be informed of the issues and the carriers fully advised of the nature and extent of the case they are called upon to defend.[14]

The order which is finally issued must not include matters of which the person complained of has not been informed by the complaint. The Supreme Court in the early history of the Federal Trade Commission said: "an order should follow the complaint; otherwise it is improvident and, when challenged, will be annulled by the court," for "the thing which may be prohibited is the method of competition specified in the complaint."[15]

---

[12] 15 U.S.C. §45 (b).

[13] The Attorney General's Committee on Administrative Procedure has called attention to the importance of the adequacy of notice (Sen. Doc. No. 10, 77th Cong., 1st Sess. [1941] pt. 13, pp. 37, 44–51), but in discussing the Federal Trade Commission it comments on the point that preliminary discussions will have informed the defendant as to the points at issue (Sen. Doc. No. 186, 76th Cong., 3rd Sess. [1940] pt. 6, p. 13).

[14] *Brooks Coal Co.* v. *Wabash R. R. Co.,* 39 I.C.C. 426, 428–429 (1916).

[15] *Federal Trade Commission* v. *Gratz,* 253 U.S. 421, 427 (1920).

The agency is not, however, held in a straitjacket by this rule, since amendments are freely permitted subsequent to the filing of the original complaint. Nevertheless the principle, that the defendant must have sufficient notice of any amendment to enable him to prepare his defense, is not affected, and only if the amendment is properly introduced may the issues therein be included in the order.[16] The object of assuring a full opportunity to present testimony and of preventing surprise is served by the readiness of the agency or the trial examiner to adjourn the hearing, either to places at which evidence can be more easily obtained or to a later date to give a party time to assemble his proofs to establish a point or to meet evidence already presented. The essential point is that the defendant be not taken by surprise so that, if it is clear that he understood the issues, especially if he met them at the hearing, he cannot take advantage of a technical defect in the complaint rendering it doubtful whether a particular point was included. The courts have taken a liberal position on this point:

The next objection to the validity of the order is that it is not confined to the issues raised. . . . If this order were a judgment of a court, we should without hesitation say that the facts alleged in the petition did not support it. The Interstate Commerce Commission is, however, an administrative tribunal dealing with practical problems. So long as parties affected by its orders appear and are fully heard, we think it would be most unfortunate to deny its power to grant such relief as the facts shown upon the investigation should call for, even though such facts might be presented by evidence technically outside the issues raised. Notwithstanding, therefore, that the commission has established rules of practice analogous to those in courts, notwithstanding that its rules even provide that hearings shall be had upon issue joined, we are of the opinion that the strict rules of pleading should not be held applicable to it. Before we declare an order of the commission invalid as being outside the issues, we think that we should be satisfied that it is outside the issues actually presented to the commission and upon which the parties were heard. We have, therefore, thought it our

[16] There should be less need of detailed charges in the complaint in that the defendant will have discussed the subject with the investigator before formal action is commenced.

duty to examine the evidence and consider the claims of the parties made upon the hearing before the commission. Through such examination we find that the milling company and the carriers appeared before the commission, and that the various phases of the discriminations claimed to exist against the milling company were fully inquired into. . . . As the hearing progressed, its scope apparently widened, and at its conclusion we are satisfied that the real question before the commission in the minds of all the parties was whether it was proper and practicable to afford relief like that granted by the order.[17]

Intervention

In nondisciplinary cases and occasionally even in disciplinary cases there may be others than the principal parties who have an interest in the proceeding, and they should be notified and given a right to participate. Controversies between private parties will not often concern others; but in some situations, as in the determination of reparations cases before the Interstate Commerce Commission, permitting intervention may avoid multiplicity of suits, and the rate involved in the case will be a matter of interest to various persons. Where the ques-

[17] *New York Central & H. R. R. Co.* v. *Interstate Commerce Commission,* 168 Fed. 131, 138–139 (C.C.N.Y., 1909).

In a case before it the Interstate Commerce Commission said: "The carriers in their answers do not demur to the obvious technical defect in pleading. They made no objection at the time of hearing to the introduction of testimony the avowed purpose of which was to prove damages by discrimination. In view of the manner in which defendants' counsel have met the real issue it can scarcely be seriously contended that they were not fully advised of the nature and full extent of complainant's case." *Brooks Coal Co.* v. *Wabash R. R. Co.,* 39 I.C.C. 426, 429 (1916).

In a National Labor Relations Board case the Supreme Court dismissed a technical argument based on a change in the wording of a complaint on the ground that there could have been no doubt in the defendant's mind as to the meaning of the pleading. *National Labor Relations Board* v. *Mackay Radio & T. Co.,* 304 U.S. 333 (1938).

The Securities and Exchange Commission has, in one case, disaffirmed findings made by the trial examiner which "exceeded the scope of the violations charged in the order" that started the proceeding. *In the Matter of Michigan–Utah Consolidated Mines Co.,* 3 S.E.C. 126, 128 (1938).

tion involved is whether or on what terms a privilege shall be granted, others than the applicant will often be affected. Public bodies are frequently concerned, and an opportunity should be afforded them to express their points of view. For example, whether a license for a radio station shall be granted, or on what terms, depends on the public convenience and necessity and not chiefly on the interest of the applicant. Other license holders, too, will be affected by the grant and under the statute may appeal, so they should have an opportunity to take a part in the hearing.

The procedure under the National Labor Relations Act dealing with unfair labor practices is another instance in which intervention is permitted on a showing of sufficient interest. Employees who claim back wages because of the loss of their positions as a result of the unfair labor practice set forth in the complaint may intervene. More important than the right of individuals is the right of labor organizations other than that which made the original charge to protect their positions when the matter at issue concerns them. This is notably the case where an organization is alleged to be a company union, or where an alleged unfair labor practice consists in favoring another union against the complainant, or where the intervenor labor organization itself is concerned in the designation of the proper bargaining unit.

The Securities Exchange Act of 1934 and the Public Utility Holding Company Act of 1935 are liberal in authorizing intervention,[18] and the Securities and Exchange Commission is liberal in permitting intervention "upon proper showing of sufficient interest in the subject matter."[19] In other agencies, particularly in disciplinary proceedings, intervention is infrequent, for example, in cases under the Federal Trade Commission.

As a result of intervention the hearing may often resemble a contest between private parties in which the agency assumes "the burden of exploring the facts and of counseling the parties with reference to

[18] 15 U.S.C. §§78l(f), 79s.
[19] Securities and Exchange Commission, *Rules of Practice,* Rule XVII (1938).

the nature of the issues that may be involved."[20] Even without formal intervention, and so without making them parties to the proceeding, the Securities and Exchange Commission has at times permitted private parties to take part in the hearings in respect to a question as to which they had a special interest.[21] These few instances illustrate the variety of conditions under which the problem of intervention presents itself. The tendency appears to be toward permitting public bodies and persons who can show an interest to intervene. Particu-

[20] Landis, *The Administrative Process*, p. 40.

[21] The Commission's trial examiners are liberal in permitting participation in the hearings by almost any persons, whether or not they become formal parties to the action. In a proceeding to determine whether the registration of certain securities should be suspended or withdrawn, both the issuer and the issuer's preferred and common stockholders were represented by counsel at the hearing, although the issuer's preferred and common stockholders were, of course, not parties to the proceeding. *In the Matter of Prima Co.*, 3 S.E.C. 246 (1938); see also *In the Matter of Connecticut Railway and Lighting Co.*, 2 S.E.C. 21 (1937). In a proceeding upon an application for approval of the acquisition of certain stock in exchange for stock of the applicant, a holder of ten shares of stock of the applicant asked leave and was permitted to testify in connection with a certain contract between the applicant and the company whose stock it sought to acquire, such a contract being then involved in litigation brought by stockholders of the applicant. *In the Matter of the Applications of Commonwealth Edison Co.*, 2 S.E.C. 709 (1937). In a stop order proceeding, counsel for the United Mine Workers of America, who had entered no formal appearance at the hearing, asked and received leave to appear as *amicus* and to file a brief and affidavits in support of exceptions to the trial examiner's report. Members of the United Mine Workers were employed in Indiana mines competing with those of the respondent. *In the Matter of American Terminals and Transit Company*, 1 S.E.C. 701, 705 (1936).

In a stop order proceeding involving a registration statement including an appraisal to which objection was made by the Commission as containing untrue statements, the appraisal company was represented by counsel at the hearing before the trial examiner and treated "as a party in all respects," although not made a formal party to the record. Counsel for the appraisal company examined and cross-examined witnesses, made objections to the admission of evidence, and filed suggestions for findings of fact and exceptions to the findings of fact made by the trial examiner, although respondents consented to the issuance of a stop order. *In the Matter of Continental Distillers and Importers Corporation*, 1 S.E.C. 54, 56 (1935).

larly in cases in which policy determination plays an important part, or in which a public interest is involved, the agency will be aided by a reasonable liberality in permitting parties to intervene and present their views.

Evidence

The conditions surrounding the taking and weighing of evidence before an agency are very different from those under which the common law rules of evidence grew up in trials before a jury controlled and directed by an experienced judge and managed on both sides by trained lawyers.[22] The statutes setting up the various administrative agencies contain little on the subject of evidence. Occasionally they indicate the intention of Congress not to limit an agency in the kind of evidence which may be introduced in proceedings before it by providing expressly that the common law rules of evidence shall not be controlling.

Although the common law rules of evidence are not required by the statutes to be applied in administrative cases, some of them, such as the hearsay rule and the rule of best evidence, serve as useful guides. Many of the persons administering these rules as trial examiners are lawyers who are accustomed to their application in courts and therefore find it natural to follow them during a hearing. There is, furthermore, insistence by the courts that the parties be given a fair hearing and, in determining the elements of what is a fair hearing and what is arbitrary action, the judges are influenced by the treatment of evidence by the trial examiner or by the agency which issues the order.[23] The hearsay rule, for example, is not rigorously ap-

[22] "The greatest and most remarkable offshoot of the jury was that body of excluding rules which chiefly constitute the English 'Law of Evidence' . . . [it was] this judicial oversight and control of the process of introducing evidence to the jury, that gave our system birth; and he who would understand it must keep this fact constantly in mind." Thayer, *A Preliminary Treatise on Evidence at the Common Law*, pp. 180–181.

[23] See *John Bene & Sons* v. *Federal Trade Commission*, 299 Fed. 468, 471 (C.C.A. 2d, 1924), in which the court said that the record contained little "legally competent, relevant, pertinent, and material" evidence, but that the Commission

plied by administrative agencies to the admission of evidence. However, a finding of fact would rarely be based wholly on hearsay. The courts disapprove dependence on hearsay, and it is looked upon as a weak support for a finding of fact.

While the agencies should not be required to enforce the substantive rules of evidence in their hearings, it is otherwise with the vital method of bringing out the truth by cross-examination. It is true in proceedings before administrative tribunals, as it is in proceedings before courts, that the "belief that no safeguard for testing the value of human statements is comparable to that furnished by cross-examination, and the conviction that no statement (unless by special exception) should be used as testimony until it has been probed and sublimated by that test, has found increasing strength in lengthening experience."[24]

Cross-examination is not only necessary in the interest of the parties involved but is an efficient means of checking the facts, even those presented by the agency's own investigators, and of giving to the agency, when it gets its report of the hearing, a well-tested basis upon which it may rely for its decision and for findings of fact on which to base its order. Even the evidence produced by the agency from its own or other government experts should not be permitted to go into the record until it has been tested in the fire of cross-exami-

could, nevertheless, receive and consider legally incompetent evidence if it was the kind "that usually affects fair-minded men in the conduct of their daily and more important affairs," and if "fairly done." The requirement of fairness was not here observed. In *National Labor Relations Board* v. *Union Pacific Stages,* 99 F. 2d 153, 176 (C.C.A. 9th, 1938), *reh. denied* (1939), the court said that the National Labor Relations Act was not intended "to encourage loose practices or set aside or abandon the rules of evidence which the test of experience has proven are the best suited to ascertain the truth of a controversy." Cf. *Tri-State Broadcasting Co.* v. *Federal Communications Commission,* 96 F. 2d 564, 567 (App. D.C., 1938), *reh. denied* (1938), where the court, in reversing a Commission order of improper findings, criticized the admission of certain hearsay testimony because its "admission deprived the appellant of the right to cross-examine those a composite of whose views" were being reflected into the record.

[24] Wigmore, *A Treatise on the Anglo-American System of Evidence in Trials at Common Law,* vol. 5, p. 29.

nation, or at least the opportunity given to the parties of testing in this fashion the accuracy of the experts' conclusions. A court may enforce this requirement where it has been disregarded by sending the case back to the agency if the statute authorizes cross-examination expressly or by implication from the requirement of a hearing.[25]

The concept of fair hearing includes the right to compel the attendance of witnesses. Most administrative agencies have the power

[25] The importance of cross-examination is emphasized in a Securities and Exchange Commission case: "In the interest of expedition, a stipulation was entered into at the outset of the investigation, between respondents and counsel for the Commission, which provided that the testimony of witnesses 'properly admitted' in the investigation, including the exhibits made a part of the record, might be considered competent evidence 'in any subsequent proceeding involving the parties thereto, subject to the right of the parties herein to introduce further evidence, and to explain, control or rebut the testimony so offered.' During the investigation, respondents were allowed to introduce witnesses in their own behalf and to cross-examine witnesses. It should be noted at this point that the cross-examination was obviously necessary to safeguard the validity of testimony which would, by the terms of the stipulation, be competent in any formal proceedings which might ensue after the preliminary investigation." *In the Matter of White, Weld & Co.,* 1 S.E.C. 574, 576 (1936).

Referring to the Interstate Commerce Commission, the Supreme Court said: "The Commission is an administrative body and, even where it acts in a quasi-judicial capacity, is not limited by the strict rules, as to the admissibility of evidence, which prevail in suits between private parties. . . . But the more liberal the practice in admitting testimony, the more imperative the obligation to preserve the essential rules of evidence by which rights are asserted or defended. . . . All parties must be fully apprised of the evidence submitted or to be considered, and must be given an opportunity to cross-examine witnesses, to inspect documents and to offer evidence in explanation or rebuttal." *Interstate Commerce Commission* v. *Louisville & Nashville R. R. Co.,* 227 U.S. 88, 93 (1913).

In several instances the statute establishing the agency and its procedure contains a provision guaranteeing the right to cross-examine. For example, this right is given under the Packers and Stockyards Act, 1921, 7 U.S.C. §193 (a), and in investigations by the Bureau of Marine Inspection and Navigation for violation of the Shipping Act, 46 U.S.C. §239 (d).

Departmental regulations are another source of this guarantee. Thus the rules and regulations of the National Labor Relations Board specifically confer the right of cross-examination on both the Board and the employer. Rules and Regulations, Series 2, Art. II, §§24, 25 (1940).

of subpoena. Ordinarily they have imposed some limitations on the use of the subpoena power to protect persons wanted as witnesses. The issuance of subpoenas is discretionary; some showing of materiality is required, particularly for a subpoena *duces tecum*. There may be considerations, such as the nationwide effectiveness of process, which require limitations on administrative agencies, similar to the geographical limits on the power of the federal courts to compel the attendance of a witness at a hearing or trial.[26] On the other hand, the expense of transporting witnesses imposes a restriction on parties to proceedings before administrative agencies and provides the possibility of a definite advantage to the agency. While there is little indication of abuse by the agencies of discretionary power over subpoena, the power is one which is obviously open to the possibility of abuse. Since there is little relation between the policy-making powers of the agency and the power to examine witnesses, it is possible that the power to issue subpoenas should be given to some independent office where questions such as whether the subpoena is sought for the purpose of delay might be examined impartially and without the possibility of a determination influenced by the desire to win the litigation.[27]

Findings of Fact

Generally speaking, administrative agencies are required to make findings of fact where formal proceedings are had. The most prevalent provisions in the statutes are not that findings of fact shall be made, but are those which relate to their effect in the courts when made. Thus "findings of fact, when supported by substantial evidence, shall be conclusive." These provisions are not in uniform language, though the lack of uniformity does not seem to interfere with a likeness of consequences attributed to them by the courts.[28]

[26] Federal Rules of Civil Procedure, Rule 45 (e).

[27] The subject is discussed in Note, Subpoenas and Due Process in Administrative Hearings, 53 *Harv. L. Rev.* 842 (1940).

[28] When the Interstate Commerce Commission awards reparation, it must in-

The most precise and exacting provision of all is contained in the
Communications Act of 1934. In addition to declaring that the findings, if supported by substantial evidence, shall be conclusive, it requires the Commission to file, within a certain time after notice of
appeal is given, "a full statement in writing of the facts and grounds
for its decision as found and given by it."[29] Under this Act the Court
of Appeals of the District of Columbia has held that the Commission shall publish simultaneously with the issuance of an order a
summary and brief form of findings of fact, to be followed later by
the "full statement," in case an appeal is made. The statute requires
the petitioner to assign the reasons for his appeal. But if no grounds
for the order were stated until, say, sixty days after notice of appeal,
the appellant would be in no position to assign his reasons.[30]

clude findings of fact in its report. Similarly, the National Labor Relations Act
provides that when the Board issues a cease and desist order in respect to unfair
labor practices it "shall state its findings of fact." Findings are required by two
recent statutes, viz., the Fair Labor Standards Act of 1938, 29 U.S.C. §201, and
the Federal Food, Drug, and Cosmetic Act, 21 U.S.C. §301, in the formulation of
substantive rules and regulations. The former does not require that the findings
be based solely on the record, although the record as it leaves the Administrator
must support those findings, whereas the latter specifically requires that the rules
be based solely on the record.

[29] 47 U.S.C. §402 (c).

[30] Thus, "to hold that the statement of the grounds on which the commission
reached its decision may be disclosed for the first time sixty days after the appeal
is taken would be manifestly unfair because, if for no other reason, it would be to
require an appellant to appeal from a decision the grounds for which he would
not and could not know, and by the same token to assign reasons for the appeal
wholly different, as it might very well turn out, from the grounds which the commission later asserted as the basis of its denial of the application." Referring to
the language of the statute, that the Commission should file "a full statement in
writing of the facts and grounds for its decision *as found and given by it,*" the
Court said: "The six words we have emphasized imply, we think, that the
grounds of decision and a brief factual statement of the reasons therefor have
been previously given, that is, previously to the filing of the full statement, i.e.,
findings of fact, in this court." *Missouri Broadcasting Corp.* v. *Federal Communications Commission,* 94 F. 2d 623, 626 (App. D.C., 1937), *reh. denied* (1938),
cert. denied, 303 U.S. 655 (1938); *Heitmeyer* v. *Federal Communications Commission,* 95 F. 2d 91 (App. D.C., 1937).

Some statutes are silent on the subject of findings of fact. The Post-master General, for example, is authorized to issue fraud orders "on evidence satisfactory to him."[31] Only in recent years has he adopted the practice of making findings. Portions of the statutes adminis-tered by the Securities and Exchange Commission say merely that "if it appears" to the Commission that a registration statement is incom-plete or inaccurate on its face, or includes any untrue statement, or if it appears that any unlisted security has been withdrawn from any exchange, the Commission may act.[32] But it seems clear that these provisions, especially when taken in conjunction with the express provision relating to review, contemplate that findings shall be made.

Findings of fact serve three useful purposes: a publicity safeguard against arbitrary action, a check within the agency itself, and a basis of judicial review. They have to do with an aspect of the facts which is of uniform concern to the courts, namely, whether there is suffi-cient evidence to support the findings. A record of the evidence is the most helpful, if indeed it is not the only practicable, device for en-abling the courts to ascertain whether the findings are so supported. Thus the findings apprise the parties, as well as the courts, of the basis of the action of the Commission, and they facilitate the deter-mination whether the case has been decided upon the evidence and the law or, on the contrary, upon arbitrary or extra-legal considera-tions. This is an important point which, coupled with the related point (on which the statutes are generally silent) of stating the rea-sons for the action taken, deeply concerns the position of administra-tive agencies in public esteem. It has been suggested that findings of fact, whatever may be true as to the statement of reasons, are consti-tutional requisites; at all events the courts, in the interpretation of statutes, are quick to see the desirability of findings.[33]

---

[31] 39 U.S.C. §259.   [32] 15 U.S.C. §77h (d).

[33] A detailed discussion of the content and form of findings of fact is con-tained in an opinion in the Court of Appeals of the District of Columbia, *Sagi-naw Broadcasting Co.* v. *Federal Communications Commission*, 96 F. 2d 554, 559 (App. D.C., 1938), *cert. denied, Gross* v. *Saginaw Broadcasting Co.*, 305 U.S. 613 (1938). In an effort to "spell out the process which a commission properly

Findings of fact are intimately related to the larger problem of a full hearing, and the procedure of several agencies with regard to them has been altered or affected by the *Morgan* cases.[34] The imme-

follows in reaching a decision," Judge Stephens said: "The process necessarily includes at least four parts: (1) evidence must be taken and weighed, both as to its accuracy and credibility; (2) from attentive consideration of this evidence a determination of facts of a basic or underlying nature must be reached; (3) from these basic facts the ultimate facts, usually in the language of the statute, are to be inferred, or not, as the case may be; (4) from this finding the decision will follow by the application of the statutory criterion. For example, before the Communications Commission may grant a construction permit it must, under the statute, be convinced that the public interest, convenience, or necessity will be served. An affirmative or negative finding on this topic would be a finding of ultimate fact. This ultimate fact, however, will be reached by inference from basic facts, such as, for example, the probable existence or non-existence of electrical interference, in view of the number of other stations operating in the area, their power, wave length, and the like. These basic facts will themselves appear or fail to appear, as the case may be, from the evidence introduced when attentively considered. . . .

"We ruled in Missouri Broadcasting Corporation v. Federal Communications Commission, 68 App. D.C. 154, 94 F. 2d 623, 1937, and again in Heitmeyer v. Federal Communications Commission, 68 App. D.C. 180, 95 F. 2d 91, 1937, that findings of fact in the broad terms of public convenience, interest, or necessity, the criterion set up by Section 319 (a) of the Act, were not sufficient to support an order of the Commission. We now rule that findings of fact, to be sufficient to support an order, must include what have been above described as the basic facts, from which the ultimate facts in the terms of the statutory criterion are inferred. It is not necessary for the Commission to recite the evidence, and it is not necessary that it set out its findings in the formal style and manner customary in trial courts. It is enough if the findings be unambiguously stated, whether in narrative or numbered form, so that it appears definitely upon what basic facts the Commission reached the ultimate facts and came to its decision."

In *National Labor Relations Board* v. *Thompson Products,* 97 F. 2d 13 (C.C.A. 6th, 1938), the Circuit Court of Appeals for the Sixth Circuit said that the findings were not in the proper form; that they were mingled with statements of witnesses and expressions of opinion. The court said that no evidence should be injected nor any discussion made in the findings. Rather they should be a clear-cut statement of the basic facts, without incorporating the evidence or the reasoning by which the Board arrived at its findings. If the Board desires to discuss, emphasize any part, or give any reasons, it should do so in the form of an opinion or memorandum which should not be a part of the findings.

[34] *Morgan* v. *United States,* 298 U.S. 468 (1936); *Morgan* v. *United States,* 304 U.S. 1 (1938).

diate result of these two decisions was to induce several agencies to try to make the ultimate decider take some part in arriving at findings of fact and decisions. The first decision bears so directly on the point now under discussion that its particular passages in that regard should be noted here. The Court reversed a rate order of the Secretary of Agriculture on the ground that it did not appear that he had accorded the parties the "full hearing" required by the statute. Actually the case was remanded for a determination whether he had or not. It was alleged in the complaint that while the Secretary had signed the order, all the work in connection therewith—the taking of testimony, formulation of the findings and order, hearing of oral argument—had been done by subordinates. In the language of the Court: "The Secretary who, according to the allegation, had neither heard nor read evidence or argument, undertook to make the findings and fix the rates. The Assistant Secretary, who had heard, assumed no responsibility for the findings or order, and the Secretary, who had not heard, did assume that responsibility." The Court called attention to the fact that the conclusive weight ascribed by law to the findings "rests upon the assumption that the officer who makes the findings has addressed himself to the evidence and upon that evidence has conscientiously reached the conclusions which he deems it to justify. That duty cannot be performed by one who has not considered evidence or argument. It is not an impersonal obligation. It is a duty akin to that of a judge. The one who decides must hear." This necessary rule, the Court went on to say, "does not preclude practicable administrative procedure in obtaining the aid of assistants in the department. Assistants may prosecute inquiries. Evidence may be taken by an examiner. Evidence thus taken may be sifted and analyzed by competent subordinates."

The Securities and Exchange Commission takes the language of the *Morgan* case as indicative that the primary purpose of the examiner's findings is to narrow the issue before the Commission for decision. Under its interpretation of the case, the Commission is not bound by the findings of a trial examiner but actually must make findings "upon its own consideration of the evidence."[35] For the preparation of the findings and opinions the entire record, including a transcript of the oral argument, is transmitted to the general counsel, and a draft is prepared by attorneys in the opinion section of the office. Copies of the draft opinion are then circulated among the members of the Commission for individual consideration, and later the opinion is called for joint discussion among the draftsmen and the commissioners. By that time "each Commissioner is familiar with the record, has read the proposed opinion, has reached some decision in his own mind, and is prepared to discuss the issues and offer suggestions as to the form and content of the opinion. . . . in most cases the opinion is not acceptable in its first draft and must be rewritten in accordance with the matured conclusions of the Commission. Occasionally a completely new opinion, or even alternative opinions, must be prepared."[36]

In the National Labor Relations Board when the record, including the trial examiner's intermediate report and the exceptions thereto, is filed with the Board, it is examined by an attorney in the review

[35] Thus Rule IX (c) provides that the report of the trial examiner is advisory only and that findings of fact contained therein are not binding upon the Commission; and the same view has been expressed by the Commission in several of its decisions. However, it is difficult to say whether these adequately explain the actual practice of the Commission. Some doubt is thrown on them by other rules which provide for exceptions to the trial examiner's findings and which provide that objections not saved by exceptions are deemed to have been abandoned and may be disregarded, thus making the procedure appear to be rather in the nature of appellate proceedings than a "final hearing on the merits before the Commission." This is supported by various statements from the Commission's decisions: "Inasmuch as the registrant has not excepted to the findings of the trial examiner, it is not entitled to any extended discussion by the Commission in addition to the findings of fact," *In the Matter of Virginia City Gold Mining Co.,* 2 S.E.C. 855, 856 (1937), and "In view of the fact that no exceptions have been taken to the trial examiner's report, we need discuss the alleged deficiencies only insofar as the general interests of the investing public may be served," *In the Matter of Sunbeam Gold Mines Co.,* 3 S.E.C. 308, 309 (1938).

[36] Lane, *in* Symposium on Administrative Law, 9 *Am. L. School Rev.* 139, 154, 159 (1939).

section. He makes no recommendations or findings; he is a mere source of information for the Board. The Board deliberates and suggests the nature of the decision it desires, and the attorney then prepares a draft of the findings of fact and the order. Thus the actual decision and findings are not written by the Board or a member thereof, but by a member of the review section. This procedure indicates that the Board does not rely completely on the trial examiner's findings. However, as in the Securities and Exchange Commission, those findings are very useful and are accorded great weight. In several cases the Board has said merely that exceptions, in so far as they were inconsistent with the findings, conclusions, and order set forth below, were found to be without merit.[37]

In the Federal Trade Commission the trial examiner's report includes proposed findings of fact and recommendations as to the final disposition of the case.[38] The parties may file exceptions to the report and, although oral argument before the Commission itself is not restricted to the exceptions, the Commission assumes agreement with those parts of the report not excepted to.

The statutory provisions with regard to the effect of findings are aimed at finality of determination of the facts by the agency, but not an absolute finality, for findings must be supported by evidence, and whether they are so supported is a question of law which may be brought to the courts.[39] Some of the statutes say that the findings

[37] Thus in *In the Matter of Thompson Products, et al.,* 3 N.L.R.B. 332, 333 (1937): "With this slight exception, we find nothing in the respondent's exceptions to the Intermediate Report which requires any material alteration of such findings and conclusions. In substance, the findings of fact and conclusions of law herein made embody those made by the Trial Examiner."

[38] Dean Landis, a former member of the Commission, has said that the findings are as a matter of practice drafted by the attorney representing the Commission at the hearing. Landis, *in* Symposium on Administrative Law, 9 *Am. L. School Rev.* 139, 181, 183 (1939).

[39] Irrespective of statute, the courts have carved out a category of facts, "jurisdictional facts," as to which the findings of the agency have little weight. For further reference to "jurisdictional facts," see p. 205.

shall be conclusive "if supported by substantial evidence";[40] others omit "substantial";[41] still others say "if supported by testimony."[42] The Communications Act of 1934 has a double-barreled declaration: "Findings of fact by the Commission, if supported by substantial evidence, shall be conclusive unless it shall clearly appear that the findings of the Commission are arbitrary or capricious."[43] The Longshoremen's and Harbor Workers' Compensation Act makes them final "if in accordance with law."[44] Sometimes the courts have reached the same general result without statutory aid.[45]

The courts agree that the primary task of considering the facts, weighing the evidence, drawing inferences therefrom—in short, making findings—is for the agency itself. It is not enough to justify the overturn of such findings that the court, had it been considering the evidence independently, would have reached a contrary conclusion.[46] And notwithstanding refinements as to the judicial role, what the courts appear to be endeavoring to do is to determine, in the light of the whole record, whether the finding is an "arbitrary" one. The term "arbitrary" lacks precision, but it has the merit of putting the question before the courts after the manner of a basic problem of due process of law.

The effect of the statutory declaration that findings shall be conclusive if supported by evidence has thus been stated by the Supreme Court:

[40] Communications Act of 1934, 47 U.S.C. §402 (e); Federal Power Act, 16 U.S.C. §825*l* (b); Securities Exchange Act of 1934, 15 U.S.C. §78y (a); Public Utility Holding Company Act of 1935, 15 U.S.C. §79x (a).

[41] Securities Act of 1933, 15 U.S.C. §77i (a); National Labor Relations Act, 29 U.S.C. §160 (f).

[42] Clayton Act, 15 U.S.C. §21.   [43] 47 U.S.C. §402.

[44] 33 U.S.C. §921 (c).

[45] In the case of the Interstate Commerce Act see *Chestnut Ridge Ry. Co.* v. *United States,* 248 Fed. 791 (D.N.J., 1917), and *Louis. & Nash. R. R. Co.* v. *United States,* 245 U.S. 463 (1918). In the case of the Packers and Stockyards Act, 1921, see *Denver Union Stock Yard Co.* v. *United States,* 21 F. Supp. 83 (D. Colo., 1937), aff'd, 304 U.S. 470 (1938).

[46] *Federal Trade Commission* v. *Artloom Corp.,* 69 F. 2d 36 (C.C.A. 3d, 1934), reh. denied (1934).

But as has often been pointed out, this, as in the case of other findings by administrative bodies, means evidence which is substantial, that is, affording a substantial basis of fact from which the fact in issue can be reasonably inferred. . . . Substantial evidence is more than a scintilla, and must do more than create a suspicion of the existence of the fact to be established. "It means such relevant evidence as a reasonable mind might accept as adequate to support a conclusion," . . . and it must be enough to justify, if the trial were to a jury, a refusal to direct a verdict when the conclusion sought to be drawn from it is one of fact for the jury.[47]

And several points are deducible from the decisions in the Supreme Court and elsewhere.

Thus Congress is not endeavoring to make the courts deal with facts generally. What appeared as one effort in that direction went astray. The provision in the original Radio Act of 1927 that on appeal the court "may alter or revise the decision appealed from and enter such judgment as to it may seem just" was interpreted by the Supreme Court as conferring upon the courts an administrative rather than judicial function.[48] This decision led to an amendment of the Act, brought over into the present Communications Act of 1934, limiting the jurisdiction to questions of law and specifying finality of the findings of fact if supported by substantial evidence.

Findings must be made by the agency itself. It is not enough that the record contains sufficient evidence on which findings could have been made or which would justify the action taken. The Supreme Court has said, with regard to the Interstate Commerce Commission, that the question is not merely one of the absence of elaboration or of a suitably complete statement of the grounds of the Commission's determination, but of the "lack of the basic or essential findings re-

---

[47] *National Labor Relations Board* v. *Columbian Co.,* 306 U.S. 292, 299–300 (1939). In a later part of the opinion by Chief Justice Hughes in *Edison Co.* v. *National Labor Relations Board,* 305 U.S. 197 (1938), from which Mr. Justice Stone quoted in the *Columbian* case, the meaning of substantial evidence is elaborated further, at p. 230: "Mere uncorroborated hearsay or rumor does not constitute substantial evidence."

[48] *Federal Radio Commission* v. *General Electric Co.,* 281 U.S. 464 (1930).

quired to support the Commission's order. In the absence of such findings, we are not called upon to examine the evidence in order to resolve opposing contentions as to what it shows or to spell out and state such conclusions of fact as it may permit. The Commission is the fact-finding body and the Court examines the evidence not to make findings for the Commission but to ascertain whether its findings are properly supported."[49]

Evidence to support the findings must be in the record. Otherwise the decision might be based upon evidence never brought to the attention of the parties, thus depriving them of the opportunity to cross-examine or present countervailing evidence. In one case the Supreme Court said: "But a finding without evidence is beyond the power of the Commission. Papers in the Commission's files are not always evidence in a case. . . . Nothing can be treated as evidence which is not introduced as such." Also, that the "objection to the use of the data contained in the annual reports is not lack of authenticity or untrustworthiness. It is that the carriers were left without notice of the evidence with which they were, in fact, confronted, as later disclosed by the finding made."[50]

A deeper objection to the use of evidence not on the record was expressed by Mr. Justice Cardozo in *Ohio Bell Telephone Co.* v. *Public Utilities Commission of Ohio.* In this case the Commission had turned to documents which had not been introduced in evidence, and the company had had no opportunity to explain or rebut them.

---

[49] *Florida* v. *United States,* 282 U.S. 194, 215 (1931). And see *Atchison Ry.* v. *United States,* 295 U.S. 193, 201–202 (1935), where Mr. Justice Butler said: "This court will not search the record to ascertain whether, by use of what there may be found, general and ambiguous statements in the report intended to serve as findings may by construction be given a meaning sufficiently definite and certain to constitute a valid basis for the order. In the absence of a finding of essential basic facts, the order cannot be sustained."

[50] *United States* v. *Abilene & So. Ry. Co.,* 265 U.S. 274, 288, 289 (1924). See Henderson, *The Federal Trade Commission,* p. 63.

This rule does not appear to be adhered to as rigidly in immigration proceedings, where the whole procedure is less strictly supervised than in other agencies. Van Vleck, *The Administrative Control of Aliens,* p. 170.

From the standpoint of due process—the protection of the individual against arbitrary action—a deeper vice is this, that even now we do not know the particular or evidential facts of which the Commission took judicial notice and on which it rested its conclusion. Not only are the facts unknown; there is no way to find them out. When price lists or trade journals or even government reports are put in evidence upon a trial, the party against whom they are offered may see the evidence or hear it and parry its effect. Even if they are copied in the findings without preliminary proof, there is at least an opportunity in connection with a judicial review of the decision to challenge the deductions made from them. The opportunity is excluded here. The Commission, withholding from the record the evidential facts that it has gathered here and there, contents itself with saying that in gathering them it went to journals and tax lists, as if a judge were to tell us, "I looked at the statistics in the Library of Congress, and they teach me thus and so." This will never do if hearings and appeals are to be more than empty forms. . . . To put the problem more concretely: how was it possible for the appellate court to review the law and the facts and intelligently decide that the findings of the Commission were supported by the evidence when the evidence that it approved was unknown and unknowable? . . . "A hearing is not judicial, at least in any adequate sense, unless the evidence can be known."[51]

The Trial Examiner

Much of the responsibility for the conduct of judicial proceedings in the agencies rests on the trial examiner. A formal hearing is usually held before a trial examiner, seldom before the head of an agency whether an individual or a commission or board. The trial examiner

---

[51] 301 U.S. 292, 302–304 (1937). And, with reference to the Longshoremen's and Harbor Workers' Compensation Act the Court said: "The statute, however, contemplates a public hearing and regulations are to require 'a record of the hearings and other proceedings before the deputy commissioner.' §23 (b). This implies that all proceedings by the deputy commissioner upon a particular claim shall be appropriately set forth, and that whatever facts he may ascertain and their sources shall be shown in the record and be open to challenge and opposing evidence. Facts conceivably known to the deputy commissioner, but not put in evidence so as to permit scrutiny and contest, will not support a compensation order. . . . An award not supported by evidence in the record is not in accordance with law." Hughes, C. J., in *Crowell* v. *Benson,* 285 U.S. 22, 48 (1932).

is in most cases a member of the staff of the agency, but he may be appointed from outside the staff for a particular hearing.[52] It is common practice for the trial examiner to conduct the hearing and make his findings of fact and recommendations to the agency, which decides and issues the order.[53] Unless established by statute, his position is created by the agency itself to facilitate the performance of its statutory duties and may be abolished by the agency.

The proceedings at the hearings are formal, governed by rules which are applied by the trial examiner. He must apply these rules as they are interpreted by the agency, but he is responsible for the application of the rules at the hearing, and if there is to be satisfaction with justice as administered in the agency, his application of the rules should not be varied from case to case. The agency may itself change its policy, which may involve a modification in the procedure as it has been previously practiced; but the trial examiner has no such rule-making authority, and under the instructions of the agency he should apply the regulations as they are written and as they are interpreted by the agency.

The trial examiner must assure that ordered conduct of the proceedings before him which can only be a consequence of respect for him and his office based upon confidence in his impartiality and ability. He administers the oath to the witnesses. He must in controlling cross-examination follow the practice of his agency. He must rule on the objections to the introduction of evidence that may come up at the hearing. It is also his duty in the interest of expedition and in the limitation of the record not to admit testimony which under the rulings of the agency is inadmissible. He must of course take into consideration the policy of his agency in respect to such evidence, for example, as hearsay and the way in which it may treat the rule of the best evidence, so that the record when it goes up will con-

[52] See Landis, *The Administrative Process,* pp. 104–105.

[53] The Longshoremen's and Harbor Workers' Compensation Act sets up an exception. The deputy commissioner who conducts the hearings prepares findings and makes an order, which is effective unless modified or disapproved by a district court. 33 U.S.C. §921.

tain the information which should be before the agency in the form suited to its uses.

The trial examiner's function in regard to the evidence is not wholly that of a moderator at the hearing. He should get into the record all the facts which the agency should have in order to come to a just decision. He has to consider not so much what evidence should be excluded as that there should be in the record enough competent testimony on which the agency can base its findings. This duty makes difficult the exercise of his power to exclude redundant or incompetent evidence upon which depends keeping the record within reasonable bounds. He will be inclined to admit testimony where there is doubt and let the agency decide whether it is incompetent. If he should erroneously exclude evidence, his ruling is subject to an order by the agency to reopen the hearing and admit the excluded testimony. If he admits the evidence, however, the agency may hold it incompetent and strike it from the record. Even if it remains in the record, no harm will be done if it is not used to sustain the findings. The Supreme Court has said that the "mere admission by an administrative tribunal of matter which under the rules of evidence applicable to judicial proceedings would be deemed incompetent does not invalidate its order."[54]

The trial examiner's task as already indicated is not merely to let counsel present the evidence and then to decide whether or not it is admissible. He must if he thinks it necessary urge them to bring in other evidence or strengthen the evidence upon certain points so that the record will not be deficient when it is presented to the agency for final decision. In connection with this duty he should have the power to issue subpoenas. Even in matters involving contests over private rights it is part of the function of the trial examiner to see that the

[54] *United States* v. *Abilene & So. Ry. Co.*, 265 U.S. 274, 288 (1924). "Ordinarily the admission of incompetent testimony cannot be assigned as error in a proceeding of this kind, because the court is only concerned with the question whether there is any competent testimony to support the findings of the commission." *Hills Bros.* v. *Federal Trade Commission*, 9 F. 2d 481, 484 (C.C.A. 9th, 1926).

case of a party who is not well represented is fairly and fully presented. For example, the deputy commissioner in compensation proceedings often questions witnesses to bring out testimony favorable to
the injured employee.

The trial examiner must rule on amendments to the complaint or
other pleading which initiated the formal proceedings where the
amendments are introduced during the hearings, and at the close of
the hearing he must pass on a motion, which is frequently made, to
conform the pleading to the evidence. Especially in disciplinary matters, this step taken at the close of the hearing is of importance.

The responsibility of the trial examiner in most of the agencies
does not end with his conduct of the trial and seeing to it that a
proper record is made. Under the Longshoremen's and Harbor Workers' Compensation Act the deputy commissioner himself makes an
order to take effect if not changed on appeal and prepares the findings to support it. While trial examiners have no such authority, the
function which they often have of making suggested findings and
recommendations is only a degree less important, for except in difficult cases the findings and recommendations of the trial examiner
are usually accepted by the agency in making the order which dis-
poses of the case and the findings to sustain it.

It is important that the trial examiner exercise this function. No
one else in the agency will have the same understanding of the case
which he should have acquired. He has presided at the trial, so that
he has had the advantage not only of hearing the witnesses but of
noticing their demeanor on the stand and their willingness or unwill-
ingness to make answers. If there is conflicting testimony, he has
heard the witnesses on each side and therefore will have an opinion
as to who should be believed, based not only on what the witness actually said but upon the way he said it and his openness on the stand.
He has had to control cross-examination and has had to pass on the
admission of documentary evidence. He has ruled on motions to
amend the pleadings in order to have the issues conform to the evidence submitted at the trial, and he has ruled on other amendments

to the pleadings and other motions which may have been made in the course of the hearing. His estimate of the weight of the evidence and of what has been proved in the course of the hearing as expressed in his findings and conclusions is an important part of the procedure.

The issues may be more sharply defined and better developed if the trial examiner considers the briefs of counsel and the findings suggested by them, and hears argument. A similar advantage should come from the trial examiner's review of his tentative findings and recommendations in the light of criticism of the counsel on both sides.

The trial examiner should be independent of the legal staff of the agency, which has advised that the complaint should issue, which has prepared the complaint, and which conducts the case for the government at the hearing, thus separating as far as possible the prosecuting and the judicial functions of the agency. In conducting hearings and in the preparation of his reports the trial examiner should be treated as carrying on a judicial function and should have no other relation with the counsel for the government than with the counsel for private parties. He should be influenced by the law officers of the agency only as he would be influenced by the arguments of any lawyer and should deal with them during the hearing in the same way in which he deals with counsel for private parties. This principle is widely recognized.

The Federal Communications Commission has gone far in making its formal procedure less judicial. It has abolished the separate division of trial examiners under a chief examiner who was responsible directly to the Commission. The officer who now conducts the hearings is a member of the legal staff appointed by the general counsel. The change away from judicial procedure at the hearing is made evident by the fact that the attorney who prepares the case and represents the view of the Commission as against the applicant may be appointed to hold the hearing.[55] If the case is complicated two

[55] Monograph of the Attorney General's Committee on Administrative Procedure, Sen. Doc. No. 186, 76th Cong., 3rd Sess. (1940) pt. 3, p. 23.

persons "are selected to represent the Commission," one as presiding officer and one as Commission attorney. The purpose of the hearing, however, is to bring out the facts which will be needed to guide the Commission as an administrative body in making its decision, and the selection as presiding officer of the attorney who has prepared the case would not seem appropriate for the preparation of a record which would give fairly the position of the applicant or of other stations which might be intervenors. As the presiding officer is more an administrative officer holding a hearing as part of the administrative task of advising the Commission, it is quite logical that he does not make findings or conclusions or recommendations and that, instead of the report which was formerly given to the parties as a basis for their exceptions and argument before the Commission, he simply sends a confidential memorandum to the Commission, together with the record of the hearing, to be treated as only one of the memoranda on which the Commission will base its action.[56] There has appeared certain justification for specialization by the officers who conduct hearings in the fact that "the general counsel has discovered that some attorneys are particularly capable of handling the functions of presiding officer."[57]

An argument can be made for this change so far as it affects station permits and licenses on the ground that these proceedings are not of a disciplinary nature. The government is not proceeding against a

[56] The change has been adversely criticized. Louis G. Caldwell, first general counsel to the Federal Radio Commission, has said of the former system: "But the system was fundamentally all right. It had the merit of segregating the Commission's judicial function from its prosecutor function to a fair degree and of narrowing the issues to those really in controversy, so that the Commission was relieved of burdensome detail. The initial decision was made by a man who was present throughout the hearing, heard the witnesses and observed their demeanor. The system placed issues squarely in the lap of the Commission so that they had to be decided instead of being side-stepped." Comments on the Procedure of Federal Administrative Tribunals, with Particular Reference to the Federal Communications Commission, 7 *Geo. Wash. L. Rev.* 740, 767 (1939).

[57] Monograph of the Attorney General's Committee on Administrative Procedure, Sen. Doc. No. 186, 76th Cong., 3rd Sess. (1940) pt. 3, p. 29.

person not conforming to the law but is getting the information to enable it to determine whether or not a license should be granted. This difference, however, does not affect the judicial function of the Commission in so far as it is preparing a record for a court appeal, so that the same arguments which can be made for the judicial character of the hearings in other agencies can be made in these cases. If other station owners intervene, then the matter becomes one in which there is a controversy between private parties as well as a public question, and the Commission is making a record upon which under the statute an interested party disappointed by the order may appeal. It is in the interest of the parties, as well as of the Commission itself, to have an impartial trial officer sit in the hearing at which the record is made up.

The officer who is to carry the important function of trial examiner should be a well-trained and competent person who knows the practice of his agency, for he is bound by its policies and by its instructions. He must also have in mind many points of law. Questions whether the evidence shows that the subject matter of the controversy is within the terms of the statute—for example, whether a labor practice affects interstate commerce, whether a business practice is an unfair method of competition, or whether an employee was injured in the course of his employment—should be in the mind of the trial examiner. In cases under the Perishable Agricultural Commodities Act, where the principal questions involve quality of the product and the facts of delivery, questions of the law of agency, of the interpretation of contracts, of the statute of frauds may arise.

New trial examiners in the offices of the National Labor Relations Board in Washington are trained for a period of four to six weeks before being assigned as examiners to hearings. After a reading course of about three or four weeks, they are assigned to sit with experienced examiners for a number of hearings, after which they are assigned to the simple hearings in the usual representation cases. The Interstate Commerce Commission also has a special training course for its examiners—in the rules of the Commission, its policies, its treatment of evidence, its procedure of carrying on a hearing, and in preparing findings and reports.

Dean Landis has made a valuable comment on the training and function of trial examiners. Referring to the Securities and Exchange Commission he says:

The adequate development of these staffs would provide judges who have, as they should have, an understanding of the general policy of the administrative, indeed a proper bias toward its point of view, and yet, by having been entirely disassociated with the earlier phases of the proceeding, have no personal interest in its outcome. Today trial examiners' staffs on the whole have too little competence. The reasons for this are many, but one of the most outstanding springs in many agencies from the rigid requirements of civil service rules, rules which, in defiance of the administrative's own desires, place these important individuals within a classification that entitles them to a salary of only $4,600 a year. It is impossible to expect for that price those qualities that are necessary to make a good trial examiner—experience in the disposition of business and wide knowledge of the field of regulatory activity. Because of these limitations, the Securities and Exchange Commission was led not to use its regular trial examiners for the conduct of difficult cases but to hire outside experts for that purpose, or to assign a lawyer in the General Counsel's office to a particular proceeding. Both of these devices had their virtue but, at the same time, failed to promote the building of a permanent judicial force.[58]

The importance of the trial examiner is emphasized in the *Final Report of the Attorney General's Committee on Administrative Procedure*. It says that "these officials should be men of ability and prestige, and should have a tenure and salary which will give assurance of independence of judgment," and urges that they be appointed for terms of seven years and "be removable only upon formal charges of fraud, neglect of duty, incompetence, or other impropriety."[59] The Committee suggests a method of appointment and removal which, in its opinion, would tend to secure competent trial examiners and protect their independence. The Committee recommends that each

[58] Landis, *The Administrative Process*, pp. 103–105.
[59] Sen. Doc. No. 8, 77th Cong., 1st Sess. (1941) p. 46.

agency nominate trial examiners and that the appointments be made from the nominees by the Office of Federal Administrative Procedure, the creation of which it recommends.[60] A trial examiner would be subject to removal from office only on charges and by a trial board composed of the members of the Office of Federal Administrative Procedure who may "delegate the conduct of the hearing to the Director of the Office sitting with two other persons designated by the members of the Office. Charges might be presented either by the agency concerned or by the Attorney General of the United States acting upon complaint made by private persons and believed by him to be well founded."[61]

A further protection of the independence of the trial examiners as judicial officers is incorporated in the suggestion that in agencies employing five or more trial examiners the agency should designate one of them as chief, who should assign the examiners to sit in particular proceedings. The Committee believes that its recommendations "would insure internal but nevertheless real and actual separation of the adjudicating and the prosecuting or investigating functions."[62]

Hearing before Agency

In the great majority of cases it is on the record made before a trial examiner that the case comes to the agency for decision. Occasionally, however, the head of the agency may hear a case which in its opinion is of unusual importance. The Act setting up the Federal Communications Commission expressly provides that the agency itself must hold hearings upon cases involving certain questions, such as that of a change of policy.[63] The National Labor Relations Board

---

[60] This office would be composed "of a director to be appointed by the President and confirmed by the Senate; an associate justice of the United States Court of Appeals for the District of Columbia designated by the chief justice of that court; and the Director of the Administrative Office of the United States Courts, who is appointed by the Supreme Court of the United States." *Ibid.*, p. 47.

[61] *Ibid.*, p. 49.   [62] *Ibid.*, p. 55.

[63] The same is true in cases involving the revocation of a station license, new devices or developments in radio, or a new kind of use of frequencies. 47 U.S.C. §409 (a).

has "on occasion" exercised its power of hearing a case itself or of taking it away from the trial examiner at some stage of the proceeding.[64] This procedure may secure the quick action which may be needed to prevent an open labor disturbance.

When the agency acts on the record made before the trial examiner it tends to resemble an appeal tribunal. Indeed, it has been said that the trial examiner is in a real sense "becoming a lower administrative tribunal" and that the agency "is itself in fact, if not in theory, becoming a tribunal of second instance."[65] The record, together with the recommendations of the trial examiner, goes to the agency, where it is considered by the agency's lawyers and technical officers, who report upon it to the agency. It may be referred in an agency headed by a board or commission to one of the members of the board or commission, but even here the help of his technical and legal staff may be important in his study of the record and the report, and his duty is to suggest action by the agency, which is the ultimate deciding authority.

The members of the board or commission which heads an independent agency have many duties other than that of exercising their judicial function. The task of studying the voluminous and some-

[64] Monograph of the Attorney General's Committee on Administrative Procedure, Sen. Doc. No. 10, 77th Cong., 1st Sess. (1941) pt. 5, p. 21, n. 93.

[65] Lane, *in* Symposium on Administrative Law, 9 *Am. L. School Rev.* 139, 154, 159 (1939).

Although this may be a convenient way of visualizing the administrative process, there are a number of important features which clearly distinguish the relationship between a lower and an appellate court from that between the trial examiner and the adjudicating agency. In the first place, no sanction attaches to the findings, recommendations, or proposed order of the trial examiner, as in the case of a judgment or decree of a court of the first instance.

Secondly, the statutes specify the grounds upon which an appeal may be taken from a lower to an appellate court. Should a party be unable to bring himself within these grounds, the judgment of the lower court becomes the final step of the court proceeding. In administrative proceedings, however, the trial examiner's report is never more than advisory to the head of the agency.

Finally, the lower court, although a part of the judicial hierarchy, exists by virtue of legislative enactment and is independent of its appellate court. Such independence the trial examiners do not have.

times technical records is heavy, for one of these records may extend to a thousand pages and more.[66] To search through this great mass of testimony to determine what facts it proves so that the case can be decided fairly, even with the aid of the issues defined in the amended complaint or other pleading, would be a time-consuming task, so that the use of the trained lawyers and other technical men in the agency's staff cannot be dispensed with. They must also be depended upon for aid in drawing the findings and order after the agency has determined upon the decision. Dean Landis has commented on this point:

A further factor that makes against administrative adjudication having those qualities that it should appropriately have is that the members of an administrative agency rarely have the time and opportunity for thoroughly scrutinizing a record and coming to their own conclusions as to what it establishes. Their other functions may be so time-consuming that the actual process of adjudication is delegated, subject to only slight supervision.[67]

Memoranda from members of the staff are generally used by the agencies, and consultation with counsel and other staff members seems to be inherent in the system of administrative judicial tribunals. It has been sanctioned by the courts. In *National Labor Relations Board* v. *Biles Coleman Lumber Co.,* the Circuit Court of Appeals for the Ninth Circuit said:

It is obvious that such an administrative body, with scores of cases for its decision, many involving complicated questions of fact and often intricate questions of law, properly will rely upon its employees for assistance in their preparation. The administrative duties imposed on the Board by the Congress could not proceed otherwise.[68]

[66] Chairman Madden says that the average record before the National Labor Relations Board is over one thousand pages. Board members cannot read this amount of material, so a review attorney is used to analyze testimony and prepare the findings and order. Madden, *in* Symposium on Administrative Law, 9 *Am. L. School Rev.* 139, 144, 146–147 (1939).

[67] Landis, *The Administrative Process*, p. 105.

[68] 98 F. 2d 16, 17 (C.C.A. 9th, 1938). See also *Sanders Bros. Radio Station* v. *Federal Communications Commission*, 106 F. 2d 321 (App. D.C., 1939); re-

The Supreme Court also recognized the practical aspects of administrative law when it said in *Morgan* v. *United States:* "Assistants may
prosecute inquiries. Evidence may be taken by an examiner. Evidence
thus taken may be sifted and analyzed by competent subordinates."[69]

Oral argument, if requested, can usually be had before the agency.
Some statutes expressly confer the right.[70] It is only reasonable that a
party who desires it should have an opportunity to present to the
agency his analysis of the case and the conclusions which he draws
from it in this last effort to influence the agency. An agency cannot
help but profit from a presentation of a case by a competent person
who looks upon it from a different point of view from that of the
agency's own officers and counsel.

versed on other grounds, *Federal Communications Commission* v. *Sanders Bros.
Radio Station,* 309 U.S. 470 (1940).

[69] 298 U.S. 468, 481 (1936). The Federal Communications Bar Association
has protested against the use by the Commission of reports from its technical staff,
which are kept confidential, and requested that they be incorporated into the public record at the time of the public hearing. The Association also suggested that
the Commission might be aided by having counsel participate in the oral argument in case of a difference in opinion between the views of the law department
and those expressed by the trial examiner in his report. Federal Communications
Bar Association, Recommendations of the Federal Communications Bar Association on the Proposed Rules of Practice and Procedure, 3 *F.C.B.J.* No. 1, pp. 39–
40 (1938).

[70] Communications Act of 1934, 47 U.S.C. §409 (a). But cf. *Ullman* v. *Adams
Express Co.,* 14 I.C.C. 585, 586 (1908): "The act provides for the taking of testimony in these investigations by a single Commissioner or by an examiner. It is
probable that the Commission might, in its discretion, require the submission of
a case upon the testimony so taken and written briefs. However this may be, we
have never, in fact, yet refused, and should only refuse under peculiar and unusual circumstances, the application of a party to be heard orally. As above observed, the testimony in these investigations is often taken without the presence
of any member of the Commission. It almost never happens that a majority of
the Commission hear the testimony. The only opportunity which a party has of
stating his views to this body by word of mouth is upon the argument. The importance of these arguments is recognized, and they will ordinarily be allowed as
a matter of course. Application for such argument should, however, be made
when the testimony is concluded and not deferred as in this case, although here,
even, as soon as we learned that the parties desired to present their views orally
the proceeding was reopened and set down for argument."

Place of Hearing

The place where the hearing is held may be of importance. From the point of view of the private party it will usually be an advantage to have the hearing held near his home or place of business. Not only is the expense of a trip to Washington a consideration, especially to a person or corporation not having large means, but there is the added objection of the time which a trip would require. If it is necessary to introduce the testimony of witnesses the cost of transportation may be heavy, and it is often inconvenient to take records from an office where they may be in frequent use to a distant point. These factors were given emphatic recognition in *National Labor Relations Board v. Prettyman*[71] where the Circuit Court of Appeals refused to enforce an order of the Board on the ground that, in holding hearings in Washington with regard to the employer's practices in Michigan, the Board fell short of due consideration of the convenience of the employer and his rights under the statute. The need for adjustment to the convenience of the parties and their witnesses is met through the designation by the agency of trial examiners to hold hearings in various parts of the country. The place of hearing may be transferred from one point to another during the course of the proceeding, so that the evidence can be presented before the trial examiner in a formal hearing with full opportunity for cross-examination rather than taken on deposition.

The device of depositions is another way of making easier the taking of testimony, both on the part of the witness himself and from the point of view of the expense of transportation to the place of hearing.

Hearings on fraud orders in the Post Office Department are held in Washington, so that a person against whom a charge is pending must come or send his counsel to that city if he cannot settle the matter informally with officials. As many of the parties against whom orders are issued by the Post Office Department are not large and prosperous concerns, the expense involved in such a proceeding may

[71] 117 F. 2d 786 (C.C.A. 6th, 1941).

induce the parties charged to come to an arrangement, thereby decreasing the number of formal hearings.

In cases before the Federal Communications Commission, where the decision may depend on technical questions of electrical interference, it would be a burden on the engineering staff of the Commission if they were compelled to travel all over the country to hearings in different cities. These are reasons for holding hearings in Washington, and the use of depositions may make unnecessary the taking of testimony by a trial examiner on the spot, but there may be instances in which it would be a sufficiently substantial advantage to the parties to warrant the sending of a trial examiner to the field.

Appeals to the agency itself must necessarily be argued in Washington. It would not seem possible for an agency, with all the work which it must do, to spend much time in traveling about the country holding hearings on appeals, hearings which do not involve the taking of testimony.

Expert Staffs

Through the whole of the procedure, informal and formal, the officers of the agency have the great advantage of the help of expert staffs. Technical questions aside from legal may come up at almost any stage. The chemical analysis of a product may be the element upon which a decision will depend, and it may form the basis of a settlement before the hearing or convincing evidence in a formal hearing. Qualified accountants are essential in many of the agencies to advise upon the frequently highly complicated problems and to advise in respect to settlement of a question or to build up the case for formal procedure. The engineering staffs of many agencies, for example the Federal Communications Commission, are as essential to their functioning as is a legal staff; and in some agencies the use of physicians is necessary. Many agencies have also on their staffs economists, whose counsel may go beyond the immediate case and help to inform the officers of the agency or the agency itself as to the wider implications of a decision or of a settlement in the field of the social organization in the same way that a lawyer will advise in respect to the law.

Prior to formal procedure the agency may make use as it will of the facts as found by its staff and of their opinions, but when the matter comes to the formal stage it is met by the rule that its findings must be supported by evidence in the record. The memoranda of the technical assistants must therefore be given a more formal character and produced at the hearing, where they may be subjected to the criticism of the other parties.

The test of cross-examination should be applied to the conclusions of government scientists or engineers, as well as to those of private persons, in proceedings by an agency which is making a record and findings for the courts, and is even more necessary in checking the findings of experts in economic or social fields.

IMMIGRATION PROCEDURE

A procedure which indicates how an organ may be set up to carry on the judicial function as part of an agency itself within a Department is that created by regulation in the Immigration and Naturalization Service of the Department of Justice. So far as appeal is concerned, it emphasizes the distinction between the judicial and the administrative functions of the Immigration and Naturalization Service, including that of the prosecutor. Under the statute the Attorney General makes the final orders in respect to deportation or exclusion and passes on the fines imposed on carriers for breaches of the law; but under the regulations, before he acts the appeal must be passed upon by the Board of Immigration Appeals, which is not a statutory body but is set up by the regulations. The members of the Board have no relation to a case until the record is brought before them for their consideration, and they have no other duties than those of deciding cases, of regulating procedure, and of disciplining attorneys appearing before the Board or before any other officer of the Immigration and Naturalization Service. It has been suggested that the

Board be given statutory permanence, and the importance of its independence as a judicial body would justify the step.[72]

The other duties of the Service are vested by the regulations in a special assistant to the Attorney General, who has control not only of the field service but also of the services of the central office which are not part of the appeal procedure. As a consequence the Board has no administrative duties and no relationship to the preliminary investigations, the preparation of evidence, the issuing of the warrant in deportation cases, or even to the administrative hearing at which is made up the record which comes to it. It acts essentially as an appeal board, passing upon the record which has been prepared below with the recommendations of the administrative officers who have held the preliminary hearings. To aid the Board there is attached to its office a chief examiner and other examiners whose duty it is to study the records and reports which come from the field and to aid the Board in preparing its own opinions and conclusions. The Board thus has at its disposal a group of review attorneys whose work it controls and can supervise. The relationship is made more explicit by a provision that the chief examiner, in the absence of a member of the Board, may sit in his place.

In a deportation case the preliminary investigation is carried on by an officer of the administrative service who, if he feels the evidence justifies it, requests a warrant from the central office at Washington. This request is passed on by the warrant division in the administrative side of the Service. The issuance of a warrant is the first formal action. The warrant is served on the alien; it should contain the charges against him with sufficient distinctness for him to know the allegations which he must meet.

The next formal step in the procedure is the hearing before an immigration inspector in the immigration district in which the alien is held. It is at this hearing that the record is made up. Evidence may be

[72] Clark, *Deportation of Aliens from the United States to Europe,* pp. 387, 489; Van Vleck, *The Administrative Control of Aliens,* p. 247.

introduced by the alien. He has the right to counsel, important in view of his right to cross-examination of the government's witnesses.

After the hearing the findings and conclusions are prepared by the presiding inspector or, on the record as it goes up from the hearing, by one of the examiners attached to the Board. The presiding inspector is in a better position to make these findings and conclusions than is anyone else and for the same reasons which have been urged in respect to trial examiners in other agencies. It is especially important in deportation matters, where the evidence is so largely given by witnesses whose testimony may be sharply contradictory and where the impression made by the individual witnesses is so important. These factors can be given their true value only by the officer who has heard the testimony and cannot be as accurately assessed by a review attorney no matter how fair he may be.

In exclusion proceedings the first formal hearing is before a board of special inquiry appointed by the official in charge at the point of entry. The statute requires that the members of the board be selected from immigration officers in service designated as qualified by the Commissioner of Immigration. A permanent board may be maintained at the larger centers, but in other ports special boards may be created by the immigration official in charge.

At the hearing before the board of special inquiry the immigrant is permitted to have one friend or relative present. He may produce witnesses but cannot have counsel, so there is not likely to be effective cross-examination. If the board unanimously votes to admit, the immigrant is admitted; but if one of the members dissents he may appeal from the decision of his colleagues. The immigrant may also appeal if the decision is to exclude him. In case of an appeal the board of special inquiry sends up to the Board of Immigration Appeals the record with its recommendation containing a statement of the grounds on which it advises exclusion but without findings of fact or conclusions.

As in other appeal tribunals, the hearing by the Board both in de-

portation and in exclusion cases is on the record, although in deportation cases new documentary evidence may be incorporated into the
record unless such new evidence needs investigation in the field, in
which case it may be sent back for a reopened hearing. In exclusion
cases, however, the statute requires that the decision of the Attorney
General "shall be rendered solely upon the evidence adduced before
the board of special inquiry."[73] Consequently the case must be returned to the board of special inquiry for taking of new evidence going to the legal admissibility or inadmissibility of the alien.

The Board of Immigration Appeals is required to file its findings
and conclusions with its opinion. In deportation cases it may adopt
the findings and conclusions of the presiding inspector, either as they
come up or as modified by its examiners, or prepare its own. It may
approve or reverse the order of the board of special inquiry. The
decision, however, and the adoption of the findings and conclusions
on which the Board bases its decision must be acts of the Board.[74]

It is the Attorney General who under the statute has the responsibility of making a final decision, but in practice the Board's decision
is final in most cases. The Board refers to the Attorney General cases
in which there is dissent or in which suspension of deportation is ordered. It may also refer other cases of difficulty and must send up
any case at his direction. The alien has no right of appeal, nor has he
a right to make an argument before the Attorney General. The principle, however, that the alien shall be informed of the reasons for the
action taken, is maintained in the requirement in the regulations that
the Attorney General, if he disagrees with the action of the Board,
must state in writing his conclusions and the reasons for his decision.

Under the procedure outlined in the new regulations[75] the alien
will always be informed of the grounds for the order against him,
and the record on which he must make his argument before the

[73] 8 U.S.C. §153.

[74] The Board also hears appeals in cases on penalties imposed on carriers for
breaches of the immigration acts.

[75] The regulations are contained in 6 Fed. Reg. 65-73 (1941).

Board is open to him. The Board at the hearing has the advantage not only of the findings and conclusions of the trial inspector but also of the criticisms of its examiner and the exceptions of the alien with the reasons therefor. Even if the Board, on reviewing a proposed order to which no exceptions have been taken, makes up its mind that the order should be more rigorous against the alien than that proposed, it is required to make findings and conclusions to support its modifications and to serve them on the alien and then, if he requests it, to give him a hearing after he has had an opportunity to file his exceptions.

There is in immigration proceedings an interesting use of technical experts. The Public Health Service details officers to the ports to examine immigrants for physical or mental defects. The board of special inquiry is not bound by the opinion of the expert, though it may rely upon it; except that, if the defect is mental, the appeal from the opinion of the expert will go not to the board of special inquiry but to a special board of physicians set up by the Public Health Service, whose decision cannot be questioned by the immigration authorities. The decision of the board of special inquiry on a question of physical health, if based on a certificate of the health officer, is binding on the Board of Immigration Appeals.

The presiding inspector at a warrant hearing in deportation cases acts judicially. He not only presides at the hearing but has the task of preparing the record on appeal and should have that of making the findings and conclusions to be served on the alien. There is a strong argument in favor of his being a judicial officer subject to the Board rather than an inspector in the administrative branch. This is equally true of the presiding officer of the board of special inquiry in exclusion cases.

There would be an advantage, it would seem, in creating a group of trial examiners who could preside at all hearings, both deportation and exclusion, with probably special examiners for the difficult Asiatic cases. Members of such a panel could travel through the country holding hearings in different districts, thereby relieving the regular inspectors of a difficult judicial task. In larger ports a trial examiner could remain perhaps permanently as presiding officer of the board of special inquiry. If such a panel were created, the division between the judicial side of the immigration work and the administrative and prosecuting side would be much more satisfactory.

CHAPTER II. POLICY

THE formulation of the policies upon which it will act and the supervision of its staff to make sure that these policies will be carried out are essential activities of any administrative agency. In the statute creating an agency Congress expresses policies, which may be laid down in broad terms or contained in specific provisions. A particular statute may contain a policy expressed in broad terms—for example, that food be not adulterated, that workmen be assured the right of collective bargaining, that businessmen be protected against unfair methods of competition, that shippers be assured of equal treatment and reasonable rates—and it may contain also detailed policies which Congress intends to be applied to meet specific situations. Examples of this are the immigration acts, where in addition to the broad policies specific policies are included, and the Federal Food, Drug, and Cosmetic Act, where not only a general policy is set forth but specific situations are dealt with.

The administrative agency is created for the enforcement of these policies. Its affirmative task must necessarily affect all phases of its activity. Even when it is acting judicially, private rights cannot be its primary concern in the same sense that they are traditionally the primary concern of the courts. In the course of carrying out its task the agency must necessarily determine the policies under the Act which it will apply in its enforcement. This is important since the enforcement must be carried out through many subordinate officials spread throughout the country. If there is to be uniformity in the interpretation and application of the statute, the head of the agency must enforce the observance of its policies by its staff. It is the members of the staff who come in contact with individuals, and in the great majority of cases it is their decision which is final for these individuals.

A policy means more than the standards which are to be applied in dealing with particular cases. It extends to questions of how the agency will interpret its power, whether it will apply the statute strictly or liberally, whether it will endeavor to assume a broad control over the industry or the activity placed under its jurisdiction or will exert only the degree of control necessary to carry out the provisions of the statute narrowly construed. An agency may aim at certain purposes which it desires to accomplish and which it interprets the statute to include, and may use its power under the statute to accomplish them. On the other hand, the agency may be content to deal with cases as they are brought to its attention by opposing groups or by its own staff, and so develop its policy from case to case without setting up particular objectives.

Where the statute declares a broad policy the agency has a wide field for the exercise of its powers of interpretation, and even where the statute contains many limitations very different results will follow a policy of strict enforcement or of liberal interpretation. For example, a policy of strict or of liberal enforcement of the immigration acts or the Federal Trade Commission Act may make a great difference to the persons affected, whether or not there has been any explicit formulation of policy. In practice it is this broad policy which will be a major premise behind the regulations and the reasoning of the officials and staff of an agency, and it may often be unexpressed. Other policies less broad in character may find their expression in regulations or in instructions to the staff. The more situations these regulations and instructions can cover, the fewer will be the questions brought up to the heads of the agency for decision, the quicker and more uniform can be the settlement of cases by subordinates, and the more time the heads of the agency will have for the policy considerations with which they alone can deal.

Faced as it is with the positive task of administering a statute, an agency will inevitably be obliged often to modify its policies, both to meet new situations which arise and to meet differences of public opinion which come up from time to time. The broad policy of strict or liberal interpretation or the objects which the agency seeks to attain do not lend themselves to formulation, but will be modified with changes in the personalities who control them or under the influence of experience or public opinion.

In interpreting the broad policy of the statute the heads of an agency may be influenced by the political officers having the power of their appointment. In fact the heads of an agency may be appointed with the object of carrying out a particular policy. Where an agency is headed by an individual, and especially where he is the Secretary at the head of a Department, a policy may change when he leaves office; but in independent agencies headed by several persons, a certain continuity in policy can be assured by the system of appointments for staggered terms, so that there will always remain on the board or commission a certain number of experienced members who will be likely to permit change only slowly.

The broad policies determined by the agencies are not subject to check by technical standards, but in the making of regulations and standards for their staffs and in dealing with individual cases the agencies may need technical assistance. The heads of agencies are not usually experts, but by long service they become experienced in the many phases of the subject under their jurisdiction and they have the advice of experts on their staffs. In fact most of the important agencies deal with conditions requiring the aid of experts in several branches of knowledge, so no one member could be an expert in all the subjects which might come before the agency. It is the judgment of persons with experience in a particular field, rather than of experts in the various branches of knowledge involved in that field, that is important in the body which is to determine policies and enforce their application by subordinates. Where the policy is fixed by an individual, usually the Secretary at the head of a Department, he must rely on the experts in his staff for guidance to a greater degree than an independent commission, especially since he will have policies to make not in one but in many diversified fields.

There is a procedure quite generally in use for consultation with the public in the development of policies and the preparation of regulations. Experts or the heads of an independent agency are accustomed to consult informally with persons whom they regard as especially qualified in a particular field. It is not unusual to hold conferences of persons who will be affected by a policy under consideration—conferences which may be public or private—and in other ways to get the criticism of interested persons. When this procedure is followed the interested public will exert a certain influence at this early stage of the making of policy by the agency in respect to particular issues.

Thus, by a method resembling that of a congressional committee but with a technical staff which no congressional committee can boast, and with a concentration on one subject which is not possible for congressmen, an agency normally proceeds in making and modifying its policies.

Expression of Policy

The formal methods of defining the policy of an agency and of indicating its interpretation of the statute under which it acts are through its decisions, its regulations, and, in some agencies, the opinions of its counsel.[1] The policy of an agency will shape the orders made by the agency, and its judicial findings and opinions are a means of giving expression to its policy. They may form "an accessible collection of precedents by which its probable action in other cases can be forecast."[2]

The statements made informally by the heads of the agency or by policy-making members of its staff may foreshadow probable action on cases coming before it. Informal opinions and statements are likely to be more important in a new agency which has not yet developed a settled policy, but even in the older agencies they must

---

[1] The published decisions of the Department of the Interior contain numerous opinions of the Solicitor, which are occasionally cited in the decisions of the General Land Office.

[2] Henderson, *The Federal Trade Commission*, p. 105.

be carefully watched where the expression relates to a new situation or where it involves a reconsideration of a question believed settled. Dean Landis, formerly Chairman of the Securities and Exchange Commission, has graphically indicated the many devices employed by that agency in laying down its policy:

The most authoritative device is the Commission regulation. Another, on a slightly lower level, is the Commission opinion. A third is an opinion by the General Counsel of the Commission. The Commission can repudiate this opinion without getting into the embarrassing position of having openly to repudiate itself. This advantage, however, is more apparent than real, for when the General Counsel's opinion is issued to the public in the form of an official Commission release it has received, prior to its publication, the actual approval of the Commission. A fourth, an informal opinion of the General Counsel, has no such standing. For its quality is stamped upon its face by the concluding phraseology which declares that it represents merely the opinion of the General Counsel and should not be taken as an expression of the views of the Commission. It is commonly employed as a means of responding to inquiries. It receives no publicity nor is it normally a subject of discussion by the Commission as a whole or by any of its individual members. What weight the courts will give these various expressions of administrative judgment and practice remains to be seen. All have developed empirically in response to the needs of administration as those needs were viewed by that particular agency.[3]

Decisions

The policy of an agency may be developed through its judicial decisions. The case usually comes to the tribunal on a record made at a public hearing and already having a background of the broad policy as applied in the field. In its decision the agency can test the effect of its policies when put into practice and may maintain a

[3] Landis, *The Administrative Process,* p. 84. For an interesting statement of the point of view of the practitioner who must carefully examine all these items before advising a client or in the preparation of a case for presentation to the agency, see Caldwell, Comments on the Procedure of Federal Administrative Tribunals, with Particular Reference to the Federal Communications Commission, 7 *Geo. Wash. L. Rev.* 740 (1939).

policy already in force, modify it, or adopt a new policy. Where an agency decides a case on the basis of an established policy, it may refer to earlier opinions or to its rules, but if there is a new policy or an amendment of an old one there is much to be gained by the writing of an opinion.

One value of writing an opinion would be the clarification of the problems in the mind of the writer. The task of finding the reasons to serve as the basis of an order is an intellectual exercise which tests the validity of the course of reasoning that led to the decision. It may modify the first decision, and if it only strengthens the writer in his original opinion, it will at least have resulted in a public statement of reasons which will guard against a hasty and ill-considered change in policy in the future.[4]

The principle as expressed in a well-reasoned opinion will serve as notice to the public in the same way that a decision of a court expresses its policy in the interpretation or application of a statute.[5] When an administrative agency adopts a new policy or changes an existing one, the reasons for doing so should be clearly expressed so that the persons subject to its jurisdiction can know what has been done and so that the courts will be informed of the reasons for the agency's orders.

Another advantage of the use of opinions as a means of expressing the policy of the agency is the comparative ease with which a policy can be changed and the new policy expressed in a later opinion. The broad policy of the agency will affect the decisions in particular cases, and if that broad policy is changed it can quickly find its expression in new opinions written by men who share the new point of view and who can thus inform the public and their own staff of the policies which will in the future be applied. The burden of writing opinions in all cases, however, would be heavy and would

[4] See Frankfurter, Functions and Procedure of Administrative Tribunals, 12 U. of Cin. L. Rev. 260, 276 (1938).

[5] The Federal Trade Commission has been criticized for its failure "to write opinions explaining its rulings and analyzing the problems of unfair competition." Handler, Unfair Competition, 21 Iowa L. Rev. 175, 255 (1936).

not serve a purpose commensurate with the amount of time consumed. The agency should not therefore be required to write opinions in all cases, but it is part of its responsibility to determine whether its decision involves a new policy or a change in existing policy to such an extent that an opinion should be written.

The opinions of an agency should be published so that they will be accessible to the persons subject to its jurisdiction as well as to the members of the bar who practice before it. The published reports will not only be useful as a means of deducing the probable policy of the agency, but they will also act as a check on arbitrary decisions without depriving the agency of the latitude it must have in changing or modifying its policy. Furthermore, the influences which may be brought to bear upon an agency may be insistent, and the agency and its counselors may find the existence of a set of published reports in which their policies are contained to be a protection against suggestions of interested parties to make exceptions in their favor.[6]

The publicity which comes from published opinions would serve the additional purpose of increasing the individual responsibility of the members of the tribunal and of the tribunal itself. They are subject to comment in the trade papers and, in striking cases, in the general press or the law periodicals—comment from which the agency could profit. Deductions of the general policy of the agency from the written opinions would also serve to inform Congress and the public, so that the agency could be checked if it were taking a path which Congress was persuaded should not be pursued. Publicity under our democratic system of government, with a free press and free access to Congress and its committees, is a means of checking powerful administrative agencies. Publicity through opinions is an advantage to an agency which is only too likely to be accused of using star chamber methods and of favoring certain interests or persons who have political support. Malcontents there will always be; the disappointed suitor is rarely satisfied with the fairness of the decision against him,

[6] See McClintock, The Administrative Determination of Public Land Controversies, 9 *Minn. L. Rev.* 638, 645 (1925).

but the best proof of the fairness of the agency and of the decision is the published opinion itself.

As a means of expressing policy, the greater flexibility of the judicial opinion as compared with the legislative regulation will be apparent where a policy is still tentative. The opinion, as has been noted, may be changed from case to case, but where the agency has acted legislatively, the question is whether it should not, acting in its judicial capacity, observe the regulation until the regulation itself has been changed by the legislative method. Especially if the regulation was made after consultation with the representatives of the industry affected it should be changed by the same process, with an opportunity for the industry to be heard again and for a careful consideration of the broad field by the legislative method rather than by a decision in a single case involving a particular state of facts. Hardships may arise in particular cases from the observance of this principle, but it may well be argued that a rule established by the agency through the exercise of its legislative power should be observed by the agency in the exercise of its judicial power, until there has been a change by the legislative method.[7]

But the policy of the administrative tribunal should not be as fixed by the rule of *stare decisis* as that of a court. The agency has rule-making or legislative power as well as that of judicial decision and can by the use of its legislative power change its judicial rule, a power which the courts do not possess. Sitting as an administrative tribunal, the agency should be able to modify the principles laid down in its earlier decisions. Agencies which write opinions sometimes cite them in later opinions, an indication that while they generally declare they are not bound by the rule of *stare decisis* they are influenced by their earlier opinions. They speak of "following" prior decisions, or regard them as "controlling," "decisive," "conclusive," or they speak of "distinguishing," or "overruling" their own cases. A point may be considered as settled by a prior case or a dissent based

[7] See *Arizona Grocery Co.* v. *Atchison, T. & S. F. Ry. Co.*, 284 U.S. 370 (1932).

on an existing precedent or written because the policy set forth in the majority opinion is considered by the writer as constituting an undesirable precedent.[8]

Rules and Regulations

A formal method by which administrative agencies make and express their policies is through substantive regulations.[9] These represent the result of the exercise of legislative power and, if so provided by statute, they may have the force and effect of law. The making of such regulations, the performance of the legislative function for supplementing or rounding out the statute, falls only incidentally within the range of this study.

However, formulation of rules and regulations through the use of the procedure employed in the exercise of the judicial function has been prescribed in some instances and has been recommended for use in a wide field.[10] A beginning in this direction was made in the Federal Food, Drug, and Cosmetic Act enacted in 1938. Under that Act the Security Administrator "on his own initiative or upon an application of any interested industry or substantial portion thereof stating reasonable grounds therefor, shall hold a public hearing upon a proposal to issue, amend, or repeal any regulation contemplated by" certain sections of the statute. There must be notice of the hearing. The notice must set forth the proposal in general terms and specify

[8] For information on the practice of the Interstate Commerce Commission in this respect, see Pittman, The Doctrine of Precedents and the Interstate Commerce Commission, 5 *Geo. Wash. L. Rev.* 543 (1937). For a discussion of *stare decisis* in the National Labor Relations Board and the Securities and Exchange Commission, see Note, Administrative Law—Stare Decisis in N.L.R.B. and S.E.C., 16 *N.Y.U.L.Q. Rev.* 618 (1939); and in the General Land Office, McClintock, The Administrative Determination of Public Land Controversies, 9 *Minn. L. Rev.* 638 (1925).

[9] As distinct from procedural regulations, *i.e.,* those concerned with the internal affairs and methods of the agencies. Frederic P. Lee makes a distinction in regard to substantive regulations between "legislative" and "interpretive" regulations. Lee, Legislative and Interpretive Regulations, 29 *Geo. L.J.* 1 (1940).

[10] Logan Bill, S. 915, 76th Cong., 1st Sess. (1939).

the time and place of the hearing, at which any interested party may be heard in person or by his representative. The order making, amending, or repealing a regulation or determining not to take action must be based on "substantial evidence of record at the hearing and shall set forth as part of the order detailed findings of fact on which the order is based." This order may be reviewed on the petition of any person who would be adversely affected by it to the circuit court of appeals for the circuit where such person resides or has a principal place of business, and the court may affirm the order or set it aside, in whole or in part, temporarily or permanently. The findings of fact are conclusive "if supported by substantial evidence." At the request of the petitioner the court may order additional evidence to be taken before the Administrator, but the court must be satisfied that this evidence is material and "that there were reasonable grounds for the failure to adduce such evidence in the proceeding before the Administrator." If the Administrator in his order refuses to issue, amend, or repeal a regulation, the court may direct him to take positive action in respect to such regulation, in accordance with the law.[11]

This procedure has been in effect only a short time, so that experience on which to base a judgment in regard to it is not available. But should it be successful—and there is no reason to believe the contrary—its success will not be a final proof that it can operate in a different field, or that it is necessary or desirable in other fields in which substantive regulations are made. Where a regulation involves a technical question, the method of informal consultation of the technical staff with private specialists[12] and final decision by the agency head, advised by the technical staff, would seem a quicker and more effec-

[11] 21 U.S.C. §371 (e), (f). A similar procedure for the promulgation of substantive rules in a narrow field has been provided in the Fair Labor Standards Act of 1938. 29 U.S.C. §§208, 210.

[12] This includes the public hearings conducted informally at which experts and interested parties testify and give their opinions, and from which, as contrasted with formal hearings, there is no direct appeal to the court.

tive method of preparing such rules, especially if they do not have the force and effect of law. For example, the rules of the Federal Communications Commission concerned with technical aspects of broadcasting applying to the whole industry, and the rules in respect to accounting promulgated by the Securities and Exchange Commission were the result of informal consultation by the technical staffs of the agencies with other technical experts,[13] and there would seem little to be gained by the formality of a public hearing and immediate court appeal. The court in passing on such technical questions would have to depend on the technical evidence in the record. Congress should consider in each situation which must be met by administrative rulemaking the advantages of the judicial procedure in comparison with those of alternative methods, for example, informal consultation by the staff and the heads of the agency with private experts and experienced persons and more or less organized conferences, whether formal or informal.

Consultation with the interests subject to its jurisdiction is an important part in the process of securing the information upon which to base the policies which an agency will enforce, whether through its decisions or through its regulations or instructions to its staff. Formal conferences have been used by some agencies, notably the Federal Trade Commission, as a means both of informing the agency and of making a record on which recommendations may be based. While recommendations resulting from such conferences are not binding, they are the recommendations of members of the industry concerned and, if approved by the agency, constitute an expression of its policy. These recommendations, however, have not the effect of a regulation. In a particular case in which the agency is acting judicially, the question must be considered anew and evidence submitted upon which the agency may make findings and an order.[14]

---

[13] Landis, *The Administrative Process,* pp. 41–46.

[14] Monograph of the Attorney General's Committee on Administrative Procedure, Sen. Doc. No. 186, 76th Cong., 3rd Sess. (1940) pt. 6, p. 31.

These recommendations, however, have a moral effect in securing voluntary compliance in an industry or branch of an industry, so that the need for taking legal action will be very much lessened.[15]

The extensive use of trade practice conferences appears in a report of the Federal Trade Commission: "Since the inauguration of this work (1919), approximately 200 industries have undertaken the establishment of trade practice rules under the Commission's auspices. These industries are varied in character, with membership ranging from several hundred to many thousand."[16] Henderson comments on the effectiveness of these informal proceedings by the Federal Trade Commission:

> It is interesting to note that the reports of the extra-legal proceedings known as "trade practice submittals" are invariably more illuminating, more judicial in tone, and more imbued with the scientific spirit, than are the findings entered in formal proceedings. Distinctions are more carefully stated, and arguments reviewed and disposed of. Again it may be due to the form of the report rather than to any flaw in the justice of the decision, but the usual impression is that the man who drafts the report of the trade practice submittal is honestly searching for the truth, while the examiner or attorney who prepares the formal findings seems often to be trying to merely win the case for the Commission. The business men who attend these meetings seem to have accepted them in the same spirit, and I have no doubt that the educational influence of a single trade practice submittal is as valuable as the coercion of a host of formal complaints and orders.[17]

Such conferences have advantages, except in particular cases, over the fixing of policy by formal judicial procedure. They are not limited to a special set of facts or necessarily to a single trade practice, but they permit discussion by an assembly of persons, experi-

[15] Federal Trade Commission, *Annual Report,* 1939, p. 127.

[16] Federal Trade Commission, *Annual Report,* 1927, p. 7. Kittelle and Mostow, A Review of the Trade Practice Conferences of the Federal Trade Commission, 8 *Geo. Wash. L. Rev.* 427, 449–450 (1940).

[17] Henderson, *The Federal Trade Commission,* pp. 243–244.

enced in the trade, meeting with officers of the agency who can view practices in the trade impartially and with an eye to the protection of the consumer as well as to the safeguarding of businessmen against unfair competition. The resulting conclusions will represent a broad view in respect to particular practices against the background of the course of business in the trade—the best basis for a legislative conclusion.

While research into the expression of policy by regulation has not formed part of this study, it may be suggested that with its organization and its long experience the Federal Trade Commission might be vested with power to make regulations having the force of law, following the precedent of the Food and Drug Administration. If the purpose were to make a regulation, the procedure of trade practice conferences might well be improved, the issues made more definite. The Commission would have to prepare a project to state to the conference, and the discussions would be pointed if those present knew that out of them might come a regulation which private persons would have to obey and officers of the Commission could enforce. If the statute gave such regulation force of law, the Commission could in a prosecution allege a violation of the regulation. Furthermore, Congress might provide that the findings and record on which the regulation was based could be admitted in explanation of the regulation when the matter was presented to the court.

Such regulations could be amended by the legislative method, but while in effect they should govern the action of the agency. There would be a rule to which private persons could point in dealing with the officials of the agency and in planning their own enterprises, but a rule which could be amended easily if need appeared. This very ease of change, however, would require that the rules should not be retroactive.

In other than exceptional circumstances the individual should not have to run the risk that a change of mind by the administrative officer or agency may result in a retroactive change in regulations to his disadvantage. Retroactive legislative powers in the hands of Congress have much less likelihood of abuse than in the hands of administrative officers or agencies not content with remedying their mistakes for the future only.

In a few instances Congress has imposed statutory limitations remedying these difficulties. Thus it has provided in the Securities and Exchange Act of 1934 that: "No provision of this Act imposing any liability shall apply to any act done or omitted in good faith in conformity with any rule or regulation of the [Securities and Exchange] Commission or the Board of Governors of the Federal Reserve System, notwithstanding that such rule or regulation may, after such act or omission, be amended or rescinded or be determined by judicial or other authority to be invalid for any reason." Such a provision accomplishes two results. It necessarily leaves the statutory rule unchanged and thereby protects the individual who chooses to rely on the statute rather than on the regulation. However, if the individual chooses to rely not on the statute but on the Government's own regulation (whether it is an interpretive regulation that erroneously construes the law or for other reasons is not followed by the courts, or is a legislative regulation that is *ultra vires*), such a provision also protects the individual up to the time that the invalidity of the regulation is determined either by decision of the court or by amendment or rescission by the administrative officer or agency, and further protects the individual against retroactive amendment or rescission of the regulation.[18]

The regulations would have advantages for the public. Persons whose activities are subject to regulation by the agency would have standards to guide them in carrying on their affairs and could lay their plans in advance with more confidence. In dealings with subordinate officials of the agency private persons could point to regulations having the force of law as binding the officials of the agency as well as the private persons and so would have a protection against any tendency to arbitrary action on the part of subordinates. On the other hand, subordinate officials would have the advantage in dealing with private persons that they could point to the regulations as limiting their authority to make allowances and as fixing for them as well

[18] Lee, Legislative and Interpretive Regulations, 29 *Geo. L.J.* 1, 30–31 (1940). For criticism of the work of the Commission, see Handler, Unfair Competition, 21 *Iowa L. Rev.* 175 (1936).

as for the private person a standard from which they could not vary. In the difficult task of maintaining discipline of its subordinates over so wide an area as that covered by the United States, the heads of the agency would be aided by the regulation in checking any excess of authority or any tendency to favor one or another private person contrary to the policy of the agency as expressed in the regulations.

Regulations having so important an effect would need to be based on experience and careful consideration by the experienced staff of the agency and by the heads of the agency themselves, and their formulation would have to be preceded by conferences with the persons to be subject to them. These conferences and consultations may help achieve two desirable ends which should improve the relations between the agency and the persons subject to its jurisdiction. In the first place, they serve as a method by which the agency can acquire that understanding of a business or social situation necessary to make effective regulations. In the second place, they are convenient ways of informing the persons who will be subject to the regulations of their scope and content and of the advantage to them of their observance. One of the best ways of acquiring this information in a new agency, or in an old agency in respect to a new situation, is by the "gradual process of judicial inclusion and exclusion"[19] through hearings of a judicial character. An agency should be slow in attempting to make rules and regulations covering its activities before it has had experience. Furthermore an agency is set up to administer a law, and where it discovers infractions of what it considers the policy of the law it must take action whether or not it has formulated a regulation covering a particular point. An agency therefore should proceed cautiously in formulating regulations, but when its policy is fairly established there are evident advantages in formulating it in a regulation.

CONTROL OF AGENCY

Under our democratic system these powerful organs of government are subject to control through Congress, the courts, and the Execu-

[19] *Federal Trade Commission* v. *Raladam Co.,* 283 U.S. 643, 648 (1931).

tive, and also by the force of public opinion, either the organized public opinion of the industries and the labor unions or that of disinterested groups set up to advance the public welfare. This last form of control would, however, be far less effective were it not for the procedure of Congress which permits a strong public opinion to be reflected in hearings before committees or in debates upon the floor. It is often public opinion working through such groups that starts the congressional action which may result in modifying the policies of the agency, either directly through amendment of the statute or indirectly through the power of the Senate to refuse to confirm appointments. Public opinion may move the President to exert his influence on the agency to effect a change for which there is public pressure. Public opinion may also have a direct effect on the action of an agency. Some examination of the way in which these various checks may operate is appropriate in a study of the procedure of administrative agencies.[20]

Congress

Congress, which has created the agency and has given it power, may limit that power or even abolish the agency. This is a control which is not likely to be exercised except in regard to a matter which has aroused a very appreciable public interest, but accountability to Congress must always be reckoned with by an administrative agency. This accountability may be effective, either in producing a modification of the statute or, more often, in affording a forum in which there may be public criticism of the agency directed definitely toward suggestions for changes in the statute creating it. Criticism in Congress of an agency may begin by a speech on the floor or by the introduction of a bill and become crystallized when brought before a standing committee at hearings on the bill in which the opponents and proponents of modifications of a statute administered by

[20] For a discussion of safeguards against abuse of the rule-making power of the agencies, see Comer, *Legislative Functions of National Administrative Authorities,* Chap. VI.

the agency may have an opportunity to be heard. The agency will also have an opportunity to appear at these hearings in defense or explanation of its own position or to support its own request for change in the law, so that the committee and the public may be informed of the arguments both for and against the proposed change. When the subject of these hearings interests the public the newspapers will report them and take part in discussion, which is likely to be more than a general criticism or approval of the agency and may be focused on specific changes in its policy. Interest groups will bring pressure to bear in respect to amendments dealing with specific questions with which the public is not concerned.

As a result of the hearing, not only will the committee, Congress, and the public be informed of the objections and recommendations of all sides, but the agency itself can gain an understanding of public opinion and of the feeling of Congress. This may induce it to modify its position or its procedure, because it realizes that it has been making a mistake or because it may feel that by making the change on its own initiative it may prevent a more stringent change by Congress.

The reputation which an agency has acquired, and its consequent standing with members of the committee who are particularly concerned with the subject of its activities, and with Congress generally, may influence the acceptance of proposals to extend its powers or to limit the control of the courts over it. For instance, many statutes extending the jurisdiction of the Interstate Commerce Commission were enacted because of the record of the Commission in the administration of earlier laws committed to its jurisdiction. As it established itself in the judgment of Congress and the public, its powers were extended broadly so as to make it far more important than the original body set up to deal with complaints of individual interests against the powerful railroad companies. Similarly, the statute extending the power of the Federal Trade Commission over deceptive acts and practices and false advertising was influenced by its standing with Congress. Confidence in the administration of the

Perishable Agricultural Commodities Act, for example, was registered by Congress in passing the amendment authorizing the Secretary to enforce orders under it through revocation of licenses of
marketing agents, in addition to the already existing method of securing payment by recourse to the courts.

On the other hand, the sharp criticisms of the National Labor
Relations Board and the many suggestions for amendments to the
Act, from both employer and labor groups, amendments which
would limit rather than extend the power of the Board, are evidence
that the Board, in dealing with the highly contentious field in which
it operates, has not acquired in the legislative or public estimation
the standing of the older bodies.

Congress is not limited, however, to consideration of amendments
to the statutes as the occasion for investigating the operations of an
agency. Congress, or either house, may at any time create an investigating committee. Since an investigation is usually carried on by
an appropriate standing committee, the creation of a special investigating committee is likely to imply dissatisfaction by Congress with
the standing committee. There is also the annual opportunity for
questioning the administration of the agency, either in principle or
in detail, through the hearings conducted by the committees on appropriations of the Senate and the House of Representatives. In
these hearings the officers and heads of the agency must appear and
submit to questioning, both as to their general policy and as to their
expenditures, and the amount of the appropriation may depend on
the result of the hearing, or a particular activity may be curtailed
by cutting or omitting the item in the budget to cover its expenses.

Another way of influencing the policies of the independent agencies lies in the constitutional power of the Senate to refuse confirmation of appointments. This power the Senate is more willing to
exercise in respect to independent agencies than in respect to appointments in an executive department, particularly in case of officers upon whom the President is entitled to depend for advice and
for the carrying out of his own policies. It is proper in such case that

the Senate should be unwilling to exercise its power to prevent an appointment taking effect. In the independent agencies, however, where the agencies are carrying out a policy of Congress laid down in a statute, the Senate is readier to express its own opinion and to refuse confirmation of persons whose points of view in carrying out the functions of the board or commission to which they have been appointed are not satisfactory to it.

The Courts

Over the policies enforced by administrative agencies the courts have little control. They may interpose a certain check in determining whether Congress in enacting the statute has declared a general or basic policy with sufficient definiteness to escape the objection against delegation of legislative power and, given such a basic policy, the courts may come into play for determining whether the agency stays within the policy fixed by Congress. In practical operation neither of these aspects of control is substantial, for the reason that the basic policy itself may be stated in very wide terms. In 1935 the Supreme Court held two congressional provisions invalid as not setting a sufficiently definite standard.[21] No subsequent developments have indicated whether the Court has reduced or relinquished its former requirements on the subject of delegated power, though the evidence is abundant that the Court no longer offers a substantial check against Congress in the formulation and enforcement of policy.

Hence, persons or groups dissatisfied with the substance of statutes must seek relief through amendments to the law, just as they must seek congressional action for any extension of the powers of the agencies. As the check of the courts on the substantive provisions of statutes diminishes, the importance of the work of the congressional committees becomes more apparent. It is before these committees that representatives of the different interests may urge

[21] *Panama Refining Co.* v. *Ryan*, 293 U.S. 388 (1935), and *Schechter Poultry Corp.* v. *United States*, 295 U.S. 495 (1935).

their points of view and suggest changes in the bill to meet their objections or accomplish the purposes which they have in mind.

The President

The President has great influence in making the policies expressed in the Acts of Congress setting up controls over business and social activities. If he opposes a new control or the extension of an existing one, he can through the veto practically make it impossible to carry out, and it is with his initiative, or at least with his support, that most of the regulatory statutes are passed. When a new agency therefore is set up the President will exercise great influence on its policy, and it will be his general policy as well as that of Congress that the agency is carrying out. His views as to the scope of the power conferred on the agency and the way in which it should be exercised will have great weight. He appoints and removes, though his power of removal may be limited. In appointing heads of agencies he will select persons in general sympathy with his ideas of what the policy should be; and his influence over his own appointees, both as Chief Executive and as the head of his party, will go far toward keeping them in line with his views as to general policy.[22] Public opinion is certain to influence the action of a political officer like the President, but as against expressions by groups he may rely on the approval of his point of view as reflected in his popular majority and in the mandate which he feels was given him by the electorate. In his appointments he must furthermore take into consideration the power of the Senate, also affected by public opinion or by its own view of public policy, to refuse confirmation of his appointments.

Where, however, the head of an agency is a commission or board with overlapping terms, especially if the terms are long, the President's general policy may come in conflict with that of the majority of the board or commission, and it may be some time after he comes into office before he has an opportunity to appoint a member of like

[22] Herring, The Federal Power Commission and the Power of Politics, 15 P.U. Fort. 223, 292 (1935).

mind with his own. If the board or commission be strongly entrenched with the public, it may well be able to maintain its own policies until sufficient new appointments have been made to change the majority of the personnel, or, where the President has the power of removal, he has exercised that power.[23] A discussion of the consequences of possible diversity of policy, even of broad policy, between the President and an agency lies outside the scope of this study.[24] Both are charged with the duty of carrying out the policy of the law as laid down by Congress, but notably where the agency is performing its judicial duty or a legislative duty such as rate fixing, it would seem that the agency should act with a full sense of its independent responsibility under the law.

It is of course impossible for the President to exercise supervision over the policies of the agencies except in a general fashion. He will not often question a policy to be applied to a particular situation or in a particular case unless the decisions of the agency would have an important consequence on a general policy which he is desirous of putting into effect.

Public Opinion

The agencies must always consider the force of public opinion as a check upon their activities. Under the aegis of free speech and press this country is well equipped with the means of creating and giving expression to opinion by spoken word and printed page. Through the publicity given to hearings and decisions and through the space given to important addresses by members of the agencies, there is presented to the public a large amount of evidence of what the agency is doing, upon which adverse or friendly comment may be based. The agency has the initial advantage that it was created to cope with what was considered an evil by public opinion sufficiently strong to cause Congress to act. But the public is rarely unanimous

[23] *Humphrey's Executor* v. *United States,* 295 U.S. 602 (1935).
[24] See *Report of the President's Committee on Administrative Management,* 1937.

in its opinion, and there is always on the other side a vigorous dissent which continues to take an active part in criticizing the agency while it is being tested by its accomplishments.

As times goes on and as the agency proves itself, as has the Interstate Commerce Commission, the opposition lessens or appears only sporadically and, where it is of consequence, is devoted to an attack on details of the law rather than on the agency itself. But during the first years of an agency the opposition will reflect in its attacks the bitter feelings which marked the fight over the passage of the original Act. As the agency progresses it sometimes arouses hostility among those who favored passage of the statute but who have become dissatisfied with its administration. On the other hand, many of its original opponents may as time goes on find it on the whole useful and, while endeavoring to modify the law to make it operate more to their liking, are inclined to defend rather than attack the basic statute and its administration. This democratic process of criticism and correction may find its final expression in the committees and on the floor of Congress, or it may be brought to bear directly on the agency and so effect a modification of its policy.

A recent example of the role which may be played by the public is in the watch kept on the Federal Communications Commission in respect to censorship. Although the statute expressly forbids censorship,[25] the Commission is sometimes urged to use its powers of indirect control over a particular station whose programs or advertising have aroused the indignation of a few or many objectors. When the dramatic Orson Welles radio program depicting the attack of the Martians in New Jersey caused such a commotion, the Commission was criticized for not having prevented the sketch from being put on the air.[26] However, when in response to another complaint the Commission designated for hearing the license renewal of a station which had carried Eugene O'Neill's play "Beyond the Horizon,"[27] there was a great storm of public protest and the designation

[25] 47 U.S.C. §326.   [26] *New York Times,* November 1, 1938, p. 26.
[27] 15 *Broadcasting* 22 (Oct. 15, 1938).

was withdrawn. Criticism by the public and the trade press of the Commission's action on program complaints finally caused it to appoint a committee to investigate the complaint procedure, and changes were put into effect as a result of the committee's report and recommendations.[28] How far strong expression of public opinion influenced the National Labor Relations Board to change its rule forbidding employers to ask for elections on bargaining units cannot be stated, but it must have had effect.[29]

General criticism will go only to issues, usually dramatic issues which attract the attention of a large section of the public, but there is a special public, more directly affected by the activities of a particular agency, which is concerned not only with the important questions of general interest but also with minor policies and with detailed regulations or rulings of the agency. This is the public which functions in trade conferences, directly consulting with the agency on the policies which concern it. The specialized press also must keep informed of the operations of the agency and is an organ for criticism and suggestion by its public, bringing to bear upon the agency the opinion of the interested professional or trade or labor union group.

Criticism of an agency may be unjust and may be founded on a mistaken notion of the nature of the powers or duties of the agency. There may be deliberate misrepresentation in statements pro and con and, instead of the criticism being an honest effort to point out mistakes in law or in procedure, statements and arguments on both sides may be so highly colored as to throw an entirely unfair light on what was done. This is inevitable in the carrying out of the process

[28] On February 27, 1939, the Federal Communications Commission announced that it would no longer issue temporary licenses to stations under investigation, that complaints would be handled more judiciously, and that informal complaints would not be revealed to the public until some positive action had been taken by the Commission, at which time an informative press release would be distributed. 16 *Broadcasting* 16 (March 1, 1939).

[29] Statement of Senator Robert F. Wagner to Senate Committee, *New York Times,* April 12, 1939, p. 18: "There is wide support for an amendment which would permit employers to petition for elections."

of informing the public by advocates rather than by dispassionate students and, where opinion on both sides of a question is heated, the advocate will get a hearing that may be denied to the nonpartisan expositor of the facts or the law, whichever side he may take in the argument. Unfortunate as may be the consequences of intemperate advocacy and partisan criticism, they result from that freedom of speech and of the press which, as the mouthpiece of public opinion, is an important means of informing and warning powerful agencies.

CHAPTER III. SANCTIONS

THE term "sanction" is sometimes used to include all methods of shaping unofficial conduct in order to effectuate official policy.[1] This chapter is primarily concerned with only a small part of that great field, those sanctions which are employed by federal administrative agencies acting judicially. In order to indicate the relative position of this part of the field, some discussion of other types of sanctions is necessary.

Sanctions That Are Not Part of the Judicial Function

Many extremely effective administrative methods of shaping conduct are better classified as nonjudicial, either because they are not based upon consideration of individual situations or because they lack the formality of final determination. Exhortation, education, and propaganda, for example, are nonjudicial sanctions frequently employed by administrative agencies as methods of effectuating official policy. In the administration of the Food and Drug Act "it is believed that more effective compliance with the law may be obtained by showing reputable manufacturers how to bring their products into conformity with its terms than by imposing fines or effecting seizures and confiscations after the violation has been committed."[2] The standards developed by the trade practice conferences of the Federal Trade Commission are made effective, in so far as they are effective at all,[3] largely by methods of exhortation and education.[4] The sanc-

---

[1] "These implements or remedies to effectuate policies can appropriately be called sanctions. . . . Sanctions, or the methods that exist for the realization of policies, may be thought of as constituting the armory of government." Landis, *The Administrative Process*, pp. 89–90.

[2] *Report of the Chief of the Bureau of Chemistry*, 1926, p. 20.

[3] See Handler, Unfair Competition, 21 *Iowa L. Rev.* 175, 253–255 (1936).

[4] Members of the industry are asked to sign an "acceptance" of the rules, but the acceptance is not considered to have any legal effect as a contract or otherwise.

tion is an appeal to economic self-interest. Official action is confined to indicating the danger, encouraging action to meet it, and providing advice, information, and procedure.

Intermediate and Final Sanctions

The chronological sequence of sanctions carries with it no indication of the point at which a sanction is actually effective. Mandatory orders, both prohibitory, such as the injunctions of courts and the cease and desist orders of administrative agencies, and directive, might be thought of as intermediate. Failure to obey such orders may lead to further proceedings and, finally, to the imposition of a fine or to imprisonment. But this, too, is in a sense merely intermediate. Enforcement, the ultimate compulsion, is not with the court or the administrative agency. The path, if followed far enough, may lead to an official physical power alone as the final sanction. All action short of this will then have a prospective character. But such orders, whether directives to act or to cease from acting, or to pay damages or a fine, or to suffer imprisonment, are personal and individual compulsion, in contrast to legislative directives which are general and impersonal.[5] The application is unmistakable, the compulsion in practical effect immediate, whatever the dispute as to the part played by the tacit threat of ultimate power.[6]

Court enforcement is provided by statute for the orders of most federal administrative agencies. Violation of a cease and desist order of the Federal Trade Commission is a criminal offense punishable by

[5] "What distinguishes legislation from adjudication is that the former affects the rights of individuals in the abstract and must be applied in a further proceeding before the legal position of any particular individual will be definitely touched by it; while adjudication operates concretely upon individuals in their individual capacity." Dickinson, *Administrative Justice and the Supremacy of Law in the United States,* p. 21. See also Fuchs, Procedure in Administrative Rule-Making, 52 *Harv. L. Rev.* 259, 263–265 (1938).

[6] Compare the declaratory judgment. "The display of force is quite unnecessary to give effect to the decision. The more highly organized a society becomes, the less occasion is there to display force in order to secure obedience to its decrees and adjudications." Borchard, *Declaratory Judgments,* p. 10.

fine and imprisonment, as is operation after the refusal of a license by the Federal Communications Commission or the use of the mails to distribute securities after the Securities and Exchange Commission has issued a stop order. Some agencies, like the National Labor Relations Board, even have to apply to the court for a decree before there can be punishment for disobedience. Still, it is wholly unrealistic to speak of the courts' decrees in these cases as the "real" sanctions. The thousands of cases where conduct has been modified to accord with the orders of the administrative agencies without any action whatsoever by the courts evidence the reality of the intermediate sanctions.

There are many methods of effectuating policy by direct personal compulsion which do not involve even a threat of ultimate official power. Economic competition with those whose conduct the government seeks to influence is one such method.[7] Publication of deviations from approved conduct, the fixing of standards which become, without official prohibition, the required standards, nonexclusionary licensing as a designation of fitness are tried and effective sanctions which depend wholly on the exercise of unofficial compulsion, since from them there is no further recourse to ultimate official power.

Inspection and Investigation

Formal intermediate sanctions are usually admonitory or minatory in character; but admonishment and threat are used earlier in the sequence of sanctions than the stage of formal determination,[8] and informal preparatory sanctions are of far greater import in actual effect than is formal action.[9] The inspection and investigation functions of

---

[7] "It is not without moment that the economic effectiveness of the resort by government to this device today disturbs private enterprise far more than the employment of administrative methods of regulation. Or, to put it concretely, the private utilities fear the Holding Company Act less than they do the Tennessee Valley Authority." Landis, *The Administrative Process,* p. 121.

[8] The Federal Food, Drug, and Cosmetic Act expressly provides for a written warning as an alternative to prosecution. 21 U.S.C. §336.

[9] Landis, in a plea for a study of administrative sanctions, makes no distinc-

administrative agencies, for example, are *per se* enormously powerful weapons for effectuating official policy.[10]

In so far as inspection and investigation are preparatory sanctions, their effectiveness depends to some extent on the effectiveness of the sanctions for which they are preparatory; but they are in themselves deterrents from or correctives of the conduct at which the subsequent sanction is aimed. The scope of the supervisory inspection power is

tion between directive and preparatory sanctions: "Not even a catalogue of the devices for enforcement is to be found, far less a knowledge of the fields in which they have been employed. The legislator must pick his weapons blindly from an armory of whose content he is unaware. The devices are numerous and their uses various. The criminal penalty, the civil penalty, the resort to the injunctive side of equity, the tripling of damage claims, the informer's share, the penalizing force of pure publicity, the license as a condition of pursuing certain conduct, the confiscation of offending property—these are samples of the thousand and one devices that the ingenuity of many legislatures has produced. Their effectiveness to control one field and their ineffectiveness to control others, remains yet to be explored. Why is it that the informer's share, the traditional device of an early New England civilization, has generally disappeared from the statute books but retains its full force and vigor in the field of customs enforcement?" Landis, The Study of Legislation in Law Schools, 39 *Harvard Graduates' Magazine,* 433, 438 (1931).

After his service as an administrator with the Federal Trade Commission and the Securities and Exchange Commission, Landis repeated his plea for a study of sanctions in practically the same words. Landis, *The Administrative Process,* pp. 90–91.

[10] For examples of this type of power see Securities Act of 1933, 15 U.S.C. §77h (e); Securities Exchange Act of 1934, 15 U.S.C. §78u; Federal Trade Commission Act, 15 U.S.C. §46; Interstate Commerce Act, 49 U.S.C. §13 (2); Communications Act of 1934, 47 U.S.C. §403. The provision of the Communications Act of 1934 reads as follows: "The Commission shall have full authority and power at any time to institute an inquiry, on its own motion, in any case and as to any matter or thing concerning which complaint is authorized to be made, to or before the Commission by any provision of this chapter, or concerning which any question may arise under any of the provisions of this chapter, or relating to the enforcement of any of the provisions of this chapter."

The constitutional aspects of this power will not be considered. See Handler, The Constitutionality of Investigations by the Federal Trade Commission, 28 *Col. L. Rev.* 708, 905 (1928); Langeluttig, Constitutional Limitations on Administrative Power of Investigation, 28 *Ill. L. Rev.* 508 (1933).

immense. It includes the operation of national banks (and, in fact, almost all other banks, since practically all are insured with the Federal Deposit Insurance Corporation), railroads and motor carriers, those engaged in shipping by water and by air, telephone and telegraph companies, many gas and electric companies, bituminous coal producers and distributors, liquor producers and dealers, producers and handlers of many agricultural products, issuers of securities, stock exchanges and stock brokers, commodities exchanges and brokers, and many others. Agriculture, through visits of the county agents, is widely subject to the same sanction and, while the county agents' duties are theoretically largely educational and hortatory, other methods are available and are used in the hundreds of thousands of cases of resettlement and farm loans and subsidies.[11] The personal lives of millions of people, in both their occupational and nonoccupational conduct, have become to some extent subject to the same type of sanction with the regular visits of the government relief investigators.

On the deterrent side, the investigation sanction includes the hundreds of thousands of businesses which are subject to food and drugs legislation and to the wage and hour legislation. The inspection or investigation for violation ranges from the considerable regularity of the sampling activities of the Food and Drug Administration[12] to the formal investigations of the Securities and Exchange Commission, where there is ordinarily substantial ground for believing that the law has been violated.[13]

There are of course great differences in the extent of inspection.

[11] Cf. the Reconstruction Finance Corporation, which exercises actual control of many businesses to which it has lent money, requiring agreement to permit "supervising influence" in return.

[12] For a description of these methods see Hayes and Ruff, The Administration of the Federal Food and Drugs Act, 1 *Law & Contemp. Prob.* 16, 25–26 (1933).

[13] Formal investigations by the Commission have been said to be "somewhat analogous" to grand jury proceedings. *In re Securities and Exchange Commission,* 84 F. 2d 316 (C.C.A. 2d, 1936).

Supervision of railroads becomes affirmative regulation and finally control. On the other hand, in some of its phases the administration of the regulations of the Federal Food, Drug, and Cosmetic Act involves little more than policing for violation.[14]

Even where an industry is not subject to a single supervision, the subjection of various aspects to the inspection of different agencies

[14] The nature of an industry may make continuous supervision difficult or impossible. Cavers, discussing the legislative history of the Federal Food, Drug, and Cosmetic Act, refers to this difficulty: "The committee was charged with the task of revising the existing law within the administrative framework created for that law, not to revise that framework, even though it were thought insufficient to provide complete protection for the consumer. The F & DA has been, by and large, a policing organization, acting after the event to detect violations of the law. The prosecution of violations in the federal courts is vested in the Department of Justice. The establishment of, for example, a system of licensing controls, vested in an administration with broad quasi-judicial and quasi-legislative powers, would, if feasible, greatly augment consumer protection. Yet the legislative experience of the bill as drawn clearly demonstrates that a more ambitious undertaking would not have been politically practicable. Moreover, it is questionable that the administrative and scientific problems inherent in any comprehensive licensing system in this field are as yet susceptible of solution." Cavers, The Food, Drug, and Cosmetic Act of 1938: Its Legislative History and Its Substantive Provisions, 6 *Law & Contemp. Prob.* 2, 6–7 (1939). However, experiment is made in the direction of regulation in this field by the recent statute which provides for temporary licensing of producers and packers after a finding by the Secretary that a product is injurious to health (21 U.S.C. §344). "Following any such finding of the Secretary, manufacturers, processors, or packers of such class of food are required to obtain permits to which are attached conditions governing the manufacturing, processing, or packing methods. The system is regarded as a form of emergency control and the permits are required under the Act only for such temporary periods as may be necessary to protect the public health. However, the Act does not mention any specific time limit. While the permit system is in effect no person may introduce or deliver for introduction in interstate commerce any class of food covered by the system unless he has in effect a permit. Permits may be suspended by the Secretary immediately if any of the conditions thereof have been violated. No preliminary hearing is required in view of the necessity for prompt action, but the holder may apply for reinstatement and a prompt hearing on his application therefor." Lee, The Enforcement Provisions of the Food, Drug, and Cosmetic Act, 6 *Law & Contemp. Prob.* 70, 89–90 (1939). Regular factory inspection is also provided in the present statute. 21 U.S.C. §374.

often approaches the same result. The trend is from policing to supervision. The absence of supervisory sanctions in some of the newer fields of federal action may be merely an indication that the steps taken are only the early steps in those fields.[15]

Sanctions in Informal Settlements; the Threat of Prosecution

It is impossible to separate the influences which lead to the informal adjustments by which so many administrative controversies are settled:[16]

in many cases the imperative voice of authority is not the most effective method of approach. Something more subtle, more in the nature of mediation and influence, with authority merely in the background, may be needed in the constitution of the modern state. A somewhat ambiguous form of official action—part service and part control, part executive and part judicial, part suasion and part command, part formal and part informal—may perhaps best perform that function; . . .[17]

In many cases no doubt all that is required to influence conduct is instruction, in many others, persuasion.[18] In most cases threat is in

[15] Cf. the developments in the field of relations between the courts and the administrative agencies, Chapter IV, "The Courts." The demand for increased effectiveness probably works together with increased confidence to bring about these changes in both cases.

[16] The informal settlement of controversies which might have led to formal hearings and the imposition of formal sanctions has been described elsewhere in this study. See Chapter I, "Methods."

[17] Freund, *Administrative Powers over Persons and Property*, p. 584.

[18] Apologists for the increase of administrative power tend to emphasize the elements of persuasion and education. See, *e.g.,* Gellhorn and Linfield, Politics and Labor Relations—An Appraisal of Criticisms of NLRB Procedure, 39 *Col. L. Rev.* 339, 345–346 (1939): "In the event that the Field Examiner is satisfied that the charge filed by the union has a sufficient statutory basis, the Board does not thereupon issue a complaint, with all the publicity that would be attendant upon such issuance. Instead the Field Examiner now privately suggests to the employer that he settle or adjust the case. It will not do to say, as has Senator Burke, that those suggestions are coercive in character. One would be naive to suppose that employers have typically during the past several years been cowed by the agents of the NLRB. The truth is that the suggestion to settle is offered as

the background as a potential weapon. Whatever the justice of the adjustments which settle so many more cases than the formal hearing with its safeguards for the respondent, this informal and preparatory sanction can be used with an effect that largely nullifies the respondent's formal safeguards.[19] Dean Landis, writing of his experience as chairman of the Securities and Exchange Commission, has given a striking estimate of its effectiveness and of the value of the protection afforded by the requirement of judicial procedure:

The ability to sell a substantial block of securities depends upon creation of a belief that that issue is, like Calpurnia, above suspicion. . . . The very institution of proceedings is frequently sufficient to destroy . . . [this]

an opportunity to escape some of the humiliating consequences of past and demonstrable wrongdoing, in the expectation that the prospects for future accord will thereby be brightened. That employers generally so regard the matter is evidenced by the fact that approximately eight out of every nine to whom the opportunity is given, grasp it. Roughly a half of all the charges have been settled in this manner before the issuance of a complaint. The value of these settlements as an alternative to strikes and the latter's attendant hardship and privation need not be discussed at any length here. Suffice it to say that these settlements, substituting persuasion for tests of strength in industrial warfare, represent one of the outstanding achievements of the administration of the National Labor Relations Act."

[19] "Another example, not from my own state,—it was brought in to me by an old client, where an insurance company had set up two absolutely valid defenses to an action on a policy for some $30,000. They had been told by the superintendent of insurance that if they did not withdraw those defenses and consent to judgment and pay the claim, their license to do business in that state would be revoked. The company was over 100 years old, and very solvent,—no question about that,—but it was in the troubled days of five or six years ago, and they did not dare to face the publicity of having their charter withdrawn or revoked,—their license revoked in that particular state, and they wanted to get my notion of their defense. I told them their defenses were very good if they could prove them. But they paid the claim rather than run the risk of administrative action. It later developed, so the client told me, that the chairman of the appropriations committee of that particular state, represented the plaintiff, and the appropriation for the department of insurance was then pending before the appropriation committee, and they could not get what they wanted unless this case was settled, hence the pressure on the insurance company." Vanderbilt, Functions and Procedure of Administrative Tribunals, 12 *U. of Cin. L. Rev.* 117, 120 (1938).

quality, for the Commission's allegation that some untruthfulness attends their registration is sufficient to create grave suspicion as to their merit. . . . Administrative adjudication in these cases is, to all intents and purposes, final. But more than this, the threat of initiating a proceeding, because of its tendency to assail the reputation of an issue . . . is sufficient in the normal case to bring about compliance with the desires of the administrative.

The significant power that is exercised by the administrative in these cases is in its capacity as prosecutor rather than as judge. . . . The initiation of a complaint is public. Of itself it is an attack upon the conduct of the respondent. . . . I advert to this power to prosecute primarily to emphasize the point that the charge of arbitrariness, which is commonly made against administrative action, usually appertains to the exercise of the power to prosecute rather than to the power to adjudicate. It is restraints upon the exercise of that power that in my judgment are of far greater significance than the creation of restraints upon the power to adjudicate.[20]

Chester T. Lane, General Counsel of the Commission, says:

If nine out of ten Commission orders never reach the courts for review, ninety-nine out of a hundred business problems presented to the Commission for solution never reach the stage of formal proceedings even before the Commission. If the Commission were stripped of every vestige of judicial power, the problem of administrative fair play would remain substantially undiminished.[21]

The serious effects of prosecution by the Federal Trade Commission, regardless of outcome, give the Commission an effective sanction in the threat of prosecution.

A complaint frequently heard among business men and attorneys who have had to do with the Commission, is directed against the injustice of a formal complaint by a governmental tribunal, publicly charging serious offenses against reputable citizens, and based merely upon a provisional

[20] Landis, *The Administrative Process,* pp. 108–110.
[21] Lane, *in* Symposium on Administrative Law, 9 *Am. L. School Rev.* 139, 154, 163 (1939).

and tentative belief that the charges may be true. The complaint is given to the newspapers and naturally attracts much attention. Many months later it may be withdrawn or dismissed, but the injury to the respondent's reputation has already been done.[22]

The danger involved in the unrestricted power to employ the threat of prosecution as a sanction is not confined to agencies dealing with issue of securities and false advertising, fields where many liberals justify vigorous and even unconventional methods of control. The charge is made that the Bureau of Marine Inspection and Navigation has used the sanction to coerce striking seamen.

· Representatives of unions assert that the threat of instituting proceedings for revocation or suspension of seamen's certificates sometimes is used to intimidate the men during a labor dispute. For example, union representatives maintain that supervising inspectors have told striking seamen that, unless they immediately went back to work, proceedings would be instituted that same day to determine whether or not certificates should be suspended or revoked. In the eyes of the representatives of the union the very imminence of the threatened proceeding may constitute intimidation to end a strike.[23]

The prosecuting function of administrative agencies is not unlike the function of prosecuting attorneys, and it may be objected that "reputable citizens" such as those for whom Henderson expresses concern ordinarily feel no fear of abuse of power by these officials. Nevertheless there are differences between the power of the prosecuting attorney and the prosecuting power of administrative agencies which tend to make the threat of prosecution in the hands of the latter in some cases a more effective sanction and one for which, if restraints are required, there must be different restraints.

Differences in effectiveness depend to some extent on differences in

[22] Henderson, *The Federal Trade Commission,* pp. 330–331. Cf. Monograph of the Attorney General's Committee on Administrative Procedure, Sen. Doc. No. 186, 76th Cong., 3rd Sess. (1940) pt. 6, p. 12; Handler, Unfair Competition, 21 *Iowa L. Rev.* 175, 252 (1936).

[23] Monograph of the Attorney General's Committee on Administrative Procedure, Sen. Doc. No. 186, 76th Cong., 3rd Sess. (1940) pt. 10, p. 11, n. 13.

prestige. The prosecuting attorney is well known, an individual, a familiar figure in his community. Administrative agencies, on the other hand, are impersonal arms of the federal government; their influence is nationwide; their prestige is backed by many ideas and ideals of government which may be in fact but vaguely related to the agency in question. Moreover, the local prosecutor is usually directly accountable to the local electorate for his acts, whereas the board in Washington is far more remotely accountable.

Restraints upon the use of the prosecuting power by administrative agencies are now largely internal and subjective. Dean Landis has said of them:

Checks upon arbitrariness here must lie within the administrative itself. . . . The nature of what those restraints can be, I have referred to before —professionalism in spirit, the recognition that arbitrariness in the enforcement of a policy will destroy its effectiveness, and freedom from intervening irrelevant considerations.[24]

However, even in the national field, controls somewhat similar to those experienced by the local prosecutor are possible. With a considerable degree of conscious effort, a critical attitude toward the activities of the National Labor Relations Board has been built up and its potential prestige impaired. The public criticism of the Federal Radio Commission and the Federal Communications Commission has demonstrably served to restrain these Commissions in a number of instances.

The restraints imposed upon the local prosecutor may lead often to the opposite extreme, to refusal to proceed against citizens who, though reputable, have broken the law.[25] In the national field there has been much more alarm over the possibility of unjustified exercise of power than over unjustified failure to prosecute violators.[26]

---

[24] Landis, *The Administrative Process,* pp. 110–111.

[25] On the question of discretion not to act see Freund, *Administrative Powers over Persons and Property,* pp. 135–139.

[26] Vanderbilt gives an interesting example of this alarm in the following passage: "Before the *Hoosac Mills* case was decided I was representing the receivers of a packing concern that owed $800,000 in processing taxes. If the tax were in-

But most of the "improper influences" to which administrative agencies are said to be subject work, in individual cases, in favor of nonaction rather than in favor of action. There are occasional accusations of political persecution, but usually the accusation of politics against the agencies in their active aspects is found, when analyzed, to be directed toward the policies sought to be enforced rather than toward the choice of prosecutions. It is rarely that one hears of interference by an "outsider" in favor of prosecution. The problem of the ubiquitous congressman[27] is not one of resisting his insistence that prosecution be undertaken, but rather that of meeting his protests against "persecution" of constituents. The determination not to act arrived at as the result of such improper influences, while it does not arouse public alarm, may have far more serious consequences for the public at large than a similarly influenced decision to take action.[28] Moreover, it is a determination which is not subject to the restraints on positive action, especially because it usually does not become public.

valid the concern might be reorganized, otherwise clearly not. The question of the constitutionality of the processing tax accordingly became pertinent. I began to look into the matter. Within a few days, first one lawyer, then a second, and soon a third, began to arrive from the West. Each had a brief to prove the unconstitutionality of the Agricultural Adjustment Act. Each placed his work at my disposal. Each declined to say how he had learned of my interest in the matter or whom he represented or why his own client had not taken action to resist the payment of the processing tax. One finally did ask me what I would do if I had a client subject to nearly thirty species of federal control. I looked out my window and did not answer him. In fact, I have not answered him yet. I am, however, tremendously impressed by the fact that astute counsel permitted their clients to pay taxes running into hundreds of millions of dollars when they were convinced that the tax was unconstitutional." Vanderbilt, Functions and Procedure of Administrative Tribunals, 12 *U. of Cin. L. Rev.* 117, 144 (1938).

[27] For a condemnation of the activities of congressmen and other government officials in representing clients before official bodies, see Report of the Special Committee on Administrative Law, *Reports of Amer. Bar Assoc.,* vol. 61, pp. 720, 785–794 (1936). See also Landis, *The Administrative Process,* pp. 101–103.

[28] For the unfortunate effects of nonaction in the field of national power policy see Herring, The Federal Power Commission and the Power of Politics, 15 *P.U. Fort.* 223, 292 (1935).

The persistent (and financially able) defendant, of course, generally has his recourse to the courts for what it may be worth. And it is in this connection that both the strength and weakness of the sanction of threatened prosecution become most striking.

Landis states of the Securities and Exchange Commission that until 1938, despite the issuance of hundreds of stop orders, no effort had yet been made to review in court the Commission's issuance of any such order, and that in practically no case which "concerned a security issue sponsored by leading and assumedly reputable underwriters has there as yet been even the initiation of a stop order proceeding."[29] The history of the Federal Trade Commission is one of considerable unfriendliness toward the Commission at the hands of the courts, and many of its decisions were refused enforcement by the courts during its early period. But the danger to reputable citizens noted by Henderson continued throughout that period, and the Commission was effective in securing without prosecution thousands of agreements to desist from practices which were disapproved.

In spite of this situation, the weakness of the sanctions of both the Federal Trade Commission and the Securities and Exchange Commission has been the subject of repeated comment.[30] The sanction of threatened prosecution, whether before an administrative tribunal or a court, is ordinarily effective *only* with reputable citizens, only with those whose personal or business reputation is a valuable asset to be preserved, even, it may be, at the expense of what is conceived of as suffering an injustice. The weakness of the sanction lies in its ineffectiveness with the fly-by-night, the persistently crooked, the disreputable. It is of firms of this type that the Food and Drug Administration says:

Not infrequently firms are encountered which repeatedly violate the law, paying the fines imposed under this section whenever shipments are apprehended by the Department and legal proceedings brought, but appar-

[29] Landis, *The Administrative Process*, p. 108.
[30] "It is the weakness of the sanctions yet devised that threatens rather than their effectiveness." Landis, *The Administrative Process*, p. 119.

ently regarding those penalties as in the nature of a license fee for doing an illegitimate business. While firms of this character do not persist in business indefinitely, a more positive deterrent effect would be insured if more severe financial penalties could be imposed.[31]

In cases of this kind the threat of prosecution must depend for its effect upon the officially imposed sanctions which will result from the prosecution. If these are ineffective, the administrative agency will be strong against the reputable and weak against the disreputable. This, together with the instances where opposition aroused by the powerful can lower the prestige of the agency, is the point at which ineffectiveness becomes threatening.

It is with these sanctions that this chapter is primarily concerned, administrative sanctions which are ordinarily or traditionally imposed after a prosecution which is similar in its elements to the procedure used by courts in prosecutions. In considering this narrower field, the wider use by the same agencies and the greater effectiveness in many instances of the sanctions which do not involve judicial procedure must be kept in mind.

Administrative Judicial Sanctions

The most familiar sanctions imposed by courts are the criminal sanctions, ordinarily fine or imprisonment, and the civil sanction of damages. The major basis for this classification is the procedure by which sanctions are imposed, rather than the actual effect of the sanctions; but to some extent the classification also reflects the char-

---

[31] *Report of the Chief of the Food and Drug Administration,* 1931, p. 4.

Cf. Holmes, The Path of the Law, 10 *Harv. L. Rev.* 457, 461 (1897), reprinted in *Collected Legal Papers* (1921), pp. 167, 173: "Take again a notion which as popularly understood is the widest conception which the law contains—the notion of legal duty, to which already I have referred. We fill the word with all the content which we draw from morals. But what does it mean to a bad man? Mainly, and in the first place, a prophecy that if he does certain things he will be subjected to disagreeable consequences by way of imprisonment or compulsory payment of money. But from his point of view, what is the difference between being fined and being taxed a certain sum for doing a certain thing?"

acter of the sanction. Administrative agencies use judicial procedure for a much greater variety of sanctions than are traditionally available to the courts. The classification of these into criminal and civil or punitive and nonpunitive does not reflect the procedure followed by the administrative agencies to nearly the extent that it does in the case of the courts. However, because of the traditional and fortuitous elements in the procedure of administrative agencies, the classifica tion of sanctions in part along more or less traditional lines is useful.

Administratively imposed individualized sanctions are classified for subsequent discussion in two main groups: A, sanctions upon specific individual conduct, and, B, generalized sanctions.

A. In the first group are (1) penalties and rewards for the specific conduct involved, including imprisonment, deportation, fines, penalty taxes, monetary rewards, withdrawal of benefits, formal threat of prosecution, publicity, and withdrawal of license; (2) prescription of action, including prevention and commands to perform or cease from performing specified acts; and (3) reparational awards.

Certain punitive sanctions, which are classified under type 1, also incidentally prevent the individual against whom they are directed from repeating his offense. The withdrawal of the privilege of contracting with the government under the Walsh-Healey Act is primarily a punishment for violation of its provisions for wages, hours, and conditions of labor in the performance of government contracts, but incidentally it prevents repetition of the offense. When an owner of a steamship who has violated the provisions as to transportation of aliens is denied the privilege of transporting aliens, he is being punished for his illegal act but is also being prevented from further action of this type. Most instances of revocation or suspension of a required license, as well as those of refusal to renew such a license where the refusal is based upon disapproval of past conduct, are punishments which are also preventive. To be distinguished from these sanctions are those which are primarily designed to prevent the doing of a disapproved act or the pursuit of a disapproved course of conduct. Many sanctions classified as preventive have aspects of punishment, particularly from the point of view of the individual against whom the action is taken, though from the point of view of society as a whole prevention is the main purpose and punishment is merely incidental.

Most sanctions of type 2 are "enforced" by further sanctions in the form of punishment for failure to perform the acts directed. When the administrative action is reparational (type 3), further sanction may be provided in seizure of property or some other official performance of the reparational act. There are sanctions of type 3, such as decisions of mediation tribunals, which have no further official sanction and to this extent resemble the informal sanctions of exhortation or education. Many sanctions in reality depend for their effectiveness upon similar elements, whether or not there is provision for resort to physical power.

B. In the second group are those many activities of administrative agencies in which the question is whether an individual is entitled to a benefit or privilege offered by government or restricted to defined classes of persons. In connection with the government revenue, the determination may concern the extent of individual liability. The grant and denial of licenses, the decision of eligibility for pension and social security payments, and the fixing of taxes and tariff duties are the most common administrative functions of this type. Sanctions of this group are not primarily designed to penalize, reward, or shape the conduct of the individuals involved in particular determinations. They are methods of working out larger policies of government, such as regulation of industrial enterprise, social security, and redistribution of wealth.

Examination of these methods leads inevitably to considerations which are beyond the scope of this study. The brief attention given to these sanctions will concern principally the factors entering into determination, such as conflicting individual claims and whether an individual is within a defined class, which, resembling the factors involved in the application of sanctions of the first group, make for similarity in administrative judicial procedure.

Sanctions on Specific Individual Conduct

PENALTIES AND REWARDS

The field of punishment for legally proscribed conduct is traditionally the special field of the criminal courts, where there have been developed those safeguards against official tyranny frequently thought of as being themselves that liberty which must be defended from encroachment. Yet penal sanctions are now often administratively imposed. Certain special characteristics of administrative action have contributed to the acceptance of occupation of the field of punitive sanctions by administrative agencies. Some punitive sanctions are closely related to regulation, which is the special field of administration. Even those sanctions which are most harshly punitive, such as the revocation of a license, often the economic equivalent of capital punishment, can be considered regulatory in so far as they prevent the continuation of undesirable practices in the regulated field. Most punitive sanctions which are administratively imposed will be found to have a strong element of prevention. Moreover the sanctions are usually not in form those traditionally imposed by courts. The courts have not punished by revoking licenses or by denying such privileges as that of contracting with the government. These are sanctions similar in purpose and effect to those imposed by courts but widely different in form.

The traditional sanctions are left to the courts as the ultimate sanctions. The act of an administrative agency in revoking a license, for example, is "unenforceable." Operation without the license is the forbidden act, and that is punishable by fine or imprisonment imposed by the criminal courts. The lodging of real power in the agency has been made possible partly by leaving ultimate enforcement to the courts.

The description in the previous chapters of the general character of administrative judicial procedure will suggest many points at which it differs from the judicial procedure of courts in imposing similar sanctions. The absence of a jury in the imposition of penal sanctions is one of the most striking. Another point worthy of spe-

cial mention is the possibility of a default determination. Most statutes under which administrative agencies operate provide only for
the opportunity to be heard. When the agencies do not have the
power of arrest, the absence of respondent does not prevent their
proceeding to impose a fine or other penalty.

The power to imprison, the characteristic sanction of the criminal
courts, is not exercised by any federal administrative agency, and the
Supreme Court, in the case of *Wong Wing* v. *United States,*[32] holding unconstitutional a statute which attempted to give to immigration officials the power by summary proceedings not only to deport
but also to imprison aliens unlawfully in this country, said:

> to declare unlawful residence within the country to be an infamous crime,
> punishable by deprivation of liberty and property, would be to pass out of
> the sphere of constitutional legislation, unless provision were made that
> the fact of guilt should first be established by a judicial trial. It is not con-
> sistent with the theory of our government that the legislature should, after
> having defined an offense as an infamous crime, find the fact of guilt and
> adjudge the punishment by one of its own agents.[33]

[32] 163 U.S. 228 (1896).

[33] *Wong Wing* v. *United States,* 163 U.S. 228, 237 (1896). Cf. *Interstate Commerce Commission* v. *Brimson,* 154 U.S. 447, 485 (1894): "Such a body could
not, under our system of government, and consistently with due process of law,
be invested with authority to compel obedience to its orders by a judgment of
fine or imprisonment."

Most statutes giving to administrative agencies the power of subpoena provide for enforcement by the courts, either by contempt proceeding or by making
disobedience a misdemeanor. See Note, Administrative Sanctions—Power of
Federal Commissions to Compel Testimony and the Production of Evidence, 51
Harv. L. Rev. 312 (1937); Note, The Power of Administrative Agencies to Commit for Contempt, 35 *Col. L. Rev.* 578 (1935); Perishable Agricultural Commodities Act, 1930, 7 U.S.C. §499m; immigration laws, 8 U.S.C. §152; Walsh-
Healey Act, 41 U.S.C. §39; Communications Act of 1934, 47 U.S.C. §409; Federal Trade Commission Act, 15 U.S.C. §49; Interstate Commerce Act, 49 U.S.C.
§12 (2).

In certain Indian matters, the Secretary of the Interior is given by statute the
authority delegated to the United States courts by provision of the patent law to
enforce obedience to a subpoena "or punish disobedience as in other like cases."
25 U.S.C. §374. There are other similar provisions (see, *e.g.,* 46 U.S.C. §239 [e]),

Deportation is an administratively imposed punitive sanction which is not within the power conferred on criminal courts. The Attorney General has jurisdiction to find the fact and impose the penalty. Guilt is administratively determined, for example where the charge against an alien involves prostitution. Court conviction for the offense is not a prerequisite. Arrest, trial, and punishment are in the hands of the administrative agency.

The weakness of procedural safeguards for the accused in deportation cases has been the subject of considerable criticism.[34] In contrast with the power of the administrative to impose the punishment of deportation is the restriction of the *Wong Wing* case on the power of imposing imprisonment by the requirement of court procedure. Yet deportation in many cases falls with greater severity on the defendant. The Supreme Court has said that the sanction involves "the fundamental rights of men"[35] and may result "in loss of both property and life; or of all that makes life worth living."[36] It is the difference

but there is no indication that any administrative agency has sought to use the power to imprison or inflict other punishment under such statutory authority.

State statutes giving administrative agencies the power to imprison have been held unconstitutional as encroaching upon the judicial power. See, *e.g., People* v. *Swena*, 88 Colo. 337, 296 Pac. 271 (1931); *Langenberg* v. *Decker*, 131 Ind. 471, 31 N.E. 190 (1891). Judicial powers, including the power to imprison, are granted to some state administrative agencies by constitutional provision. See the provisions set forth in Hyneman, Administrative Adjudication: An Analysis I, 51 *Pol. Sci. Q.* 383, 392, n. 32 (1936). Under these provisions, administrative agencies which issue cease and desist orders or orders directing affirmative action themselves try cases of refusal or failure to comply, render judgment, and impose sentence. See, *e.g., Oklahoma Natural Gas Corp.* v. *Wagoner Gas Co.*, P.U.R. 1930B, 407 (1929); *Re E. L. McCapes*, P.U.R. 1927C, 98 (1926).

[34] See National Commission on Law Observance and Enforcement, Report No. 5, *The Enforcement of the Deportation Law of the United States* (1931); Clark, *Deportation of Aliens from the United States to Europe*, 1931; *Report of the Ellis Island Committee* (1934); Van Vleck, *The Administrative Control of Aliens*, 1932; Oppenheimer, Recent Developments in the Deportation Process, 36 *Mich. L. Rev.* 355 (1938).

[35] *Kwock Jan Fat* v. *White*, 253 U.S. 454, 464 (1920).

[36] *Ng Fung Ho* v. *White*, 259 U.S. 276, 284 (1922). See also *United States* v. *Davis*, 13 F. 2d 630 (C.C.A. 2d, 1926), where the court, though refusing to inter-

in the traditional and formal aspects of the two punitive sanctions, imprisonment and exile, which has led to failure to give full procedural effect to realistic factors.

A number of federal agencies have the power to impose fines or pecuniary penalties which have the effect of fines. Unlike imprisonment, a fine can be designated as remedial rather than penal or as civil rather than criminal. The constitutional limitations have proved more elastic, particularly where the penalty can be shown to be incidental to the administrative regulation of a business or where the form of collection is "civil" rather than "criminal."[37]

The Attorney General has the power to fine ship owners for a number of prohibited acts in connection with the transportation of aliens.[38] Fines were frequently imposed under these sections over a

vene in behalf of an alien ordered deported, said: "At any rate we think it not improper to say that deportation under the circumstances would be deplorable. Whether the relator came here in arms or at the age of ten, he is as much our product as though his mother had borne him on American soil. He knows no other language, no other people, no other habits, than ours; he will be as much a stranger in Poland as any one born of ancestors who immigrated in the seventeenth century. However heinous his crimes, deportation is to him exile, a dreadful punishment, abandoned by the common consent of all civilized peoples." Cf. Van Vleck, *The Administrative Control of Aliens,* p. 29.

[37] For instances of such distinctions see *Helvering* v. *Mitchell,* 303 U.S. 391 (1938); *United States* v. *One Ford Coupe,* 272 U.S. 321 (1926); *Dukich* v. *Blair,* 3 F. 2d 302 (E.D. Wash., 1925). Cases denying to state administrative agencies on constitutional grounds the power to impose fines are: *Board of Harbor Commissioners* v. *Excelsior Redwood Co.,* 88 Cal. 491, 26 Pac. 375 (1891); *Tite* v. *State Tax Commission,* 89 Utah 404, 57 P. 2d 734 (1936); *State* v. *Allen,* 2 McCord 55 (S.C., 1822); *McBride* v. *Adams,* 70 Miss. 716, 12 So. 699 (1893); *Cleveland C. C. & St. L. Ry. Co.* v. *People,* 212 Ill. 638, 72 N.E. 725 (1904).

[38] These acts include soliciting aliens to immigrate (8 U.S.C. §143), bringing in aliens suffering from certain detectable diseases or disabilities (8 U.S.C. §145), failure or refusal to make a required list of aliens transported (8 U.S.C. §150), taking money for returning aliens (8 U.S.C. §154), failure or refusal to transport deported aliens (8 U.S.C. §156), employing aliens with certain detectable diseases on passenger ships (8 U.S.C. §169), failure to furnish lists of aliens employed (8 U.S.C. §171), and transportation of immigrants without visas (8 U.S.C. §216).

period of many years by the Secretary of Labor,[39] and the penalties were regarded by the Department as effective sanctions.[40]

The fines provided range in amount from ten dollars to one thousand dollars. The fine is fixed for each type of violation without provision for discretion in fixing the amount, though in some instances there is provision for mitigation or remission under certain defined conditions. The statute provides for administrative enforcement of fines in giving the power when the fine has not been paid to refuse clearance papers to ships.

Other examples of the power to impose fines are found in the Longshoremen's and Harbor Workers' Compensation Act and the Federal Power Act.[41] The Comptroller of the Currency has the power to "assess" a penalty of one hundred dollars a day for failure of national banking associations to make reports[42] and for refusal to

---

[39] The Immigration and Naturalization Service was transferred to the Department of Justice under Reorganization Plan No. V, 5 Fed. Reg. 2132 (1940).

[40] *Oceanic Navigation Co.* v. *Stranahan,* 214 U.S. 320 (1909); *Lloyd Sabaudo* v. *Elting,* 287 U.S. 329 (1932).

[41] Under the former the United States Employees' Compensation Commission may assess a civil penalty in the amount of one hundred dollars for failure to notify that final payment has been made (33 U.S.C. §914 [g]), and where installments of awards are over fourteen days late, ten per cent is to be added to the amount of the installment unless nonpayment is excused by the deputy commissioner (33 U.S.C. §914 [e]). In the latter case the amount added to the award would be recovered by the action on the award as provided in the statute. The civil penalty is collected by civil suit brought by the Commission (33 U.S.C. §944 [g]). The Federal Power Commission has the power to fix a forfeiture in an amount not exceeding one thousand dollars, which forfeiture is to be in addition to any other penalty prescribed by the Act, in the case of any wilful failure of any licensee or public utility to comply with any order of the Commission, to file reports, to submit information, or to respond to a subpoena (16 U.S.C. §825n [a]). The Commission has never used the power granted under these provisions. Letter of Leon N. Fuquay, Secretary of the Commission, April 29, 1939: "No reason can be assigned for this fact other than that no case has been presented in the past which seemed to call for the application of this section rather than other enforcement measures." The Commission also may assess a penalty on delinquency in the payment of annual charges (16 U.S.C. §810 [b]).

[42] 12 U.S.C. §164.

permit examinations.[43] Provision is made for administrative enforcement of the first of these penalties by deduction of the amount from interest accruing on bonds deposited with the Treasurer of the United States to secure circulation of notes.

The extensive and important power to remit and mitigate statutory penalties is closely similar to the power to fine.[44] Under the Federal Alcohol Administration Act, for example, the Secretary of the Treasury may "compromise" fines for violations, which are defined as misdemeanors.[45] A compromise is limited to "a sum not in excess of $500 for each offense." The compromise procedure employed in thousands of cases is considered one of the regular administrative sanctions. Statutory penalties for violation of various provisions of the navigation laws[46] can be remitted or mitigated by the Secretary of Commerce.[47] The Federal Communications Commission has similar power over mitigation of penalties for violation of the statutory

[43] 12 U.S.C. §481.

[44] Administrative agencies frequently are given extensive powers over the sanctions imposed by courts. Such powers include the power of the Federal Board of Parole to grant and revoke paroles. 18 U.S.C. §§716, 719. The President (31 U.S.C. §197), the Secretary of the Treasury (31 U.S.C. §196), and the Postmaster General (5 U.S.C. §385) have the power to discharge from imprisonment persons imprisoned upon execution for debt due to the United States.

[45] 27 U.S.C. §207. Prior to Reorg. Plan No. IV, §2, eff. June 30, 1940, 5 Fed. Reg. 2421 (1940), 54 Stat. 1234, the Administrator of the Federal Alcohol Administration (abolished by Reorg. Plan No. III, §2, eff. June 30, 1940, 5 Fed. Reg. 2108, 54 Stat. 1232) with the approval of the Attorney General could compromise fines for violations. Under the Reorganization Plan this power of the Attorney General was transferred to "the Secretary of the Treasury, to be exercised by him or under his direction and supervision by such officer in the Department of the Treasury as he shall designate: Provided, that exclusive jurisdiction to compromise cases arising under [the Federal Alcohol Administration Act] which are pending before the courts or which have been or may hereafter be referred to the Department of Justice for action shall be vested in the Attorney General, and may be exercised by him or by any officer in the Department of Justice designated by him."

[46] 46 U.S.C. §320.

[47] Monograph of the Attorney General's Committee on Administrative Procedure, Sen. Doc. No. 186, 76th Cong., 3rd Sess. (1940) pt. 10, p. 24.

requirements as to radio equipment on ships.[48] The General Accounting Office, with the written consent of the Postmaster General, has a very extensive power over remission and mitigation of fines, penalties, and forfeitures, and has power to remove disabilities, compromise, release, and discharge claims arising under any provision of law in relation to the officers, employees, operations, or business of the postal service.[49]

The aid of a court must be invoked for the collection of such penalties and forfeitures, so that theoretically at least the respondent has an opportunity to resist their imposition with the safeguards of judicial procedure; and this is advanced as justification for the absence of judicial procedure in the fixing of the penalties administratively. However, the availability in fact of judicial protection depends, as in other situations, on the alternative to submission to the administrative order. In the Federal Alcohol Administration the threat of suspension proceedings is sufficient to enforce payment. The possibilities of abuse have been pointed out by the Attorney General's Committee on Administrative Procedure:

The potentiality of abuse is always present as long as permittees dread the mere possibility that suspension proceedings may be instituted. Such fear provides a potent inducement to settle cases, particularly if the compromise figure is so small that it occasions no greater expense than would be involved in the defense of suspension proceedings. The temptation to solicit settlements even of cases where the Administration's case is weak must be almost irresistible under such psychological conditions.[50]

Of the procedure of the Bureau of Marine Inspection and Navigation, the Attorney General's Committee says:

No standards are prescribed by statute to guide administrative discretion in remitting or mitigating. The power is one which because of its very

[48] 47 U.S.C. §§504 (b), 351–362.
[49] 5 U.S.C. §383.
[50] Sen. Doc. No. 186, 76th Cong., 3rd Sess. (1940) pt. 5, p. 10. See *supra*, n. 45.

nature is likely to be exercised with some degree of arbitrariness. . . .
One who is content to submit a written application for mitigation or remission is likely to pay a much larger fine than the individual or corporation which sends a representative to Washington to address argument to
the officials. It is undeniable that pressures substantially affect the ultimate
conclusion. . . . Partly because pressure from organized labor was sufficiently strong, not a single fine imposed upon owners in connection with a
recent tanker strike was mitigated.[51]

Penalties imposed by the Bureau of Internal Revenue and by the
Bureau of Customs for violation of the revenue laws are thought of
as additional taxes or duties rather than as fines. However, it is on
these administratively imposed sanctions more than on the criminal
sanctions also provided by statute that the government relies for the
enforcement of the revenue laws. The power to impose these administrative penalties is generally upheld by the courts as constitutionally unexceptionable.[52] Distraint and seizure provide administrative
enforcement of the penalties imposed.

The imposition of a penalty under the guise of a tax is a sanction
closely resembling a fine in all except certain formal aspects.[53] Though
neither the problems of the social uses of taxation in their broader
aspects nor the question of constitutional power to regulate through
the use of taxation will be discussed here,[54] it must be noted that it is
the lack of power in the National Government to forbid certain activities and impose a criminal penalty as a sanction which has led
Congress to disguise regulation as taxation. The Supreme Court, in

[51] Sen. Doc. No. 186, 76th Cong., 3rd Sess. (1940) pt. 10, pp. 26–27, and n. 27.
[52] *Bartlett* v. *Kane,* 16 How. 263 (U.S., 1853); *Passavant* v. *United States,* 148
U.S. 214 (1893); *Origet* v. *Hedden,* 155 U.S. 228 (1894).
[53] See Hale, Force and the State: A Comparison of "Political" and "Economic" Compulsion, 35 *Col. L. Rev.* 149, 163 ff. (1935).
[54] See Reuschlein and Spector, Taxing and Spending: The Loaded Dice of a
Federal Economy, 23 *Corn. L.Q.* 1 (1937); Brown, The Excise Tax as a Regulatory Device, 23 *Corn. L.Q.* 45 (1937); Grant, Commerce, Production, and the
Fiscal Powers of Congress, 45 *Yale L.J.* 751, 991 (1936); Cushman, Social and
Economic Control through Federal Taxation, 18 *Minn. L. Rev.* 759 (1934).

attempting to define this power, has drawn tenuous distinctions between "true" taxes and "penalties," some of which are important here in indicating that there are limitations on the procedure of administrative imposition of tax sanctions. For example, the increase in the basic tax provided for violation of the National Prohibition Act was held to be a penalty[55] and therefore "subject to the constitutional limitations placed upon prosecutions of crimes and . . . not collectible by the free and easy processes of the revenue acts."[56] If the substance rather than the form of such sanctions be considered, many which are legislatively and judicially designated taxes will be found to be penalties upon specific individual conduct.

The administrative procedure for imposing most sanctions of this type, such as the taxes on oleomargarine,[57] firearms,[58] and cotton futures contracts,[59] is the ordinary procedure of the Bureau of Internal Revenue. From the point of view of a study of administrative judicial procedure, the most interesting of the penalty tax provisions is that of the Bituminous Coal Act of 1937.[60] A heavy tax is imposed upon the sale of bituminous coal by producers who do not become members of a code under which they are subject to regulation as to prices and marketing practices.[61] The Bituminous Coal Commission certifies membership to the Commissioner of Internal Revenue, and the Commission is empowered to revoke code membership and the "right to an exemption" from the tax upon finding, by designated judicial procedure, violation of the code or regulations.[62] In order to recover membership in the code and to be relieved of the tax, a producer whose membership has been revoked must pay

[55] See *Lipke* v. *Lederer,* 259 U.S. 557 (1922); *Regal Drug Corp.* v. *Wardell,* 260 U.S. 386 (1922).

[56] Brown, The Excise Tax as a Regulatory Device, 23 *Corn. L.Q.* 45, 50, n. 25 (1937).

[57] 26 U.S.C. §971 (c) (2).   [58] 26 U.S.C. §1132b.

[59] 26 U.S.C. §1098.

[60] For a discussion of the provisions of this Act see Reeder, Some Problems of the Bituminous Coal Industry, 45 *W.Va. L.Q.* 109 (1939).

[61] 15 U.S.C. §830.   [62] 15 U.S.C. §835 (b).

double the amount of the tax on the sale price of coal sold in violation of the code, the amount of the latter to be fixed by the Commission. Thus the Commission has the power to impose what is in effect
a fine and, at least in part, the power to fix the amount of the fine.
Moreover a method of enforcement of the fine is provided through
the threat of increasing tax liability. Collection is effected by the ordinary administrative procedures for the collection of taxes, though
the provisions for review of the Commission's orders[63] afford an opportunity for judicial intervention which was lacking under the provisions of the National Prohibition Act referred to above.

The converse of the penalty sanction on conduct which is disapproved is the award or benefit for approved conduct.[64] Hale has
pointed out that such an affirmative sanction may be no less coercive
than its negative.[65] The tax sanction may be in the form of a tax as a
penalty upon disapproved conduct, or in the form of an exemption
from a tax as a reward for refraining from disapproved conduct. Under the Bituminous Coal Act of 1937 it is stated as an exemption.

Administration of benefit sanctions differs in method from administration of penal sanctions, partly because the benefit sanction has
never been available to the courts. However, the coercive nature of
the award and the detriment suffered in earning it lead on the one
hand to the use of administrative judicial procedure and on the other
to the treatment of the situation as involving a contractual claim,
either in all cases or at least in those cases in which denial is contemplated. The contractual aspect is emphasized by the absence in most
such situations of provisions for denial or withdrawal of the benefit
as a penalty for disapproved conduct not directly connected with the
activity sanctioned by its award. Withholding of subsidy payments
in connection with merchant shipping where there is violation of the

[63] 15 U.S.C. §836 (b).

[64] Such infrequent bounties as rewards for the apprehension of criminals and
the informer's share are of limited significance, and administration is largely informal. The granting of patents is a long standing and socially important sanction, and elaborate procedure has been devised for its administration.

[65] Hale, Our Equivocal Constitutional Guaranties, 39 *Col. L. Rev.* 563 (1939).

unfair and discriminatory practices provisions is one of the few examples of the punitive use of the benefit sanction.[66]

The benefit sanction has been widely employed in recent years in the control of agricultural production through payment for restriction as, for example, under the Agricultural Adjustment Act of 1938.[67] Under the Sugar Act of 1937 the benefit payments are a sanction upon the employment of child labor and the payment of minimum wages, in addition to restriction of production, preservation and improving of the fertility of the soil, and the prevention of soil erosion.[68] With the continuation of these controls beyond an emergency period and with their increasing economic and social significance, adequate administrative procedure for the protection both of the government and of the hundreds of thousands whose conduct is sanctioned by the proffered benefit is required. In actual effect the administration of the benefit sanctions approaches in importance the court administration of contract remedies. From the point of view of claimants, the necessity for adequate administrative procedure is particularly pressing because of the impossibility of remedy in the courts under statutes, such as the Sugar Act of 1937,[69] which provide that the administrative determination shall be final and conclusive.

The use of government loans, particularly in the same field of agricultural control, as a benefit sanction on individual conduct is extensive in practice and is occasionally formally recognized, as under the Agricultural Adjustment Act of 1938[70] and the Agricultural Marketing Agreement Act.[71] Formal administrative procedure is completely lacking, though here again the scope of the sanction and its social importance are sufficiently great to justify careful and impartial determination of rights.

Only the formal distinction between sanctions of the benefit type

[66] 46 U.S.C. §1227. Compare the power of the Secretary of the Interior to refuse grants to colleges which fail to conform to requirements as to racial equality, etc., 7 U.S.C. §326.

[67] 16 U.S.C. §590h.

[68] 7 U.S.C. §1131.

[69] 7 U.S.C. §1136.

[70] 7 U.S.C. §1302.

[71] 7 U.S.C. §608b; 50 Stat. 246.

and such sanctions as denial or withdrawal of a license can explain —and such a distinction cannot justify—the difference in required procedure.

Sanctions employed by the government as a source of benefits are of two types. Benefits may be given in order to induce individuals to perform certain officially desired acts. Approved conduct is rewarded. On the other hand, benefits may be given to certain classes of citizens without specific intent to encourage others to become members of the class. The withdrawal of a benefit of the second type is sometimes used as a sanction upon individual conduct. Continuation of a payment to which an individual is entitled by reason of status may be made conditional upon his following an approved course of conduct, or there may be provision for termination of benefits as punishment for misbehavior. Under the Social Security Act, for example, the Board may decrease or withdraw old age and survivor's insurance benefit payments which are payable in respect to children between sixteen and eighteen, if the children fail "to attend school regularly and the Board finds that attendance was feasible."[72] Rations or cash payments can be denied to Indians who do not send their children to school.[73] Violation of regulations by a pensioner in a veterans' hospital can be punished by a "fine" of a part of the pension to which the veteran is entitled.[74] On the other hand, provisions such as those prescribing termination of pension where a widow of a veteran is guilty of "open and notorious adulterous cohabitation,"[75] or for the termination of pension or social security payments where a widow has abandoned her children,[76] are primarily intended further to define the status entitling the widows to benefits and only secondarily, if at all, as sanctions upon the conduct involved. The possibilities of using withdrawal of pension, relief, and social security rights as sanctions are enormous. There are, however, notably few provisions of this type in the present legislation.

[72] 42 U.S.C. §403 (d) (2).   [73] 25 U.S.C. §§283, 285.
[74] 38 U.S.C. §439.   [75] 38 U.S.C. §199.
[76] 38 U.S.C. §200; 42 U.S.C. §403 (d) (3).

The principal development in the use of governmental benefits and privileges as sanctions has taken place in the field of government contracts. The extensive effectiveness of the denial of the privilege of contracting with the government first became apparent in the administration of the codes under the National Recovery Administration. With a great reluctance to attempt court enforcement and the increasing weakness of the publicity sanctions such as withdrawal of the Blue Eagle, sanctions upon violation became less and less effective. By the beginning of 1935 the Administration was practically powerless to enforce the codes except in the case of one notably large group, those who were contracting or hoping to contract with the government. With these the threat of withdrawal of the privilege was sufficient to force compliance. After the demise of the National Recovery Administration, the experience gained there led to the enactment of the Walsh-Healey Act, using withdrawal of the privilege of government contract as a sanction upon labor practices, though the scope of the prohibited activity was greatly narrowed. Under the National Recovery Administration the privilege of contracting with the government could be denied for any violation of the code, whereas under the Walsh-Healey Act the violation must occur in the work on a government contract which, if it is for an amount in excess of $10,-000, contains required stipulations as to wages, hours, and conditions of labor. Where such a violation is found, the contract may be cancelled and the violating firm blacklisted for a period of three years after the breach.[77] Other sanctions are "liquidated damages" of ten dollars a day for violation of the child labor stipulations and reparations for wage and hour violations. Jurisdiction to determine violations is in the Secretary of Labor, who also has discretion to mitigate the penalty.

During the first two and one-half years of the administration of the Act, only two firms were blacklisted; 85 per cent of the instances where violations were found were settled, usually by payment of re-

[77] 41 U.S.C. §37. A similar provision confined to wage violation is found in the Davis-Bacon Act, 40 U.S.C. §276a-2.

quired wages, without formal procedure.[78] While the severity of the sanction no doubt plays a large part in the willingness of employers to make such settlements, it also frequently results in violations going unpunished, since the Secretary is reluctant to impose a penalty which may mean serious damage to, or even destruction of, the contractor's business. The Department of Labor, recognizing this weakness in the sanctions now available, approved a bill providing for monetary penalties as an alternative to blacklisting. Instead of being permitted to purge himself by paying the stipulated wages, the contractor would be liable upon repetition of the offense for double the amount involved and for triple the original amount for each subsequent offense.[79]

The contract sanction on violation of the collective bargaining provisions of the Bituminous Coal Act of 1937 is much less extensive than the sanctions of the Walsh-Healey Act. Termination of government contracts upon finding of violation by the Commission is applicable only to contracts for coal, and the prohibition on dealing with violators extends only to coal "produced at any mine" where violation was occurring at the time of production.[80] Violation has been found by the Commission in only one case. The sanctions of the National Labor Relations Act are also applicable to violators, but a finding of violation by the National Labor Relations Board does not automatically bring about the termination of a contract for coal; the Bituminous Coal Commission must also find the violation. However, the Act would apparently authorize rejection of a bid as the result of finding of violation by the National Labor Relations Board.

In the absence of the requirement of competitive bidding or other measures designed to protect the privilege of dealing with the government, the working out of official policy through contract sanctions would have no need for express statutory authorization. The purposes served by the legislation could be accomplished by exercise of

[78] Gellhorn and Linfield, Administrative Adjudication of Contract Disputes: The Walsh-Healey Act, 37 *Mich. L. Rev.* 841, 846, 853 (1939).

[79] S. 1032, 76th Cong., 1st Sess. (1939).   [80] 15 U.S.C. §839.

election in entering into contracts and by the terms of the contracts. The legislation is directive of official action (witness the absence of criminal penalties) and gives recognition to the power of administrative sanctions, not only in its enabling features but also in regulating administrative activity.

Still more striking in the development of a law which is purely administrative are provisions such as those of the Federal Reserve Act regulating cancellation of federal deposit insurance contracts. The contract entered into between the Federal Deposit Insurance Corporation and the bank provides for termination upon violation of the laws to which the bank is subject. State banks which are not members of the Federal Reserve System enter into such contracts without official coercion, and wrongs resulting from their breach might be left to such remedies as are ordinarily provided for breach of consensual agreements. But the statute, recognizing the official nature of the sanction of termination, requires an elaborate procedure of notice, hearing, and written findings,[81] with the board of directors of the Corporation or their designee sitting in a judicial capacity. Through the year 1938 the insurance status of three banks had been terminated in this manner.[82]

The power to report a violation for prosecution in the courts has been given formal standing as a sanction by the inclusion of express provisions in the legislation administered by several agencies. The Federal Power Act, for example, provides that the Commission may transmit evidence of violation to the Attorney General, who in his discretion may institute criminal proceedings.[83]

[81] 12 U.S.C. §264 (i).

[82] Federal Deposit Insurance Corporation, *Annual Reports,* 1934–1938.

[83] 16 U.S.C. §825m (a). See also Agricultural Adjustment Act of 1938, 7 U.S.C. §610 (h); The Naval Stores Act, 7 U.S.C. §97. Cf. 26 U.S.C. §1645 (b), which provides that it is "the duty of every collector of internal revenue" to report knowledge of wilful violations of the revenue laws to the district attorney. A similar provision in the Federal Trade Commission Act authorizes the Commission, if it has reason to believe that there has been a violation of the false advertising provisions which involves a criminal penalty, to certify the facts to the Attorney General. 15 U.S.C. §56; see also §65.

In some provisions of this type the directive force appears to be upon the prosecuting authorities rather than upon the administrative agency. The agency is authorized to report violations, an authority which presumably it would have without the statute, but the district attorney is directed to prosecute "without delay."[84]

Where the authorization to report violation concerns civil penalties, as under the Perishable Agricultural Commodities Act,[85] the same questions arise since, where no special mode of procedure is prescribed for the collection of a civil penalty, civil action at law brought by the district attorney is ordinarily the proper method.[86]

The most interesting of these provisions require judicial procedure prior to report of violation.[87] Under the Agricultural Adjustment Act of 1938,[88] the Insecticide Act,[89] and the Federal Caustic Poison Act,[90] a hearing is to be held and violation found before the Secretary of Agriculture reports the violation to the district attorney.

Presumably, in the absence of special authorization, any administrative agency would be at liberty to make reports of violations and the prosecuting authorities could proceed against violators whether or not they received such reports. The effect of the express statutory provisions as sanctions is, then, largely *in terrorem*. In *United States v. Morgan*[91] the defendant contended that such a provision constituted a limitation on the power to begin a prosecution, that the administrative procedure was a prerequisite to action by the district at-

---

[84] See, *e.g.*, Perishable Agricultural Commodities Act, 1930, 7 U.S.C. §499*l*; Packers and Stockyards Act, 1921, 7 U.S.C. §224; Communications Act of 1934, 47 U.S.C. §401 (c).

[85] 7 U.S.C. §499*l*.

[86] See *New Jersey Fidelity & Plate Glass Insurance Co.* v. *Van Schaick*, 236 App. Div. 223, 259 N.Y. Supp. 108 (1932), *aff'd without opinion*, 261 N.Y. 521, 185 N.E. 721 (1933).

[87] The Federal Food, Drug, and Cosmetic Act requires the Secretary, before any violation is reported to any United States Attorney for institution of criminal proceedings, to give the person against whom such proceeding is contemplated "appropriate notice and an opportunity to present his views, either orally or in writing, with regard to such contemplated proceeding." 21 U.S.C. §335.

[88] 7 U.S.C. §608a (7).   [89] 7 U.S.C. §128.

[90] 15 U.S.C. §409.   [91] 222 U.S. 274 (1911).

torney. However, the Supreme Court held that it was the duty of the district attorney to prosecute all violations brought to his attention whether or not an administrative hearing was held in accordance with the statutory provision. As a result of this decision, there is no method available to a respondent under such a statute to prevent the administrative agency from reporting the violation or the district attorney from proceeding against him without previous hearing.

In situations where, as under the Food and Drugs Act prior to the recent legislation,[92] a companion provision requires the district attorney to proceed without delay, the use of the hearing procedure might have some effect on the action of the district attorney, since he would then be without statutory discretion as to whether to institute the prosecution, whereas if the hearing procedure were not followed, he might, upon his own investigation, decide not to prosecute. Though theoretically the hearing requirement constitutes no limitation on prosecution, in the practice of the Department of Agriculture at least protection is actually afforded since the district attorney rarely proceeds except upon report by the Secretary, and under the practice of the Department opportunity for hearing is given in all cases.[93]

Publicity has become one of the most effective administrative sanctions. The press release of the Federal Alcohol Administration Act, for example, "has virtually added to the statute another enforcement sanction."[94] The Securities and Exchange Commission has occasionally refrained, after finding violation, from imposing statutory sanctions on the ground that the publicity sanction was sufficient.[95]

The sanction of publicity is generally unrestricted by formal procedural safeguards, although its effect in damaging or destroying an enterprise is in many instances equivalent to the effect of suspension

[92] 21 U.S.C. §§11, 12.

[93] Lee, The Enforcement Provisions of the Food, Drug, and Cosmetic Act, 6 *Law & Contemp. Prob.* 70, 73–76 (1939).

[94] Gaguine, The Federal Alcohol Administration, 7 *Geo. Wash. L. Rev.* 844, 864 (1939).

[95] Monograph of the Attorney General's Committee on Administrative Procedure, Sen. Doc. No. 10, 77th Cong., 1st Sess. (1941) pt. 13, p. 9.

or even revocation of a license. While enforcement is by the community at large or by special groups in the community rather than by official action, the formal distinction fails to reflect the actual effect of the two types of sanction.

The limitations on the effectiveness of publicity already noted are equally applicable to the more formal use of publicity. The prestige of the administrative agency involved is a factor, as is the prestige of the enterprise against which the sanction is employed. Publicity by any agency, however weak, is a stronger weapon against the established and reputable enterprise than it is against the ephemeral and disreputable. But publicity by a weak agency or an agency weakened by a concerted campaign is comparatively ineffectual even against established and reputable enterprises.

Statutory provisions authorizing or directing the use of publicity are found particularly in the legislation administered by the Secretary of Agriculture. Under the Federal Food, Drug, and Cosmetic Act, for example, the Secretary is directed to publish "reports summarizing all judgments, decrees, and court orders which have been rendered under this chapter, including the nature of the charge and the disposition thereof."[96] These reports of the Secretary are "seldom

---

[96] 21 U.S.C. §375 (a). For a similar provision see the Insecticide Act, 7 U.S.C. §128.

The coercive effect of the threat of publicity is illustrated by the sampling activities of the Food and Drug Administration, where samples are "voluntarily" furnished in order to avoid the injury to trade which might result from a large number of samples being purchased by enforcement officers. "Nearly always the manufacturer will make samples available, rather than have inspectors take samples after shipment. While from the legal standpoint the furnishing of samples by the manufacturer is usually voluntary, in fact there is a considerable amount of coercion involved. The manufacturer grants the samples to avoid certain more injurious sampling activities by the Department. Thus sampling at the source avoids likelihood of seizures after the manufacturer has gone to expense of shipping the article. It also avoids injury to the manufacturer's trade that might occur if wholesalers and retailers found a large number of samples of the product of a particular manufacturer were being purchased from them by enforcement officers." Unpublished MS of Frederic P. Lee, *Administration of Federal Agricultural Commodity Standards,* pp. 494–495.

"Voluntary" factory inspection depends at least in part on the same considera-

noted by periodicals of general circulation, but trade journals tend to inform their readers of such actions."[97]

The main purpose served is that of an additional deterrent to violations of the Act, for in general it may be said that the publicity resulting from the notices of judgment is frequently superior in its deterrent effect to that of the penalties imposed. This follows because public knowledge that the product has been involved in a violation of the law serves to prejudice it in the eyes of wholesalers and retailers and to some extent the consumers, and the data contained in the notices of judgment are doubtless made use of by trade competitors.[98]

By the same section of the statute the Secretary is authorized to issue "information regarding food, drugs, devices, or cosmetics in situations involving, in the opinion of the Secretary, imminent danger to health or gross deception of the consumer."[99] These warnings "usually cover types of violations that come to the Food and Drug Administration's attention and that it expects the trade to correct, or in regard to which it desires to warn the public for its own protection."[100]

Under the Perishable Agricultural Commodities Act the Secretary is authorized to publish the facts and circumstances of any violation

tions. "Without specific authority of law, except in the case of seafood, the Food and Drug Administration has maintained under the old Act a voluntary system of inspection of factories in which are manufactured food and drugs for interstate shipment. Most manufacturers do not object to inspection of their factories, although their acquiescent attitude may be induced in part by the same considerations mentioned earlier that lead them to furnish 'voluntary' samples." Lee, The Enforcement Provisions of the Food, Drug, and Cosmetic Act, 6 *Law & Contemp. Prob.* 70, 87 (1939).

There is provision in the present legislation authorizing the Secretary to conduct inspections. 21 U.S.C. §374.

[97] Hayes and Ruff, The Administration of the Federal Food and Drugs Act, 1 *Law & Contemp. Prob.* 16, 33 (1933).

[98] Lee, The Enforcement Provisions of the Food, Drug, and Cosmetic Act, 6 *Law & Contemp. Prob.* 70, 90 (1939).

[99] 21 U.S.C. §375 (b).

[100] Lee, The Enforcement Provisions of the Food, Drug, and Cosmetic Act, 6 *Law & Contemp. Prob.* 70, 90 (1939).

of the fair trade practice provisions, including situations in which a reparations order has been issued.[101] Publication is a sanction upon violation found by judicial procedure and is either additional to or an alternative for the sanctions of suspension and revocation.[102]

Publicity is the sole administrative sanction prescribed for violation of the grading provisions of the United States Grain Standards Act[103] and the Tobacco Inspection Act.[104] Under the former the findings of the Secretary are to be published only after opportunity for hearing. Publication of the results of tests is a sanction upon violation of the standards for naval stores.[105]

Under the Commodity Exchange Act the Secretary is authorized to publish such reports "as he may deem necessary" of the transactions of any person "found guilty," by administrative judicial procedure, of violation.[106] Moreover, under another provision of the same Act power is expressly given to publish "the full facts . . . including the names of parties" concerned in transactions which in the judgment of the Secretary are harmful to the "best interests of producers and consumers."[107]

[101] 7 U.S.C. §499h.

[102] Publication as a sanction additional to revocation or suspension is provided in cases involving licensed dealers in live poultry (7 U.S.C. §218d) and licensed warehouses (7 U.S.C. §265). It is the practice of the Secretary to order publication in all cases where a license is suspended or revoked and in most cases in which reparation is awarded. Mimeographed summaries of decisions of the Secretary are distributed to a mailing list of licensees, attorneys, and others who have requested copies, and particularly to the trade papers of the fruit and vegetable industry. They are either printed in full or "listed in part" by the trade papers. Letter of C. W. Kitchen, Chief, Agricultural Marketing Service, August 9, 1939. Under other provisions of the same Act, the Secretary may publish without prior judicial proceeding the facts and circumstances of refusal to keep records in the manner ordered by the Secretary and to permit inspection of records, either with or without other sanction. 7 U.S.C. §§499i, 499m (a).

[103] 7 U.S.C. §77.   [104] 7 U.S.C. §511j.   [105] 7 U.S.C. §97.

[106] 7 U.S.C. §12. The sanction can be imposed either with or without other sanctions such as revocation of registration, and under a liberal reading of the statute the Secretary can publish reports of transactions of persons found guilty whether or not the transactions are connected with the violation involved in the judicial proceeding.

[107] 7 U.S.C. §12a.

In a sense, publicity is the statutory sanction upon which the whole theory of the Securities Act of 1933 depends, since the requirement of full disclosure is the protection afforded to investors.[108] However, the formal device provided under the Act for preventing the offering for sale of securities without full disclosure is the issuance of a stop order or refusal order. If such an order is issued, a security cannot legally be sold or offered for sale. Publicity as to the character of the issue or of the issuer is ordinarily not a necessary adjunct to the action of the Commission, since the sale of the issue is effectively prevented by the formal order. The function of such publicity, as the Commission has recognized, is to protect the public, not against the sale of the securities involved in the case, but against subsequent practices of fraudulent issuers. While the stop order and refusal order are preventive measures,[109] the publicity attendant upon the issuance of such an order is wholly punitive as far as concerns the particular securities involved. The punitive aspect is particularly apparent in those stop order proceedings in which the Commission makes findings and issues extensive opinions although there is a stipulation that the deficiencies charged exist and there is a consent to the issuance of a stop order. The Commission believes that it has a duty to make the details public.[110] Publicity is deemed to be necessary in the public interest.[111] In a proceeding where, at the outset of the hearing,

[108] The Securities Exchange Act of 1934 contains express provision for publication of information concerning violations investigated under the authority of that Act. 15 U.S.C. §78u (a).

[109] See *In the Matter of Haddam Distillers Corp.,* 1 S.E.C. 48 (1934).

[110] For a comment favorable to this position of the Commission and criticizing the majority opinion in the *Jones* case (discussed *infra,* pp. 116–118) for failure to recognize this implied duty of the Commission, see Withdrawal of Registration Statements—the Jones Case, 31 *Ill. L. Rev.* 369, 376 (1936): "If the majority meant, however, to construe 'protection of investors' to mean only those possibly interested in the particular security, its interpretation is unwarranted. The Commission was established primarily to obtain a full disclosure of information to protect the investing public and not merely for specific investors who may be affected by the registration statement in question."

[111] *In the Matter of Oil Ridge Oil & Refining Co.,* 1 S.E.C. 225 (1935); see also *In the Matter of Continental Distillers and Importers Corp.,* 1 S.E.C. 54 (1935).

the respondent submitted a stipulation stating its willingness to make
such deletions or modifications as the Commission might require, the
Commission said that "to permit such a retraction without full publication of the facts and circumstances surrounding this case would be
inconsistent with the duty imposed upon the Commission by the Securities Act of 1933."[112] In another similar proceeding the Commission said:

Despite the registrant's consent to the issuance of a stop order, the nature of this case, in essence, an enterprise to deal in an irresponsible fashion with the small savings of city and county school teachers, makes it not
only desirable but imperative to file these findings and this opinion so that
the untruthfulness and the unfairness of the registrant's officers should be
a matter of public record.[113]

In another case, although the registrant requested withdrawal of
his registration statement and later consented to a stop order, the
Commission stated that it deemed it in the public interest to issue an
opinion "in order to transmit to the public generally evidence of the
registrant's disregard of important legal and ethical standards."[114]

The case of *Jones* v. *Securities and Exchange Commission* involved
an attempt by the respondent to withdraw his registration statement
after the institution of stop order proceedings. The Commission's
reason for refusing to permit the withdrawal was the desire to hold a
hearing and make public the deficiencies in the registration statement. The majority of the Supreme Court strongly condemned the
practice of the Commission, though the exact point, the unfavorable
and damaging publicity to the respondent, was not discussed in the
opinion of the Court. The minority felt that the practice of the Com-

[112] *In the Matter of American Credit Corp.*, 1 S.E.C. 230, 232 (1935). Cf. *In
the Matter of Income Estates of America, Inc.*, Securities Act of 1933, Release
No. 1480 (1937).
[113] *In the Matter of National Educators Mutual Association, Inc.*, 1 S.E.C.
208, 210 (1935).
[114] *In the Matter of Big Wedge Gold Mining Co.*, 1 S.E.C. 98 (1935); see also
In the Matter of Gold Hill Operating Co., 1 S.E.C. 668 (1936); *In the Matter of
Trenton Valley Distillers Corp.*, Securities Act of 1933, Release No. 1658 (1938).

mission was justified because, among other things, "the enforcement of the Act is aided when guilt is exposed to the censure of the world." The rule forbidding the withdrawal of a registration statement after the beginning of stop order proceedings was, in the opinion of the minority, "wisely conceived . . . to foil the plans of knaves intent upon obscuring or suppressing the knowledge of their knavery."[115]

The position of the Commission was severely criticized by Professor Gardner:

You all remember that Congress entrusted the Securities and Exchange Commission with the enterprise of seeing to it that every security offered for public investment should be truthfully described to the public and that this enterprise has been a success. It seems that one J. Edward Jones filed with this commission a description of some securities of which he proposed to make public offering, and that he would have been free to offer them twenty days later if the commission had not interfered. The commission, however, was not satisfied as to the correctness of the description and summoned Jones to testify before it in detail. Thereupon Jones withdrew his proposal to offer these securities to the public and declined to appear. One might suppose that this would have ended the matter, but it was not to be so. The commission refused to permit Jones to withdraw his proposal, but insisted that he appear before it and testify—for no other apparent purpose than to convict him publicly of having attempted a fraud. The Supreme Court of the United States ruled that this was no part of the enterprise with which the commission had been entrusted; and two of the parties to the same stock promotion were acquitted of crime after trial upon indictments in the District of Columbia Supreme Court. Yet Squire Landis seemed to me to think it a grievance that the commission was denied the privilege of substituting itself for a court and jury and that it did not have the opportunity "to establish a record of fraud after hearing and in such a manner inform the investment world of the fraud that was attempted and the character of parties to it." No skipper of a fishing vessel, no president of a steel corporation, no private investment banker would dream of claiming such a privilege to pass judgment on his fellow citizen

[115] 298 U.S. 1, 31, 33 (1936).

in a matter which concerned the success of the enterprise in which he himself was engaged. The danger to the citizen's liberty is not smaller when he is exposed to judgment by a body supported by all the resources of the revenue and fired with zeal to achieve the laudable public purpose for which it was set up.[116]

The decision in the *Jones* case was based on a technical point of procedure, rather than on the power of the Commission to use publicity as a sanction, and the Commission, by slight changes in its procedure, has continued its practice with substantially the same effect as before.

The use by many administrative agencies of the press release as an additional nonstatutory sanction, without even such formal limitations as those of the Securities and Exchange Commission's stop order proceedings, has followed upon the recognition of the immense effectiveness of publicity.

The publication of the press release is perhaps the most effective sanction which the [Federal Alcohol] Administration possesses. The consequences of such publication upon a permittee's activities is generally thought to be at least as disastrous as the entry of an order suspending the permittee. For one thing, competitors have been able to convince their customers, by distributing copies of the release or by oral republication of its contents, not to deal with persons who are sufficiently reprehensible to be respondents in suspension proceedings. Another direct effect of the press release is to place the permittee upon the black-list which some monopoly states have created for industry members who are in difficulty with the Administration. These are immediate results flowing from the mere institution of proceedings and necessarily harm both innocent permittees as well as the guilty ones.

Because the publication of a press release has an immediate detrimental effect upon the suspected permittee, there has been an increasing tendency on the part of industry members to settle cases prior to the institution of proceedings. Whether they are right or wrong on the merits of the case, they must inevitably lose something, other than the mere cost of defend-

[116] George K. Gardner, Book Review of Landis, *The Administrative Process,* 52 *Harv. L. Rev.* 336, 341–342 (1938).

ing a law-suit, by litigating the issues. While the effect of the use of the press release is thus to discourage the litigation of possibly meritorious cases, there is something to be said in favor of the practice.

There can be little doubt that fear of the press release has occasioned an extraordinary degree of compliance with the Act. The effectiveness of publicity has generally been recognized as providing an additional sanction to regulatory agencies and, as a result, the press release is now a common phenomenon.[117]

The courts generally have found no basis in law for imposing restrictions, by requiring procedural safeguards or otherwise, on the use of publicity as an administrative sanction.[118] Publicity "may be mischievous and seriously damage the property rights of innocent persons. But the opinions and advice, even of those in authority, are not a law or regulation such as comes within the scope of the several provisions of the Federal Constitution designed to secure the rights of citizens as against action by the States."[119] Usually the ground for refusal to intervene has been the absence of coercive force. In actual effect, in damage to property and reputation, publicity may be fully as coercive as many other sanctions upon which the courts impose restrictions. It is rather the form of the sanction, the unofficial char-

---

[117] Monograph of the Attorney General's Committee on Administrative Procedure, Sen. Doc. No. 186, 76th Cong., 3rd Sess. (1940) pt. 5, p. 16.

Of the use of the press release by the Federal Alcohol Administration, the Attorney General's Committee on Administrative Procedure says: "it is arguable that the additional deterrent effect of the publicity sanction does not warrant the sacrifice of meritorious cases. The sanctions provided by the statute, particularly the power to suspend the permit, should, if utilized, provide sufficient discouragement to the potential lawbreaker. Nor is there need, in the usual case, for the taking of rapid action in order to safeguard the public health or to prevent gross deception of consumers. In the absence of these considerations, therefore, no real necessity for continuing the indiscriminate use of the press release appears to exist." P. 17.

[118] See *Standard Scale Co.* v. *Farrell*, 249 U.S. 571 (1919); *Pennsylvania R. R. Co.* v. *United States R. R. Labor Board*, 261 U.S. 72 (1923); *United States* v. *Los Angeles & S. L. R. R. Co.*, 273 U.S. 299 (1927); *Arrow Distillers* v. *Alexander*, 24 F. Supp. 880 (D.C. 1938), *aff'd* 306 U.S. 615 (1939).

[119] *Standard Scale Co.* v. *Farrell*, 249 U.S. 571, 575 (1919).

acter of the application of coercion, which puts the sanction outside the field of judicial intervention.

The absence of any external restraint upon the enormous power exercised by the Securities and Exchange Commission through the publicity sanction has been forcefully stated by Dean Landis and by the General Counsel of the Commission.[120] Dean Landis has said: "It is restraints upon the exercise of that power that in my judgment are of far greater significance than the creation of restraints upon the power to adjudicate."[121]

In a few instances administrative agencies have adopted a principle of internal restraint on use of the publicity sanction. The Department of Agriculture in the administration of the United States Grain Standards Act has carefully refrained from publicizing the bringing of charges "because the mere fact that a charge had been brought, if generally known, would have been damaging to the business of the respondent."[122] The Federal Deposit Insurance Corporation avoids all publicity in connection with proceedings to terminate insured status. The power of the Comptroller of the Currency to publish reports of examinations of banks which have failed to make changes suggested by the Comptroller has never been exercised, "since it is felt that the results in terms of public reaction might be disastrous."[123]

The Attorney General's Committee on Administrative Procedure remarks on the practice of the Department of Agriculture: "In this respect there is a sharp departure from the practice of some Federal agencies which rely heavily upon the press release as a means of publicizing the issuance of complaints."[124]

There has been little attempt to use the converse sanction, favorable publicity for approved conduct, except in so far as publication of a list of cooperators, such as the lists issued by the Securities and Exchange Commission of public utility companies registering with the

---

[120] See *supra*, pp. 86–87.

[121] Landis, *The Administrative Process*, p. 110.

[122] Monograph of the Attorney General's Committee on Administrative Procedure, Sen. Doc. No. 186, 76th Cong., 3rd Sess. (1940) pt. 7, p. 18.

[123] *Ibid.*, pt. 13, p. 17.   [124] *Ibid.*, pt. 7, p. 18.

Commission during the period of doubt as to constitutionality, constituted such a sanction. Most activities of this type are not actually direct sanctions upon the approved conduct, but rather methods of securing compliance by others, either through the bandwagon appeal or the tacit threat. The Blue Eagle of the National Recovery Administration, in spite of attempts to make it a badge of honor, merely indicated absence of discovered violations and finally became of no value even in its negative aspect.

There are said to be 149 instances in the federal statutes "where a license, permit, certificate or other formal authorization is made a prerequisite to the carrying on of a business or the engaging in an activity or the doing of an act."[125] More than fifty of these statutory provisions are said to be accompanied by power to revoke or suspend "and in many, perhaps most, of the others, the power is implied and in any event is claimed and exercised."[126] There are a few instances in which power is given to the courts to revoke licenses granted by an agency. Under the Federal Power Act revocation is accomplished by action in equity brought by the Attorney General.[127] The Comptroller of the Currency must bring an action in the district court in order to effect a forfeiture of the franchise of a national banking association.[128]

The Federal Alcohol Administration Act provides for annulment of a license where the disapproved conduct, such as fraud or misrepresentation or concealment of material fact,[129] is connected with the procuring of the license. Presumably annulment differs from revocation in that the effect of the annulment is to make the activities un-

---

[125] Report of the Special Committee on Administrative Law, *Reports of Amer. Bar Assoc.,* vol. 61, pp. 720, 749 (1936).

[126] *Ibid.,* p. 750. Where the power to revoke does not expressly accompany the power to grant a license, the courts have held that it may be implied in some cases from the nature of the grant or from other provisions of the statute. In other cases the power to issue licenses has been held to imply no power to revoke. See Freund, *Administrative Powers over Persons and Property,* pp. 117–118.

[127] 16 U.S.C. §820.

[128] 12 U.S.C. §93.

[129] 27 U.S.C. §204 (e).

der the purported license actually unlicensed activities, with the result that there could be prosecution for operation without a license. Other statutes provide for revocation under the same circumstances.[130]

Under the Motor Carrier Act modification of a license is an alternative to revocation as a sanction upon violation.[131] There is no indication that this power has been exercised. It appears to be inappropriate as a punitive sanction. Under the Communications Act of 1934, revocation of a station license is the prescribed sanction for violation, but the license may be modified where such modification will promote the public interest, convenience, and necessity.[132]

The drastic and effective character of the license sanction has recently been given recognition in the pure food legislation[133] and the live poultry sections of the Packers and Stockyards Act,[134] where statutory provision is made for the institution of a licensing system when an emergency occurs. The contemplated emergency is of course the breakdown of other sanctions.

Revocation of license is frequently prescribed without discrimination as a sanction upon all violations of the statute and of the rules and regulations of the administering agency. For example, under the Communications Act of 1934 a station license can be revoked "for violation of or failure to observe any of the restrictions and conditions of this chapter or of any regulation of the Commission authorized by this chapter or by a treaty ratified by the United States."[135]

---

[130] See Communications Act of 1934, 47 U.S.C. §§312, 325; Perishable Agricultural Commodities Act, 1930, 7 U.S.C. §§499d (e), 499h (c).

[131] 49 U.S.C. §312 (a). See also Communications Act of 1934, 47 U.S.C. §359: "If the holder of such certificate violates the provisions of the safety convention, or of this chapter, or the rules, regulations, or conditions prescribed by the Commission, and if the effective administration of the safety convention or of sections 351 to 362 of this title so requires, the Commission, after hearing in accordance with the law, is authorized to request the modification or cancellation of such certificate."

[132] 47 U.S.C. §312.   [133] 21 U.S.C. §344.   [134] 7 U.S.C. §218a.

[135] 47 U.S.C. §312 (a). For similar provisions see: Commodity Exchange Act, 7 U.S.C. §7b ("The failure or refusal of any board of trade to comply with any of the provisions of this chapter, or any of the rules and regulations of the Secretary of Agriculture thereunder"); navigation laws, 46 U.S.C. §239 (g) ("incompetent

In a few instances the statutes confine the sanction of revocation to the more serious offenses. Under the Perishable Agricultural Commodities Act licenses are revocable only upon conviction in court for certain violations or upon administrative determination that the licensee has engaged in statutorily specified unfair trade practices, has after notice continued to employ an individual whose license has been revoked, or has obtained his license fraudulently.[136] Where the charge involves either of the first two grounds, the violation must be flagrant or repeated in order to justify revocation rather than suspension. The revocation of a license of a live poultry dealer under the Packers and Stockyards Act also requires a finding of flagrant or repeated violation.[137] Revocation as distinguished from suspension is confined to "intentional" violations under the Civil Aeronautics Act.[138] This type of provision is ordinarily found in situations where only a few aspects of a business are the subject of regulation, and the blanket provision for revocation is common where there is detailed and extensive regulation.

Under another type of limitation on the drastic sanction of revocation, found in the Motor Carrier Act[139] and the Civil Aeronautics Act,[140] a certificate, license, or permit can be revoked only for wilful failure to comply with an order commanding obedience to the provi-

---

or . . . guilty of misbehavior, negligence, or unskillfulness, or has endangered life, or has willfully violated any of the provisions of this title or any of the regulations issued thereunder"); Civil Aeronautics Act of 1938, 47 U.S.C. §359 ("If the holder of such certificate violates the provisions of the safety convention, or of this chapter, or the rules, regulations or conditions prescribed by the Commission, and if the effective administration of the safety convention or of sections 351 to 362 of this title so requires"); Securities Exchange Act of 1934, 15 U.S.C. §78s ("has violated any provision of this chapter or of the rules and regulations thereunder or has failed to enforce, so far as is within its power, compliance therewith by a member or by an issuer of a security registered thereon"); United States Grain Standards Act, 7 U.S.C. §80; United States Warehouse Act, 7 U.S.C. §246.

[136] 7 U.S.C. §499h.   [137] 7 U.S.C. §218d.
[138] 49 U.S.C. §481 (h).   [139] 49 U.S.C. §312 (a).

[140] 49 U.S.C. §481 (h). This provision applies to certificates of public convenience and necessity. Certificates issued in connection with safety regulations may be revoked without such limitation. See 49 U.S.C. §559.

sion or order found to have been violated.[141] The provision of the
Motor Carrier Act was included in the bill at the request of the representative of the industry, who feared the grant of unrestricted
power of revocation to the Commission which "would hang like the
sword of Damocles over our heads" and permit virtual confiscation
of property for minor infractions of the regulations.[142] At their insistence a provision delaying revocation for ninety days was also included. In connection with the limitation on revocation, Senator
Wheeler, who introduced the bill, said:

The committee amended that so that if they made this willful failure it
could only be revoked after a reasonable time was given to them and they
were notified to that effect. There has been a suggestion made to me that
it probably should be amended to give them at least a 3-month period in
which they could comply with the order. As a matter of fact, I have no particular objection to that suggestion. Neither has the Commission any objection, in my judgment. However, the Commission feels that it is imperative that they do have the right to revoke, because it said that the experience of the State commissions has been that revocation is one of the most
effective ways of getting compliance with the law and with the rules and
regulations.

Criticism was directed against the power of revocation thus conferred
upon the Commission. It was suggested that the effect is to put the future
of countless operators wholly in the hands of the Commission, which
might act arbitrarily, and that the penalties elsewhere provided are ample
to secure compliance. As I just stated, practically all State laws contain

---

[141] For similar provisions see steamship inspection legislation, 46 U.S.C. §435;
Perishable Agricultural Commodities Act, 1930, 7 U.S.C. §499h (b). See also
Freund, *Administrative Powers over Persons and Property,* pp. 146–147.

[142] *Hearings before Committee on Interstate Commerce on S. 1629,* 74th
Cong., 1st Sess. (1935), particularly pp. 200, 281, 327, and 354. See Legislation,
Federal Motor Carrier Act, 36 *Col. L. Rev.* 945, 959 (1936), where it is remarked
that the revocation sanction "is perhaps unnecessarily drastic, since such power
over railroads has not been found necessary, and by Section 222 (a), (b) violation is punishable by fine and may be enjoined." The questionableness of the
analogy with railroads is apparent, and it is precisely the ineffectiveness of criminal and injunctive sanctions which has given rise to administrative sanctions of
this type.

similar provisions, and they have been found the most effective means of enforcing regulations. The revocation provisions in the State statutes have not operated to hamper the growth of the motor-vehicle industry. However, it is fair that operators should have warning and an opportunity to comply before any revocation occurs. The committee has therefore amended paragraph (a) to provide that the Commission shall issue an order commanding obedience to any provision of this part or to any rule or regulation of the Commission thereunder which is alleged to be violated, and that revocation shall occur only where there is failure to comply with such an order within a reasonable time.[143]

Suspension of license is usually provided as an alternative for revocation. However, under the Communications Act of 1934 there is no administrative sanction upon violation alternative to revocation in the case of station licenses.[144] The Federal Communications Commission in 1935 proposed that the statute be amended to permit suspension for a period not to exceed thirty days, saying:

There are many instances where the revocation of a license is too drastic a punishment, but where some admonitory action should be taken. In most cases these are instances of violations of Commission regulations which could be properly punishable by a short suspension. Under the existing law, however, the Commission does not have power to suspend, but only to revoke or deny a renewal application, if and when filed.[145]

On the other hand, under the Packers and Stockyards Act the Secretary of Agriculture may suspend the registration of a stockyard but cannot revoke, except in certain instances where a department or agency of a State is involved.[146] Suspension is for "a reasonable specified period." Similarly, there is no provision for revocation of operators' licenses by the Federal Communications Commission, though

[143] 79 *Cong. Rec.*, pt. 5, p. 5654 (1935).
[144] 47 U.S.C. §312 (a).
[145] Federal Communications Commission, Mimeo. 11855, Additional Legislative Recommendations (1935), quoted in Sen. Doc. No. 137, 75th Cong., 3rd Sess. (1937), p. 3, n. 11.
[146] 7 U.S.C. §§204, 205.

there is no limitation on the period for which they may be suspended.[147] There have been numerous suspensions under each of
these Acts. After fifteen years of experience with the provision of the
Packers and Stockyards Act, the Secretary has not found it necessary
to seek the power of revocation. Suspension pending compliance is
sometimes provided as the sole sanction on violation of supervisory
regulations such as those requiring submission of reports or permitting inspection of records.[148]

Where suspension is provided as an alternative to revocation, it is
usually made a universal alternative, leaving to the administrative
agency uncontrolled discretion as to the extent of the penalty. However, in addition to the limitations already described, there are statutory provisions such as that of the Federal Alcohol Administration
Act, under which a permit cannot be revoked for the first violation,
though it can be suspended "for such period as the administrator
deems appropriate."[149]

In some situations suspension is not actually a less drastic alternative. Even a short suspension may be the equivalent of revocation in
having the effect of destroying the licensed enterprise.[150]

At the hearings on the amendment to the Packers and Stockyards
Act to give the Secretary of Agriculture the power to suspend regis-

[147] Communications Act of 1934, 47 U.S.C. §303 (m) (1). "As a rule operators are suspended for from 3 to 6 months, depending upon the seriousness of the
offense. If it is a second or third offense, the suspension period is made more
drastic." Monograph of the Attorney General's Committee on Administrative
Procedure, Sen. Doc. No. 186, 76th Cong., 3rd Sess. (1940) pt. 3, p. 51.

[148] See, *e.g.*, Perishable Agricultural Commodities Act, 1930, 7 U.S.C. §499m.

[149] 27 U.S.C. §204 (e). This subsection also provides that in cases of non-user
of the permit, suspension is not an alternative to revocation. See *supra,* n. 45.

[150] "Through the suspension or revocation of basic permits, the Federal Alcohol Administration holds a life and death power over those engaged in the
alcoholic beverage industries. During the suspension period, it removes the
offender from the highly competitive market always present in the alcoholic
beverage field, wholesalers and retailers look elsewhere for their products and
oftentimes contacts lost during the suspension periods are never recovered."
Gaguine, The Federal Alcohol Administration, 7 *Geo. Wash. L. Rev.* 844, 862,
n. 62 (1939).

tration,[151] much stress was laid by members of the industry on the drastic nature of the penalty:

a concern may have spent years in building up the good will of the business, and if you suspended him, for some reason you might be very sorry for it afterwards; you might suspend him immediately and then in three days his business would be gone into thin air.[152]

Upon the large established units in practically every field, suspension will fall with much the same effect as revocation. The disruption of organization, loss of customers, and blow to prestige are fatal. On the other hand, with the small persistent violator, suspension may be merely a temporary inconvenience, and revocation alone will be really effective.

In the case of licenses for officers of ships, suspension may also be a very drastic remedy. "Sometimes the suspension for sixty days of a master's license means that the master will never again command a vessel and his career will be ruined."[153] Moreover, there may be great differences in the severity of the penalty. "For example, when the ship happens to be in port for 11 days, a 10-day suspension is almost meaningless. If, on the other hand, the vessel happens to be in port for only 9 days the sentence may be an unexpectedly heavy one because the unfortunate officer or seaman will miss the entire voyage."[154]

Practically all provisions for revocation or suspension of a license require notice and hearing.[155] However, in a number of instances the

---

[151] See 7 U.S.C. §204.

[152] *Hearings before the Committee on Agriculture, House of Representatives, on Packer Act Amendments*, 68th Cong., 1st Sess. (1924), p. 148; see also pp. 68, 69, 140, 143.

[153] Monograph of the Attorney General's Committee on Administrative Procedure, Sen. Doc. No. 186, 76th Cong., 3rd Sess. (1940) pt. 10, p. 7.

[154] *Ibid.*, p. 21.

[155] Under the Securities Exchange Act of 1934 trading in any registered securities on any national securities exchange may be summarily suspended without notice or hearing for a period not exceeding ten days and, with the approval of the President, all trading on any national securities exchange may be so suspended for a period not exceeding ninety days. 15 U.S.C. §78s (a) (4).

license may be suspended, and in a few revoked, without a *prior* hearing and with or without prior notice. The situations where such procedure is permitted are those which are conceived to be emergencies requiring prompt cessation of the licensed activity, usually in order to halt a violation immediately threatening to health or safety. For example, certificates issued in connection with safety regulations under the Civil Aeronautics Act may be suspended in cases of emergency for a period not in excess of thirty days "without regard to any requirement as to notice and hearing";[156] and there is no hearing prior to revocation of a ship's certificate where the ground is failure to obey an order for the correction of certain dangerous conditions.[157] Prior hearing may be dispensed with where the violation is of a supervisory regulation such as the requirement of submitting reports or permitting inspection of records.[158]

A peculiar situation, somewhat similar to the revocation sanction, occurs where, as under the administration of the Federal Reserve System, membership entails certain privileges, but operation without membership is neither prohibited nor in practice impossible. Revocation of membership then becomes a kind of publicity sanction. The bank, for example, whose membership in the Federal Reserve System is forfeited by formal proceedings may receive a death blow; though if its withdrawal is voluntary, it may continue to operate successfully.[159] The effects of such a sanction may sometimes be avoided by withdrawal prior to the institution of proceedings.

It is often said that the revocation of a license is a self-executing sanction, but this is not strictly true as far as official compulsion is concerned. Ordinarily the official sanction for revocation of a required license is criminal prosecution for operation without a license. This sanction depends for its enforcement on the action of the criminal courts and to a large extent on the prosecuting authorities of the criminal courts, though participation of representatives of the agen-

---

[156] 49 U.S.C. §559.   [157] 46 U.S.C. §435.

[158] See, *e.g.,* Motor Carrier Act, 1935, 49 U.S.C. §312 (a); Perishable Agricultural Commodities Act, 1930, 7 U.S.C. §499m.

[159] 12 U.S.C. §327.

cies in the preparation of criminal cases is increasingly a matter of routine. Both the insistent trend toward sanctions which are predominantly administrative and the desire to avoid the procedure of criminal courts are illustrated by the frequent inclusion of provisions permitting the administrative agencies to secure injunctions as an alternative to criminal proceedings.

In most cases of license withdrawal, of course, as in the great majority of administrative sanctions, no further action will be necessary because of acquiescence in the decision. Moreover, such provisions as those found in the Commodity Exchange Act[160] and the Securities Exchange Act of 1934,[161] which require exchanges to discipline their own members and deny trading privileges to those whose licenses have been revoked, are "enforcement" sanctions, or sanctions on sanctions, which are purely administrative in character.

There are a number of provisions prohibiting dealing with or employing persons whose licenses have been revoked, the penalty being revocation of license.[162] However, the field of interaction of government agencies in the use of sanctions is largely unexploited. The revocation of licenses upon conviction by a court of an offense related to the supervised activity is fairly common.[163] An immense extension of administrative power could be effected by making those many enterprises which are supervised in different phases of their activity by several administrative agencies subject to administrative sanctions by the licensing agency for violation in the fields of the other supervising agencies.

The short-duration license with requirement of frequent renewal has been used as a sanction device particularly by the Federal Communications Commission, where it is widely considered a weapon of censorship. Under the statute the Commission is empowered to grant

---

[160] 7 U.S.C. §§8, 9.   [161] 15 U.S.C. §§78s (a), 78o–3 (l).

[162] See, e.g., Perishable Agricultural Commodities Act, 1930, 7 U.S.C. §499h (b).

[163] Securities Exchange Act of 1934, 15 U.S.C. §78o (b). Cf. Federal Alcohol Administration Act, 27 U.S.C. §204; Communications Act of 1934, 47 U.S.C. §311.

broadcasting station licenses for periods up to three years.[164] The first regulations set the license period at six months. Together with warnings by the Commission,[165] and even with frowns and headshakings by the commissioners, the renewal requirement apparently amounted in its practical effect upon broadcasters to a standing threat, renewed every six months, to revoke licenses.

The present system gives the Commission the power of life and death over the station every six months, and as a result, every order, every finding of fact, every press release of the Commission, even every statement of a single member of the Commission must be watched by the licensee for indications of the current policies of the Commission as to program quality.[166]

Public criticism is largely responsible for the extension of the license period to a year.

Except for its use as a sanction, the short license period seems to have little to recommend it.[167] As a sanction, when renewal is not

---

[164] 47 U.S.C. §307 (d).

[165] "The Radio Commission reported that 'it is believed that this warning [on lottery programs] had the effect of materially limiting this class of program, and in such instances as came to the attention of the Commission after its issuance the programs were discontinued voluntarily by the station after the matter had been brought to its attention.' Federal Radio Commission, Annual Report (1931) 9. Protests were made in the House of Representatives that the action of the Radio Commission in issuing a news release warning radio stations to observe the 'proprieties' in broadcasting liquor advertising was unjustifiable and bordered upon censorship. 78 Cong. Rec. 2646 (1934); 78 Cong. Rec. 10991 (1934). . . .

"It is reported that following the action of Commissioner Harold A. Lafount in sending a letter to all stations urging them ' "as their patriotic, if not bounden and legal duty" to refuse their facilities to advertisers who are "disposed to defy, ignore or modify the codes established by the N.R.A.," ' and reminding them that their continued existence depended on the good will of the Radio Commission, the Columbia network took the warning so seriously that it cancelled the broadcasting of a speech by Fred J. Schlink when it discovered that the text submitted criticized the N.R.A." Note, Radio Censorship and the Federal Communications Commission, 39 *Col. L. Rev.* 447, 455, nn. 58, 59 (1939).

[166] *Ibid.*, pp. 454–455 (1939).

[167] See Freund, *Administrative Powers over Persons and Property,* pp. 109–111.

merely routine,[168] it is theoretically more effective than the threat of revocation. The frequent examination lends vigor to the supervisory aspects of regulation, in addition to its *in terrorem* effect on the licensee. To both the administrative agency and the licensee it is more vital than the routine report or the regular inspection. It differs from revocation in the very important respect of putting the burden on the applicant of proving to the satisfaction of the Commission his right to a renewal.[169]

PRESCRIPTION OF INDIVIDUAL ACTION; PREVENTION; THE DISPENSING
    POWER

Prescriptive orders of administrative agencies direct either the cessation or the performance of an act or course of action. They are definitional and admonitory in purpose, applying to the individual case the statutory provisions, which are sometimes general, and warning of punishment upon performing or not performing the act which is prohibited or required. Whether the orders are prohibitory or affirmative and whether primarily definitional or merely admonitory, the application of the statute to the individual concerned is generally thought of as a judicial determination. However, the statutory provisions, especially with reference to the affirmative orders of regulatory agencies, may be so general in their requirements that the order will actually be legislative in character, requiring performance in accordance with what is really a novel policy of administration. Thus, the point for determination may be at the one extreme whether or not a specific act was performed, and at the other whether a performance in the future will be in the public interest with past performance a matter of admission.

Where the statutory requirement is specific, an order which is prospective in operation may bear little resemblance to legislation,

---

[168] Over ninety per cent of the renewals under the Communications Act of 1934 are routine. *Hearings before the Subcommittee of the Committee on Appropriations, House of Representatives, on Independent Offices Appropriation Bill for 1940,* 76th Cong., 1st Sess. (1940), p. 1536.

[169] See Freund, *Administrative Powers over Persons and Property,* p. 60.

being largely admonitory in purpose. Prohibitory orders against contemplated acts such as several agencies have the power to issue are frequently of this type.[170] Their purpose is to prevent the performance of the disapproved act by advance determination of its unlawful character.

Prevention by advance determination is particularly effective where specific goods or persons are involved. Inspection either by police methods or in the course of regular supervision provides a method for bringing them to the attention of the agency, which may then determine whether they are equal to the statutory standards.

Some administratively imposed preventive sanctions, such as those on imports and immigration, can be based, because of the nature of the subject matter, on regular inspection. In other cases, such as the postal service, inspection would not be feasible, and administrative supervision is confined to police regulation. In interstate commerce, regular supervision, except in a few instances such as meat inspection and security regulation, has not been considered feasible or desirable, and the policing method is that usually employed.

In a number of instances administrative preventive sanctions are administratively enforced. An order excluding imports or immigrants or for confiscation of lottery tickets, for example, requires no judicial intervention. In other instances, such as violation of the Meat Inspection Act by shipping meat which has been disapproved or using the mails for distribution of a security after issuance of a stop order by the Securities and Exchange Commission, the official sanction is punishment imposed by the criminal courts. The exclusion of adulterated and misbranded food and drugs or insecticides,[171] caustic poison not branded as required,[172] seeds which are adulterated or unfit for use,[173] and tea below the prescribed standard[174] is accomplished by regular inspection and refusal by the Secretary of Agricul-

---

[170] See, e.g., Communications Act of 1934, 47 U.S.C. §205; Packers and Stockyards Act, 1921, 7 U.S.C. §213 (b).

[171] 7 U.S.C. §134.   [172] 15 U.S.C. §405.
[173] 7 U.S.C. §111.   [174] 21 U.S.C. §45.

ture (in the case of tea by the Board of Tea Appeals), of a permit for admission to the country. Examination and denial of entry permit is the method of the Attorney General under the immigration law.[175]

While formal procedure of a judicial nature is ordinarily available in the cases described in the preceding paragraph, the administration of preventive sanctions in the case of imported milk and meat shipped in interstate commerce does not include formal procedure. Milk is regularly inspected at the border[176] and is rejected or admitted by the informal action of administrative agents. Meat is regularly inspected at the packers' and is stamped as approved or rejected by the inspectors.[177]

Under the postal law certain matter is not mailable either because of its physically dangerous character or for moral or social reasons.[178] Mailing material of proscribed classes is usually punishable by criminal sanction,[179] but exclusion by the Postmaster General is often effective preventively. Mail which is contrary to law may be seized by the post office.[180] The sanction of the fraud order operates in a different manner, preventing the receipt of mail by one who is found to be engaged in the perpetration of fraud or conducting a lottery.[181] The Post Office Department, by the use of this sanction, has had considerable success in stopping the operation of lotteries and in preventing some of the more blatant fraudulent practices.[182]

The refusal order procedure of the Securities and Exchange Commission calls for preliminary examination of a security issue and collateral representations.[183] Where registration is refused after required judicial procedure, the use of the mails or facilities of interstate commerce in distribution of the security is prohibited. The operation of

---

[175] 8 U.S.C. §§151, 152, 154. [176] 21 U.S.C. §143.
[177] 21 U.S.C. §72.
[178] See *United States Official Postal Guide*, July 1936, pp. 22–23.
[179] See, *e.g.*, 18 U.S.C. §§334, 335, 338, 341, 343, 344.
[180] 39 U.S.C. §§498, 499. [181] 39 U.S.C. §259.
[182] Handler, Unfair Competition, 21 *Iowa L. Rev.* 175, 229 (1936).
[183] 15 U.S.C. §77h (b).

the stop order is substantially similar, except that it may be issued after the registration has become effective.[184]

Some sanctions of this type depend mainly on the power of the National Government to stop the movement of goods or persons from place to place and on its control over communication. They are most effective in the fields of importation and immigration and in the administration of the postal service. In interstate commerce administrative intervention is more limited, and criminal penalties or judicially imposed preventive sanctions, as under the Federal Food, Drug, and Cosmetic Act, are usually provided. The movement of persons within the country, although it is potentially an effective method, for example, of disease control or economic coordination, is not subjected to either judicial or administrative prevention because of the high value set on freedom of movement. Other sanctions on free movement in behalf of economic coordination may be found in such activities as resettlement projects and residence restrictions on relief payments. The clash between freedom of expression and judicial or administrative repression, as well as the protection of privacy of communication, has limited the scope of government intervention in the use of the postal service and regulation of interstate telephone, telegraph, and radio communication.

Summary seizure or destruction of goods by administrative agencies is a preventive sanction occasionally available under the federal statutes. Opium may "be seized and summarily forfeited to the United States Government without necessity of instituting forfeiture proceedings of any character."[185] Diseased plants[186] and animals[187] may be destroyed. Seizure and destruction of goods, especially where no payment is made, is a punitive as well as a preventive sanction. Where prevention alone is intended, as in the exclusion of imports, the goods themselves are usually returned to their owners.

The cease and desist order is often thought of as the administrative counterpart of the ordinary equity injunction.

[184] 15 U.S.C. §77h (d).

[185] 21 U.S.C. §173.

[186] See, *e.g.*, 7 U.S.C. §164a.

[187] See, *e.g.*, 21 U.S.C. §103

Cease-and-desist orders are nothing more nor less than injunctions in effect, and the fact that formal recourse to the courts is necessary before enforcement machinery is set in motion simply means that the administrative agency, like the court itself, must eventually look to the executive branch of the government to execute its decisions. . . .[188]

In both their definitional and admonitory aspects, the similarity of the two sanctions far outweighs in importance their differences, which are largely formal.

Freund sought to make a distinction between the warning order and the cease and desist order on the basis of the definiteness of the statute.[189] If a statute is definite, the administrative order serves, he felt, merely to warn, while if the statute is indefinite, its purpose is to make the "generic statutory prohibition or requirement definite." Administrative law is not so unlike judicial law as this distinction would imply. The traditional concept would have it that the issuance of every injunction is the result of some definite rule of law. This is about equally valid with the notion that those against whom cease and desist orders are issued find in the orders the first news of the applicability of an indefinite statute to the activity which the orders prohibit. Some injunctions and some cease and desist orders make definite previously indefinite law. Most injunctions and most cease and desist orders have no such definitional aspect. They are merely warnings to lawbreakers who are well aware of the illegality of their activities. Administrative agencies as well as courts follow rules of law, whether or not there are definite statutes, just as courts as well as administrative agencies legislate by putting definite content into indefinite statutes and common law rules.

The concept of unfair methods of competition, even when first included in the Federal Trade Commission Act, was not completely devoid of content. The prohibitions of the Clayton Act[190] are quite

---

[188] Report of the Special Committee on Administrative Law, *Reports of Amer. Bar Assoc.,* vol. 61, pp. 720, 749 (1936).

[189] Freund, *Administrative Powers over Persons and Property,* pp. 146–149.

[190] 15 U.S.C. §§13, 14.

definite. Moreover, the Federal Trade Commission "had the benefit of the experience of the regulation of competition at common law and under the Sherman Act,"[191] to say nothing of the various criminal statutes on certain phases of trade practices. A decision of the Federal Trade Commission was hardly required to show that commercial bribery, for example, was included in the concept; the first respondent to be ordered by the Commission to cease and desist from that practice was not taken by surprise. The function of the order was not to make definite the statute, any more than any finding of illegality makes definite any rule of law. The order merely warned of impending penalty for a practice that could equally as well have been defined by statute and punished immediately by criminal sanction.

Moreover, whatever vagueness there may have been as to the content of the concept of unfair competition in 1914 at the time of the enactment of the Federal Trade Commission Act, it "has been fairly well defined through interpretations of the Commission and the courts over a period of twenty-five years."[192] The Commission itself in its annual reports defines a large number of unfair trade practices.[193] The great majority of its orders today are admonitory rather than definitional.

It is the mildness of the cease and desist sanction which has led to its adoption in many cases rather than "because the legislator finds himself incapable of foreseeing the precise duty of the individual."[194] The reason for the use of the cease and desist sanction in the control of false advertising is not difficulty in the definition of the offense.

Those members of the House Committee who had unsuccessfully opposed the denial of jurisdiction of advertising to the F & DA [Food and Drug Administration] resolutely sought to secure the amendment of this bill so as to provide that persons violating the above provisions of the Act

[191] Handler, Unfair Competition, 21 *Iowa L. Rev.* 175, 237 (1936).

[192] Lindahl, The Federal Trade Commission Act as Amended in 1938, 47 *J. Pol. Econ.* 497, 523 (1939).

[193] See, *e.g.,* Federal Trade Commission, *Annual Report,* 1938, pp. 70–75.

[194] Freund, *Administrative Powers over Persons and Property,* pp. 148–149.

should be subject to a civil penalty of not more than $3000 or, if the commodity advertised were injurious to health, of not more than $5000. The purpose of this move was to give to the FTC Act the deterrent effect which the advertising provisions of the food and drug bill would have possessed. Under the bill proposed by Mr. Lea, no advertiser would have cause to fear more than an order to stop falsifying unless either his commodity were intrinsically dangerous or the government could succeed in the difficult task of proving intent to defraud.

Unfortunately for the minority committeemen, they were seeking to provide the FTC with teeth it did not want. Mr. Lea, speaking against the amendment after having "conferred with a representative of the Federal Trade Commission," said, "Its judgment is very decidedly opposed to this amendment because it would tend to be destructive of the successful operation of the Federal trade law. It would, in effect, convert the federal trade act, in effect, to a criminal statute primarily as to advertisements. . . . This is not the practical way to deal with business men."[195]

In some cases the cease and desist order is a sanction upon any violation of definite statutory prohibitions. Under the Commodity Exchange Act, for example, the Secretary of Agriculture may issue a cease and desist order, as an alternative to revoking the designation of a contract market, upon finding either a continuing or a past violation of any of the provisions of the Act or of any of the rules and regulations thereunder.[196] Under the Bituminous Coal Act of 1937, the Bituminous Coal Commission may order a code member to cease and desist from violation of the code as an alternative to revoking his code membership.[197] Orders of this type actually serve the same purpose as orders to comply with the statute under the Motor Carrier Act or the Civil Aeronautics Act.[198]

All cease and desist orders, even those which are in fact definitional, are admonitory in character in that they impose no punitive sanction and merely warn of punishment to come. However, to say that they are admonitory in character is not to say that in themselves

---

[195] Cavers, The Food, Drug, and Cosmetic Act of 1938: Its Legislative History and Its Substantive Provisions, 6 *Law & Contemp. Prob.* 2, 19 (1939).
[196] 7 U.S.C. §13a.   [197] 15 U.S.C. §835.   [198] See *supra*, pp. 123–125.

they are ineffectual. There can be no doubt that even under the old procedure under the Federal Trade Commission Act which required in effect two warnings (the cease and desist order of the Commission and, upon subsequent violation, a court injunction) the cease and desist order was effective in a great many cases. But cease and desist orders are subject to the common weakness of admonitory sanctions. They have little effect upon the consciously and persistently crooked unless they are backed up by ultimate punitive sanctions. This weakness was vividly illustrated in the experience of the Federal Trade Commission, before the 1938 amendment of the statute, with violators who could continue their violations with impunity until the Commission secured a court order to enforce its order.[199] Enforcement procedure for cease and desist orders against monopoly and restraint of trade, by the Secretary of Commerce in the case of the fishing industry[200] and by the Secretary of Agriculture in the case of producers' associations,[201] is even less forceful than the old procedure of the Federal Trade Commission. Under these provisions, the Secretary must apply to a court for enforcement, and the order is only prima facie evidence of the facts of violation found as a basis for its issuance.

The only sanction under the Packers and Stockyards Act as first adopted was the cease and desist order. The theory of the Act as explained by Chester Morrill, then Assistant Secretary of Agriculture, was "that every man has a right to enter into business and to continue in that business as long as he behaves himself and that the action of the Secretary of Agriculture should be limited to the removal of the misbehavior and not the removal of the man who is guilty of the misbehavior, and that that could be accomplished in most cases by the cease and desist procedure."[202] After a short period of operation under the Act, the Secretary applied to Congress for the further sanc-

[199] For a description of the new procedure for enforcement see pp. 184–185; Legislation, The Federal Trade Commission Act of 1938, 39 *Col. L. Rev.* 259, 270–272 (1939).

[200] 15 U.S.C. §522.   [201] 7 U.S.C. §292.

[202] *Hearings before the Committee on Agriculture, House of Representatives, on Packer Act Amendments,* 68th Cong., 1st Sess. (1924), p. 145.

tion in the case of stockyards of suspension of registration. Not only had the cease and desist sanction fallen far short of achieving its purpose of curbing abuse in the industry, but, Mr. Morrill testified before a House committee considering the proposed amendment, the publicity given the orders was a great handicap since other stockyards, upon learning about a forbidden practice through the public order of the Secretary, immediately adopted it in their own businesses.[203] The power of suspension was eventually granted, and the regular practice of the Bureau of Animal Industry is to impose suspension in addition to the cease and desist sanction.[204]

Variation in the effectiveness of the cease and desist sanction makes it inappropriate for some types of conduct, except perhaps as an alternative for revocation or some other punitive sanction. Its use as the sole sanction is proper when confined to those situations where definition is actually needed. That there is not always such need for definition even in the field of monopolistic practices, restraints of trade, and unfair competition, commonly considered the proper field for the cease and desist order, is indicated by the provision of revocation as an alternative in the Commodity Exchange Act and the Bituminous Coal Act of 1937 and of suspension as an alternative in the Packers and Stockyards Act, and by the use of other sanctions such as the denial of right of entry by the Secretary of Commerce under the Shipping Act[205] and exclusion of goods by the President under the Tariff Act of 1930.[206] Criminal sanctions are applied under the Wheeler-Lea Act to certain types of false advertising.[207] Of the application of the cease and desist order to this field, Cavers says:

The principal objections voiced to FTC control were directed to the fact that its "cease and desist" procedure had little or no deterrent effect

---

[203] *Ibid.*, p. 193.

[204] Bureau of Animal Industry, *Annual Report,* 1936, p. 33; 1937, p. 36; 1938, p. 49. In these years, respectively, 23, 12, and 30 orders to cease and desist coupled with orders of suspension were issued, whereas no orders merely to cease and desist without suspension are reported.

[205] 46 U.S.C. §813.   [206] 19 U.S.C. §1337 (e).

[207] 15 U.S.C. §54 (a).

on the advertisers' tendency to hyperbole, since the most rigorous penalty for an offense would be a Commission order not to do it again, an order which if violated could lead to nothing more drastic than a judicial order not to do it again.[208]

Handler believes the sanction inappropriate even under the new procedure of the Federal Trade Commission:

Will the modified procedure deter the dissemination of false advertising? The Commission must undertake a preliminary investigation before issuing a complaint in order to satisfy itself that grounds exist for the institution of proceedings. This naturally takes time. Hearings cannot be held sooner than thirty days after service of the complaint. Various jurisdictional requirements, such as proof of interstate commerce, tend to prolong the trial. The examiner must take the matter under advisement and prepare his report. The case is then put on the Commission's calendar for argument. After argument, findings of fact and a cease and desist order must be prepared. Sixty days must then elapse before the order becomes binding.

In the meantime the advertiser may have discontinued the challenged advertisement and may have embarked upon a new advertising campaign which is equally deceptive. The proceedings before the Commission may therefore relate to a controversy which has become essentially moot. A cease and desist order does not penalize the advertiser for his previous derelictions and does not prevent him from indulging in new and different misrepresentations. This procedure thus permits an unscrupulous advertiser to "play fast and loose" with the Commission. He can reap the profits of his misrepresentations until compelled to desist, and then by adopting new copy, continue his depredations of the public until again forced to stop. A prohibition which operates prospectively, and then only after the lapse of considerable time, cannot have much deterrent effect on wrongdoing.[209]

The difficulty connected with the scope of the prohibitory order which Handler indicates in the quoted passage is not confined to the

[208] Cavers, The Food, Drug, and Cosmetic Act of 1938: Its Legislative History and Its Substantive Provisions, 6 *Law & Contemp. Prob.* 2, 14 (1939).

[209] Handler, The Control of False Advertising under the Wheeler-Lea Act, 6 *Law & Contemp. Prob.* 91, 105 (1939).

field of false advertising, though it is particularly acute there and particularly important, since about nine-tenths of the cease and desist orders of the Federal Trade Commission have been directed toward the control of false advertising.[210] A commission employing the cease and desist sanction must steer a course between the Scylla of generality and the Charybdis of too great specificity. An order merely directing the respondent to cease and desist from all unfair trade practices would not meet the requirement that the sanction define the offense. On the other hand, an order defining the practice too specifically will leave him free to make a change in some minor particular and to proceed in substantially the same way as before. Freund pointed out the difference in this respect between "qualitative" and "quantitative" orders, showing that a qualitative order, as, for example, an order to desist from charging a specific rate, is entirely ineffectual, since the slightest change would be a literal obedience to the order. However, he imputed too great strength to the quantitative order which, he said, "may leave a theoretical liberty to indulge in other equally obnoxious practices; but it will take time to develop them; and the cease-and-desist order may in these cases practically accomplish its purpose, while it would not in a matter of quantity."[211] The very admonitory character of the cease and desist sanction, together with the procedural safeguards provided, gives the respondent the time required to develop the new practices, as the situation described by Handler indicates.

Henderson noted the difficulties of the Federal Trade Commission in drafting orders which were at the same time sufficiently specific to be effective and sufficiently general to cover the substance of the offense and gave examples of the orders drafted to meet these difficulties.[212] The practice of the Commission has varied, but in some cases its orders have prohibited a designated type of unfair practice, such as paying commissions to any employee of any customer or pass-

[210] McLaughlin, Legal Control of Competitive Methods, 21 *Iowa L. Rev.* 274, 285 (1936).

[211] Freund, *Administrative Powers over Persons and Property*, p. 148.

[212] Henderson, *The Federal Trade Commission*, pp. 72–77.

ing off goods as the goods of a competitor, without further specification such as the particular employees or competitors. The courts have found some orders of this type too general.[213] In so far as the orders are admonitory, there appears to be no reason for narrow limitation of their scope. The application of the definition of the offense found by the Commission to the subsequent offense for which the respondent may be punished could be better left to the trial of the subsequent offense. It is difficult to say how the respondent could be injured by such a procedure. Probably the limitation arises from the tendency to put excessive emphasis on the definitional aspects of cease and desist orders. It is true, for example, that an order to cease and desist from unfair competition without further definition might leave it to the respondent to act at his peril with no clear idea of the limits of the action which would subject him to penalty. But an order to cease and desist from bribing a customer's employees or from passing off goods as the goods of a competitor sufficiently defines the offense for the purpose of subsequent imposition of a punitive sanction.

The power to issue a cease and desist order does not carry with it any power to issue an affirmative order.[214] A respondent who is ordered to give up a practice cannot be commanded to substitute another unless there is statutory authority for the affirmative part of the order. An order issued under the authority of such a statute is very different in character from an exclusively prohibitory order. The Communications Act of 1934, for example, provides that the Commission may issue an order to cease and desist from "any charge, classification, regulation, or practice . . . [which] is or will be in violation of any of the provisions of this chapter" and may

---

[213] See, *e.g., Federal Trade Commission v. Beech-Nut Packing Co.*, 257 U.S. 441, 445–446 (1922); *Raymond Bros.–Clark Co. v. Federal Trade Commission*, 280 Fed. 529 (C.C.A. 8th, 1922); *Federal Trade Commission v. Kay*, 35 F. 2d 160, 163 (C.C.A. 7th, 1929), *cert. denied*, 281 U.S. 764 (1930).

[214] See *J. W. Kobi Co. v. Federal Trade Commission*, 23 F. 2d 41, 43 (C.C.A. 2d, 1927); cf. *Cream of Wheat Co. v. Federal Trade Commission*, 14 F. 2d 40, 50 (C.C.A. 8th, 1926).

determine and prescribe what will be the just and reasonable charge . . . and what classification, regulation, or practice is or will be just, fair, and reasonable, to be thereafter followed, and to make an order that the carrier . . . shall not thereafter publish, demand, or collect any charge other than the charge so prescribed . . . and shall adopt the classification and shall conform to and observe the regulation or practice so prescribed.[215]

The Secretary of Agriculture has the same power to issue affirmative orders under the Packers and Stockyards Act.[216] The administrative power under such provisions becomes a power substantially to direct operation rather than merely a power to prevent or punish violation.

Comment on the National Labor Relations Board has frequently been based on the theory that the Board's sanction is merely the order to cease and desist, the implication being that the Board has only approximately the same power as the Federal Trade Commission. But the National Labor Relations Act provides that the Board, in addition to an order to cease and desist from unfair labor practices, may order the person involved "to take such affirmative action, including reinstatement of employees with or without back pay, as will effectuate the policies of this chapter."[217]

An examination of the orders issued by the Board lends support to the view that the Board's power to issue affirmative orders, its power to direct, is far more important and effective than the merely admonitory power to order cessation of unfair labor practices. Among the affirmative orders issued by the Board are orders to bargain collectively and to embody the understanding reached by the collective bargaining in an agreement for a definite term,[218] to reinstate employees,[219] to post notices stating that the employer will not engage in specified unfair labor practices,[220] to inform personally every em-

---

[215] 47 U.S.C. §205 (a).   [216] 7 U.S.C. §211.

[217] 29 U.S.C. §160 (c).

[218] See, *e.g., In the Matter of St. Joseph Stock Yards Co.,* 2 N.L.R.B. 39 (1936).

[219] See, *e.g., National Labor Relations Board* v. *Remington Rand,* 94 F. 2d 862 (C.C.A. 2d, 1938).

[220] See, *e.g., National Labor Relations Board* v. *Mackay Radio & T. Co.,* 304 U.S. 333 (1938); *National Labor Relations Board* v. *Santa Cruz Fruit Packing*

ployee that his contract with the employer constitutes a violation of the Act and that the Board is therefore obliged to discontinue such contract,[221] and to "disestablish" a company union.[222]

Most important of the affirmative orders of the Board is that to pay back-wages. Not only does the possibility of such an order serve as an effective deterrent upon wrongful discharge, since every employer acts at the peril of having these wages accumulate as a penalty, but the back wage provision is an effective sanction upon prompt compliance with the order once it is issued.[223] "The provisions . . . were designed to insure that an employer would cease unfair labor practices."[224] The punitive aspect is especially apparent in the practice of the Board as to strike benefits. Although the employees have been reimbursed to some extent by the strike benefits for their loss of wages, this amount is not deducted from the back-wage order.

Affirmative orders issued by a number of agencies which do not issue formal cease and desist orders resemble the cease and desist orders in having both definitional and admonitory aspects. At the one extreme are orders to comply with the provisions of the statute where

Co., 91 F. 2d 790 (C.C.A. 9th, 1937). See Recent Cases, Labor Law—National Labor Relations Act—Power to Order Employer to Post Notices that It Will Cease and Desist from Unfair Trade Practices, 52 Harv. L. Rev. 1016 (1939).

[221] See, e.g., In the Matter of Carlisle Lumber Co., 2 N.L.R.B. 248 (1936).

[222] See, e.g., National Labor Relations Board v. Pennsylvania Greyhound Lines, 303 U.S. 261 (1938); Comment, National Labor Relations Act: Employer Domination of or Interference with a Labor Organization, 26 Calif. L. Rev. 611, 616–620 (1938).

[223] See Note, Back Pay Orders under the National Labor Relations Act, 48 Yale L.J. 1265 (1939).

[224] National Labor Relations Board v. Carlisle Lumber Co., 99 F. 2d 533, 537 (C.C.A. 9th, 1938). See also National Labor Relations Board v. Biles Coleman Lumber Co., 98 F. 2d 18, 23 (C.C.A. 9th, 1938). On the character of the damage sanction as compulsive and deterrent, see Hale, Force and the State: A Comparison of "Political" and "Economic" Compulsion, 35 Col. L. Rev. 149 (1935), for example, p. 162: "While the law seems to concentrate its attention, when assessing damages, on the function of compensating plaintiffs, it most likely welcomes the deterrent effect on the former class of defendants. If it did not, there would be no reason for picking them out to bear the plaintiffs' losses. . . ."

those provisions are entirely definite; at the other are the regulatory orders of such agencies as the Interstate Commerce Commission or the Federal Power Commission.

The affirmative order defines the duty imposed by the statute by directing the individual concerned to perform the act which the statute requires, whereas the cease and desist order defines the statute by directing him to refrain from an act which the statute forbids. Both are admonitory in that they warn of punishment unless the statute is complied with by acting or refraining from acting in the manner ordered.

The affirmative order is the formal sanction by which regulatory power is exercised. It is a typical method of prescribing rates, regulations, and practices of regulated enterprises, but detailed consideration of regulatory supervision is beyond the scope of this study. Some of the statutes of regulatory agencies contain very broad provisions for the issuance of affirmative orders. For example, the Federal Communications Commission is given the power to "issue such orders . . . as may be necessary in the execution of its functions"[225] and the United States Maritime Commission, "such order as it deems proper."[226] Another type of general provision is that already described which gives the administrative agency the power in connection with cease and desist orders to prescribe the rate, regulation, or practice which must be substituted for the forbidden activity.[227]

Power is frequently given to issue particular orders in connection with equipment and operation. Very extensive regulation of transportation involves in its formal aspects the issuance of such affirmative orders. The regulatory power of the Interstate Commerce Commission is summarized by Sharfman as follows:

the Commission's powers are not confined to the regulation of rates and the limitation of profits. It is authorized to regulate safety of operation,

---

[225] 47 U.S.C. §154 (i).   [226] 46 U.S.C. §821.

[227] See, *e.g.*, Communications Act of 1934, 47 U.S.C. §201. See also Interstate Commerce Act, 49 U.S.C. §§1 (9), 6 (13) (a); Federal Power Act, 16 U.S.C. §824a.

service practices and the utilization of facilities, extensions and abandon-
ments of line, the issuance of securities and assumption of obligations, in-
terlocking directorates and pooling arrangements, acquisitions of control
and actual consolidations; and it is empowered to prescribe and police carrier accounts, to require regular and special reports, and to enforce publicity of all carrier operations.[228]

Where the agencies have licensing power over the regulated enterprises, revocation and suspension of licenses and other administrative
sanctions are usually available for the enforcement of affirmative orders. Other agencies must depend for enforcement on the criminal
courts or on mandamus proceedings. The "recommendations" of the
Federal Trade Commission for the adjustment of the business of an
export trade corporation found by the Commission to be restraining
trade are enforced by reporting the restraint to the Attorney General.[229]

Liability to private citizens for damages caused by failure to obey
an order is sometimes found as an enforcement sanction. Disobedience of an order issued by the Secretary of War to owners or persons
operating a bridge over any navigable waters, to repair damage or
prevent danger to property caused by the placing of the bridge, entails liability for a sum double the amount of the injury to be recovered in court.[230] The Secretary's order under this statute resembles
the reparational sanction in that, unlike the situations where affirmative orders are issued by regulatory agencies, the controversy is formally between private citizens.

The permissive order power and the so-called dispensing power of
the regulatory agencies differ from the licensing power only in the

---

[228] Sharfman, *The Interstate Commerce Commission,* pt. I, p. 4.
For statutory provisions giving the Commission power to issue affirmative
regulatory orders, see, *e.g.,* 49 U.S.C. §§1 (9), (21); 3 (4); 5 (10), (11); 6 (13)
(a), (b); 313 (b) (2).
For similar express powers to issue affirmative regulatory orders, see Communications Act of 1934, 47 U.S.C. §§201, 214 (d), 220 (a); Federal Power Act,
16 U.S.C. §§824f, 825a (a); Civil Aeronautics Act of 1938, 49 U.S.C. §487 (a).
[229] 15 U.S.C. §65.   [230] 33 U.S.C. §500.

specificity of the conduct involved. The statutory provisions forbid certain activity, such as consolidation or merger[231] or issuance of stocks or bonds,[232] except with the authorization of the regulating agency. There are numerous and important instances of this dispensing power, especially in the regulation of transportation by the Interstate Commerce Commission.[233] Enforcement sanctions include in some cases, as for example the Motor Carrier Act, administrative revocation or suspension of license. Judicial criminal sanctions are also provided.

REPARATIONS

The reparational sanction, damages to the injured party for the injury done him, is the ordinary sanction of the courts in civil cases. Several administrative agencies have the power to award damages on claims by private citizens against other private citizens, including situations in which claims would be classified by the courts as tortious as well as contractual. In this phase of their judicial power the determinations of administrative agencies are often strikingly similar in method to the methods of the courts. The Secretary of Agriculture, in dealing with damage awards under the Perishable Agricultural Commodities Act, must interpret the terms of a written contract and decide many and difficult questions of law.

In applying the principles of conflicts of law, contracts, agency, and sales, whether of common law origin or statutory modifications of the common law, the Secretary of Agriculture has the same task as a court.

---

[231] See, e.g., Motor Carrier Act, 1935, 49 U.S.C. §313 (a).

[232] See, e.g., Interstate Commerce Act, 49 U.S.C. §20a (2); Federal Power Act, 16 U.S.C. §824c (a).

[233] See, e.g., Interstate Commerce Act, 49 U.S.C. §4 (1), long and short haul rate; §6 (3), §317 (c), minimum time for publication of change in rate; §303 (b), §309 (a), exemptions from statutory requirement of certificate; §310, exemptions from prohibitions against holding certificates as both common carrier and contract carrier; §311 (b), exemption from the requirement of a broker's license. See Freund, *Administrative Powers over Persons and Property*, pp. 128–135; Note, The Power of Dispensation in Administrative Law—A Critical Survey, 87 *U. of Pa. L. Rev.* 201 (1938).

Judicial precedents and State statutory provisions are controlling. Interstices in the law must be filled by novel decisions. He is guided by his own prior decisions.[234]

The grant of power to the administrative agencies to determine claims for damages in controversies between private citizens was due, in general, to dissatisfaction with the operation of the courts. It is interesting to note, however, that practically every objection advanced against court procedure in the arguments in favor of giving administrative agencies this jurisdiction has stressed the difficulties of recovering on claims. The advantage claimed for administrative procedure, reduced to its essentials, is that plaintiffs will have less difficulty in securing awards of damages.[235] Those against whom claims are made apparently find little fault with the procedure of the courts. The situation which led to the enactment of the Perishable Agricultural Commodities Act, giving to the Secretary of Agriculture the power to award reparation for damages caused by unfair trade practices in the shipping of fruits and vegetables, has been described as follows:

Recourse could be had to the courts for relief from most, if not all, of the fraudulent and unfair practices, but the remedy at law was found to be seriously inadequate. Individual losses were small; the buyer and the seller were often hundreds and frequently thousands of miles apart; the commodities were highly perishable; and, in case of a dispute, immediate disposition thereof was necessary, especially in view of the fact that, pending the outcome of the dispute, storage and demurrage accrued against the

[234] Unpublished MS of Frederic P. Lee, *Administration of Federal Agricultural Commodity Standards,* p. 398.

[235] In speaking of the reparations procedure of the Interstate Commerce Commission, Sharfman says: "The purpose of Congress in imposing the reparations function upon the Commission was largely to render somewhat less formidable the task of obtaining redress for injuries sustained in consequence of violations of the Act by the carriers, particularly since individual claims are usually small." Sharfman, *The Interstate Commerce Commission,* pt. III, vol. B, p. 333.

"The idea in authorizing the [Interstate Commerce] Commission to award reparation apparently was to afford a direct and inexpensive way for the complainant to secure a decision on that point." Interstate Commerce Commission, *Annual Report,* 1916, p. 75.

shipper, and the products deteriorated rapidly. Litigation was expensive and slow, and the hope of recovery was not bright enough to justify resort to the courts in most instances. Therefore, it was an easy matter for commission merchants, dealers, and brokers to take advantage of the farmer, small cooperative, etc., and to obtain concessions of all kinds.[236]

It is such considerations as these, which concern the failings of the courts, rather than any special abilities of administrative agencies, that have led to the grant to them of power to award damages. The distinction between "cases where the knowledge and judgment of experienced technicians is required" and "cases where the decision depends only upon ordinary fact determinations and the application thereto of the rules of the common law"[237] is apparently felt by the Interstate Commerce Commission to have little validity in the decision of cases as distinguished from the fixing of rates. Decisions on contract violations under the Walsh-Healey Act would not "be beyond the competence of even the most pedestrian judge."[238]

Differences in the effectiveness of administrative action of this type might be thought to depend to some extent on the differences in methods of enforcement of the damage awards. Entirely apart from further enforcement, all such determinations have some effect merely as declaratory rulings, adjudicating the rights of the parties.[239] The extent of this effectiveness varies with the agencies involved, depending upon such factors as prestige, extent of regulatory supervision,

[236] Sellers, *Administrative Procedure and Practice in the Department of Agriculture under the Perishable Agricultural Commodities Act, 1930*, pp. 2–3.

[237] Brown, Administrative Commissions and the Judicial Power, 19 *Minn. L. Rev.* 261, 296 (1935), citing Fletcher, Power of the Interstate Commerce Commission to Award Damages, 25 *Yale L.J.* 489 (1916).

[238] Gellhorn and Linfield, Administrative Adjudication of Contract Disputes: The Walsh-Healey Act, 37 *Mich. L. Rev.* 841, 873 (1939).

[239] Of administrative declaratory rulings, Borchard says: "In Anglo-American jurisdictions, administrative tribunals have not yet obtained the authority to issue declarations as such, though the effect of their ruling is often purely declaratory. . . . There is manifest a growing tendency by statute and decision to expand the power of administrative tribunals to render declaratory judgments." Borchard, *Declaratory Judgments,* pp. 593–594.

and the availability of unofficial enforcement methods. Even where official enforcement sanctions are available, enforcement is sometimes left almost entirely to unofficial pressure.

The reparations orders of regulatory agencies such as the Interstate Commerce Commission,[240] the United States Maritime Commission,[241] and the Federal Communications Commission[242] are enforceable by court action brought by the successful party, in which the order is merely prima facie evidence of the facts found. However, the general powers of these agencies over the regulated industries tend toward infrequent resistance to their damage awards. While reparations orders of regulatory agencies usually may be issued for any violation of the statute, most of them are concerned with overcharges.[243]

The reparations orders of the Secretary of Agriculture under the Packers and Stockyards Act can be enforced by court action in the same manner,[244] but the Secretary's power to suspend registration for any violation of the Act[245] gives him an effective administrative enforcement sanction.

The Perishable Agricultural Commodities Act, in addition to enforcement by the suit *de novo,* provides for automatic suspension of license where it is not shown within a designated period that the damage award has been paid.[246] The Act as originally passed contained only the provision for court enforcement, and dissatisfaction because of its ineffectiveness led to amendment providing the administrative enforcement sanction.

Under the Federal Power Act, besides its power to order refund after a decision that rates are not justified,[247] the Commission can fix

---

[240] See 49 U.S.C. §16.   [241] See 46 U.S.C. §829.

[242] See 47 U.S.C. §407.

[243] For the Interstate Commerce Commission see Sharfman, *The Interstate Commerce Commission,* pt. III, vol. B, pp. 330–331.

[244] 7 U.S.C. §210 (f). The power applies only to the provisions concerning stockyards.

[245] 7 U.S.C. §204.   [246] 7 U.S.C. §499g (d).

[247] 16 U.S.C. §824d (e).

the amount which is to be paid by the owner of a water power project benefited by head water improvement.[248] The Act contains no special provisions for the enforcement of award orders of the Commission as distinguished from other orders which are enforceable by the usual injunction and mandamus provisions and criminal penalties for violation.[249] If the violator is a licensee, the revocation of his license is available as a sanction, but this also requires court action.[250] The Act provides in the case of licensed public utilities for a forfeiture to be fixed by the Commission for wilful failure "to comply with any order of the Commission,"[251] and presumably this penalty could be inflicted as an administrative sanction on violation of an award order. The Commission has never resorted to the use of this power.[252]

Awards under the Longshoremen's and Harbor Workers' Compensation Act become final after a designated period unless proceedings are brought to set them aside. Enforcement is effected by filing the award in court and by judgment and execution thereon.[253] There are no exclusively administrative enforcement sanctions except such as may be found in the penalty provisions on delinquency in payment of awards, when these provisions are taken together with the power of a deputy commissioner to excuse such delinquency.[254]

Frequently the payment of claims is secured by the requirement, statutory or administrative, of posting a bond or depositing security.[255] Recovery on such a bond requires judicial intervention, but there are statutory provisions in the case of deposits, such as those giving the

---

[248] 16 U.S.C. §803 (f). The power of the Commission to make such awards has been involved only twice. Monograph of the Attorney General's Committee on Administrative Procedure, Sen. Doc. No. 10, 77th Cong., 1st Sess. (1941) pt. 12, p. 17.

[249] 16 U.S.C. §825m.   [250] 16 U.S.C. §820.   [251] 16 U.S.C. §825n (a).

[252] Sen. Doc. No. 10, 77th Cong., 1st Sess. (1941) pt. 12, p. 39.

[253] 33 U.S.C. §918.

[254] See 33 U.S.C. §§914 (e), 918. The deputy commissioner can suspend payment of compensation for unreasonable refusal to submit to medical treatment. 33 U.S.C. §907 (a).

[255] See, e.g., Packers and Stockyards Act, 1921, 7 U.S.C. §204; United States Warehouse Act, 7 U.S.C. §247.

Comptroller of the Currency the right to settle claims,[256] where the payment of damages is wholly administrative. Probably in some instances the agencies would require a judgment of a court before proceeding to pay out money, whereas administrative judicial procedure would suffice in others.

The punitive aspect of the award of back wages by the National Labor Relations Board has been described.[257] The award also has for its purpose the reimbursement of workers for damage done them by violation of the Act.[258] Back-pay awards are enforced by the same procedure as are other orders of the Board, the enforcement sanctions being judicially rather than administratively imposed.

Back-pay awards under the Walsh-Healey Act can be paid out of any balance owed by the government on the contract in connection with which the violation occurred, or they may be recovered in an action brought by the Attorney General.[259] Up to March 1, 1939, only two cases had been turned over to the Attorney General under this provision.[260]

The money awards of the National Railroad Adjustment Board are officially enforced by action in the courts, in which the determination of the Board is merely prima facie evidence of the facts found.[261] In practice, unofficial pressure is the enforcement sanction.

The statute gives no right of appeal to either carriers or unions from an adverse decision of the Board. The Board has no powers of enforcement, and therefore non-compliance by a carrier may continue with impunity unless the union acts to obtain compliance. This the union can do in two

---

[256] 12 U.S.C. §137.   [257] *Supra*, pp. 143–144.

[258] Back-pay orders are described as remedial by the Commission in: *In re Art Crayon Co., Inc.,* 7 N.L.R.B. 102, 119 (1938); *In re Colorado Milling & Elevator Co.,* 11 N.L.R.B. 66 (1939); National Labor Relations Board, *Annual Report,* 1938, pp. 199–200. See also *Consolidated Edison Co. of New York* v. *National Labor Relations Board,* 305 U.S. 197 (1938).

[259] 41 U.S.C. §36.

[260] Gellhorn and Linfield, Administrative Adjudication of Contract Disputes: The Walsh-Healey Act, 37 *Mich. L. Rev.* 841, 845, n. 11 (1939).

[261] 45 U.S.C. §153 (p).

ways: first, by petitioning the appropriate United States District Court for an order enforcing the Board's award, pursuant to the procedure laid down by the statute; and secondly, by economic pressure. The first course has not been adopted. Out of 1,616 awards handed down by the four Divisions up to July 30, 1936, of which considerably over half must have been in favor of the employees, not one was taken to court for an enforcement order, and the presumption is either that the carriers willingly complied in all these cases, or that, in some of the cases where the carriers did not at first comply, compliance was brought about by threatened strikes.[262]

It is for protection against this unofficial compulsion rather than against official power that the railroads demand provision for judicial review at the instance of the losing party; the unions oppose such review.[263]

Controversy between the government and a private citizen over the performance of a contract is not essentially different from controversy between two private citizens. The government as contractor is appearing in a quite different role from that in which it appears in the determination of controversies or the prosecution of cases. Apart from the power to withdraw its consent to be sued, it stands in practically the same position as any party to a contract. The determination of disputes arising out of government contracts is then on the same order as the determination of controversies between private citizens, and the government might simply withhold payment where it believed that the contract had been breached and permit the matter to be settled by the courts.

However, in fact the government has set up a system for administrative determination with judicial and appellate procedure administered by the contracting officers, the heads of departments, and the Comptroller General,[264] or, in the case of war risk insurance, by the

---

[262] Garrison, The National Railroad Adjustment Board: A Unique Administrative Agency, 46 *Yale L.J.* 567, 591 (1937).

[263] Monograph of the Attorney General's Committee on Administrative Procedure, Sen. Doc. No. 10, 77th Cong., 1st Sess. (1941) pt. 4, p. 6.

[264] See McGuire, *Matters of Procedure under Government Contracts.*

Veterans' Administration, or, under the Walsh-Healey Act, by the Secretary of Labor.

A number of administrative agencies, including most of the cabinet officers, have the power to adjust claims, usually with a limitation as to amount, made against the United States for damages caused by the operations of the various departments.[265] Ordinarily these are to be certified to Congress for payment, but under some of the provisions the administrative agency is empowered to pay the claims.[266]

Arbitration and mediation activities by the National Government are an increasingly important device for the determination of controversies between private citizens. Official arbitration, because of the potential official pressure to submit the controversy and the prestige attaching to the official award, is a more effective sanction than its "voluntary" nature would indicate. It is most important and effective in the field of labor disputes, but there are other instances such as arbitration by the Secretary of Agriculture between cooperative associations and purchasers of milk under the Agricultural Marketing Agreement Act of 1937.[267]

The potentially compulsive character of official arbitration has been recognized by the Railway Labor Act under which, when the parties refuse to submit a controversy to arbitration, the President may appoint an Emergency Board to investigate the controversy and report.[268] No change may be made in the conditions involved in the dispute during the thirty-day period designated for the Board's investigation, or for thirty days after it has made its report. While there is no official sanction upon failure of the parties to accept the report, it has in practice ordinarily led to the settlement of the controversy along the lines suggested by the administrative board. The procedure

---

[265] For example, Secretary of the Treasury, 14 U.S.C. §40; Secretary of Commerce, 33 U.S.C. §721; Secretary of State, 31 U.S.C. §224a; Secretary of the Navy, 34 U.S.C. §599; Secretary of War, 5 U.S.C. §208; Postmaster General, 5 U.S.C. §392; Secretary of the Interior, 25 U.S.C. §388 (no limitation on amount of the individual claim).

[266] See, e.g., 34 U.S.C. §600; 25 U.S.C. §388; 5 U.S.C. §392.

[267] 7 U.S.C. §671 (a).   [268] 45 U.S.C. §160.

tends to resemble compulsory arbitration because of the prestige attached to its official character and to the appointment of the Board
by the President.

Administrative Determinations That Are Not Sanctions on Specific Individual Conduct

Many administrative determinations involving the rights of individuals are not sanctions on specific individual conduct, though in
some cases conduct may be one of the factors considered in reaching
the determination. While the granting of permits under the Federal
Alcohol Administration Act is to some extent dependent on past
conduct in that such a permit is not granted if the applicant has been
convicted of a felony or misdemeanor within a designated period
prior to the application,[269] in no realistic sense can the grant of such
a license be thought of as a reward for refraining from the commission of crimes or denial be considered as punishment for a crime. Licensing under the Act is primarily a means for bringing the industry
under regulation, and the conduct test is a device for keeping out of
the industry persons whose future conduct, judged by their past,
might make them undesirable licensees. The licensing of officers of
merchant ships is not based on any desire to encourage others to follow the course leading to the license, nor is exclusion on the ground
of "habits of life and character"[270] in purpose a penalty for bad habits
or immoral character. Obviously, the granting of relief payments or
W.P.A. employment is not intended to encourage the conduct which
makes applicants eligible to receive such payments. Taxation of certain activities is not designed to discourage those activities except in
the rare instances where, usually because of constitutional inhibitions,
a prohibitory statute is disguised as a revenue measure.

A regard for balance makes it necessary for us to remember that the
motivation of specific human conduct is not always the *raison d'être* of a
given tax. It may be rather that the imposition is for the purpose of securing some broader social policy. Any government fiscal system which taxes

[269] 27 U.S.C. §204 (a) (2).   [270] See 46 U.S.C. §226.

the rich and spends the proceeds for the moral and physical welfare of the masses is obviously engaged in a method of wealth redistribution.[271]

Tariff duties are often fixed with the purpose of burdening certain types of goods, but this is a part of a larger social policy, the protection of domestic industry, and not a sanction upon the special individual conduct of the importer.

The grant of social security benefits is not intended to sanction past conduct, even where employment is a required prerequisite. The purpose of excluding certain types of employment, such as agricultural and domestic work, is obviously not to discourage engaging in these occupations.

Military and naval pensions perhaps have some slight effect as sanctions. The anticipation of St. Crispin's Day may be more pleasant if it is thought of as coinciding with the date for the receipt of the monthly pension check. But the aspect of such pensions as rewards for past conduct and therefore sanctions for the future is certainly secondary to other aspects. In so far as pension distributions to war veterans are not merely payment for political support, they are principally to be justified as welfare assistance measures, though the classification is very roughly arrived at for the purpose.

As government licensing and government assistance grow increasingly important and extensive in scope, there is a corresponding increase in the social necessity of assurance that those who are entitled to receive such grants do receive them and, on the other hand, that the conduct of enterprises in which a general public interest is involved is not imperiled or the public treasury mulcted by grants to those who are not entitled to receive them. The right to receive such grants becomes for the individuals concerned a property right no less valuable than any other claim which receives official recognition. There is the same need for procedure that leads to fair and impartial determination of these rights and liabilities as there is where a punitive sanction is imposed.

---

[271] Reuschlein and Spector, Taxing and Spending: The Loaded Dice of a Federal Economy, 23 *Corn. L.Q.* 1, 5, n. 16 (1937).

In the field of government assistance, especially in the form of loans, there has been a great increase in the use of the corporate device.[272] The advantages gained by the use of the corporation form from the point of view of internal administration[273] cannot be permitted to obscure the official nature of the application of sanctions. Provisions such as those of the Federal Reserve Act which require elaborate administrative judicial procedure for the termination of a contract of the Federal Deposit Insurance Corporation indicate recognition of the necessity for appropriate safeguards in the relationship between such official corporations and individuals dealing with them.[274] Similar recognition is strikingly lacking in the procedure for the award and denial of government loans, potentially and actually a sanction of immense coercive force.

Where the sanction is an official grant which is not exclusive, that is to say, a grant to which all applicants of certain specified status are entitled, the right to the grant is a question wholly between the applicant and the government. Military and naval pensions, some social security payments, and many kinds of licenses[275] are of this type. In all cases of licensing prior licensees have a certain interest adverse to subsequent applicants in limiting the field of competitors; but, with

[272] Among the corporations administering measures of government assistance are the Reconstruction Finance Corporation, Federal Deposit Insurance Corporation, Home Owners' Loan Corporation, Emergency Housing Corporation, Tennessee Valley Authority, Commodity Credit Corporation, and Federal Subsistence Homestead Corporation. For a survey of government corporate activities see McIntire, Government Corporations as Administrative Agencies: An Approach, 4 *Geo. Wash. L. Rev.* 161 (1936); Note, The Corporation as a Federal Administrative Device, 83 *U. of Pa. L. Rev.* 346 (1935).

[273] See Dimock, *Modern Politics and Administration,* pp. 363–366.

[274] 12 U.S.C. §264 (i).

[275] Where licensing is merely a taxation device and where, as in the case of milk licenses under the first Agricultural Adjustment Act, all enterprises in the industry are automatically licensed, there is, of course, no occasion for exercise of administrative discretion. See Freund, *Administrative Powers over Persons and Property,* pp. 65–70; Black, Does Due Process of Law Require an Advance Notice and Hearing before a License Is Issued under the Agricultural Adjustment Act? 2 *U. of Chi. L. Rev.* 270 (1935). Registration of trademarks likewise involves no exercise of administrative discretion.

the exception of those instances where there is legislative declaration of policy permitting monopoly, that interest is not a proper factor in administrative determination. Pressure for exclusionary requirements is of course exercised upon the legislature.

The nature of the public interest involved in the administration of this type of sanction makes desirable a procedure for determination which resembles as little as possible the "cock fight" aspect of judicial procedure. A nonexclusive license, for example, is often granted without anything in the nature of judicial procedure, though where such a license is denied, the interest of the applicant is usually protected by hearing requirements. The grant or denial of a privilege such as classification of mail by the Postmaster General is a determination of this type. Where the claim is by the government in connection with the revenue, the judicial nature of the determination adverse to the taxpayer is similarly recognized. The absence of requirements for formal procedure when the determination is to grant the application is based upon the possibility of safeguarding the public interest by procedure within the administrative agencies. Where the statute clearly specifies the standards so that there is a minimum of administrative discretion, the propriety of leaving the determination to internal administrative procedures is reasonably clear. However, where a determination in favor of a claimant involves the exercise of relatively unguided discretion and especially where the determination concerns matters of great importance such as, for example, large tax refunds, a noncontroversial judicial procedure provides more effective safeguards for the public interest. Frauds on the relief agencies may be left to police methods and punitive sanctions, but Teapot Domes could be profitably avoided by formal requirements as to methods of determination.

On the other hand, where the grant is exclusive in the sense that it is limited to one or a few, conflicting individual interests appear in addition to the public interest. The procedure of the General Land Office for the determination of claims is largely devoted to controversies between claimants for the same piece of land. In the grant of exclusive rights in air waves the Federal Communications Commission must consider conflicting individual claims. Where, although the subject matter is not physically limited, the grant of a license is made to depend upon a finding of public convenience and necessity, as, for example, under the Motor Carrier Act, the object is in part to protect the field from competition. Both prior grantees and those who hope for future grants may have interests conflicting with the applicant's. These conflicting interests are factors to be considered in the determination of the claim. The allowance of the claim of one becomes in a sense a sanction upon others, since its effect is to deny their prospective claims or, in some cases, to diminish the value of rights previously granted.

The public interest as a factor in the determination of rights of these types may be either in the assurance that the privilege claimed will be exercised in an approved manner or, more frequently, that it will not be exercised in a disapproved manner. There is also a public interest in seeing to it that the claimant receives a fair hearing and in the determination of whether he is entitled to the claimed benefit by reason of being in a defined class.

The administrative determination of eligibility for benefits, such as pensions or social security payments, affords comparatively limited scope for the exercise of discretion, since the standards are usually specifically defined in the legislation. However, the elaborate procedure of the Veterans' Administration and the questions already arising under the old age insurance provisions of the Social Security Act indicate that application of the legislative standards to individual cases involves not only determination of doubtful fact situations but also extensive administrative interpretation of the statutory provisions. Similarly, the detailed statutory provisions of the revenue laws do not prevent genuine controversies over tax liabilities requiring administrative determination, even where the facts are admitted.

Where the question is whether the privilege will be exercised in the public interest, the standards are occasionally set forth with such specificity that very little is left to administrative discretion in the determination of whether the statutory requirements are met. In the administration of grants of public land, for example, the question for the administrator is whether the claimant has performed the acts required by the statute, since the performance of the prescribed acts is the only standard fixed for securing assurance that the land will be used in a manner deemed to be in the public interest. However, the legislative standards ordinarily leave a wider sphere to administrative discretion. Even in the grant of licenses which depend mainly upon considerations of technical competence, such as the licenses for officers of ships, the standards are not ordinarily defined by the statute. Standards of technical competence are often fixed by administrative regulations rather than left to discretion in the decision of individual cases; but the precision of administratively prescribed tests will vary, so that administrative application of standards to particular cases will involve a varying amount of discretion. Moreover standards of moral fitness, which are usually coupled with requirements of technical competence, are largely subjective in practice.[276] An extreme example of unguided administrative discretion is found in the issue of passports by the Secretary of State, where moral considerations have sometimes been determinative.[277]

Particularly interesting examples of administrative determinations depending upon technical considerations are found in the application to individual cases of the standards for certain commodities fixed by the Secretary of Agriculture. The decision that particular goods are or are not of the fixed standard entails no grant or denial of any public right or privilege; but the classification is itself a valuable right, since sales are made in accordance with it, and contract remedies may be available or unavailable on the basis of the Secretary's decision.[278]

[276] See Freund, *Administrative Powers over Persons and Property*, p. 100.

[277] *Ibid.*, pp. 520–521. See Sigler, The Problem of Apparently Unguided Administrative Discretion, 19 *St. Louis L. Rev.* 261 (1934).

[278] See, *e.g.*, 7 U.S.C. §54, cotton; §78, grain; §492, farm products; §499n (a), perishable agricultural commodities; §511f, tobacco; §585, apples and pears.

Administrative determinations with similar important consequences on private rights are made in the grant, denial, and withdrawal of licenses under the United States Warehouse Act. There is no official requirement that warehouses be licensed, but warehouses which meet certain standards are entitled to a license.[279] They are regularly inspected and the license may be withdrawn if the warehouse falls below the required standard.[280] Although any warehouse may operate without such a license, the license is a valuable right, since the acceptability of warehouse receipts depends largely upon whether the goods represented by the receipts are stored in a licensed warehouse.

An officially noncompulsive sanction of this type is the seafood inspection service of the Department of Agriculture, which is described in the following passage:

It is voluntary although a number of inducements are embodied in the amendment and the regulations thereunder to make acceptance of the system widespread. A packer may apply for inspection for his plant and is granted it if the plant possesses suitable specified processing equipment and sanitary facilities. In order to retain the inspection service the packer must also observe sanitary requirements as to unloading platforms, equipment and plant, and prevention of bacterial spoilage, processes specified for closure of the can, and requirements as to the time and temperature for processing. . . . The cost of the service is paid by the owner of the plant. . . . Lots of canned shrimp inspected and passed as conforming to the requirements of the regulations are issued an inspection certificate to that effect, and the labels thereon are required to bear the legend "Production Supervised by United States Food and Drug Administration."

The inspection system is also interwoven with a label approval system. . . . While there is no direct prohibition against the use of an unapproved label, failure to submit labels for approval is a basis for withdrawal of inspection. The use of an unapproved label is also a basis for denying an inspection certificate. Practically, only approved labels are used. . . .

While the shrimp inspection service is not a mandatory requirement of law, practically its use for the shrimp packer has been found advantageous.

[279] 7 U.S.C. §244.   [280] 7 U.S.C. §246.

Unless the packer avails himself of the inspection service, his product, if shipped in interstate commerce, is liable to condemnation if found to be unfit for food and the packer is subject to criminal prosecution. Use of the inspection certificate avoids the likelihood of such proceedings and the trade losses that result from the attendant publicity. Also, unless the packer avails himself of the inspection service he is unable to label his products under the supervision of the government, and as a result sales resistance is met both from distributors and consumers.[281]

Decisions in representation cases before the National Labor Relations Board and the National Mediation Board have somewhat the same effect. Though they do not directly impose any duty, they give a valuable right to the group in whose favor the decision runs, since it is with the group so designated that the employer is required by the statute to bargain collectively. The determination of course also involves the denial of this right to competing groups.

In granting licenses to conduct enterprises in which there is a general public interest, administrative discretion is even less limited by statutorily prescribed standards. The factors which are to be taken into consideration are, for example, business experience,[282] financial standing,[283] trade connections,[284] fitness, willingness, and ability properly to perform the services.[285] Some administrative agencies may consider "other qualifications of the applicant."[286]

Where the purpose of licensing is restriction of competition, there is a further interest in the desirability of granting the privilege at all, particularly where there are prior licensees. The legislatively declared standard of determination is typically the vague public con-

---

[281] Lee, The Enforcement Provisions of the Food, Drug, and Cosmetic Act, 6 *Law & Contemp. Prob.* 70, 88–89 (1939).

[282] Federal Alcohol Administration Act, 27 U.S.C. §204 (a) (2).

[283] Federal Alcohol Administration Act, 27 U.S.C. §204 (a) (2); Communications Act of 1934, 47 U.S.C. §308 (b).

[284] Federal Alcohol Administration Act, 27 U.S.C. §204 (a) (2).

[285] Motor Carrier Act, 1935, 49 U.S.C. §307 (a); Civil Aeronautics Act of 1938, 49 U.S.C. §481 (d) (1).

[286] 47 U.S.C. §308 (b).

venience and necessity. Definite administrative standards in addition to those arising from conflicting individual interests are slow to develop where the determination is guided by considerations of public convenience and necessity, as in the licensing of radio broadcasting and motor transportation.

The situations presented in this section are too numerous and varied to permit of more than an attempt to point out the applicability of judicial procedure to the determination of issues involving sanctions of this type, an applicability that is frequently overlooked because of the habit of mind that links judicial procedure with sanctions traditionally imposed by courts.

CHAPTER IV. THE COURTS

P ROCEEDINGS in court, in the event that a case progresses that far, may be considered in a large sense as the final stage in the administrative process. Few cases ever reach the courts.[1] Those few have a certain effect generally on administrative methods, particularly in the agencies whence the cases come. But not much in the way of generalization is warranted, partly for the reason that the decisions are based on statutory grounds rather than on constitutional requirements. Nor can generalization be indulged in even as to the statutes, though there is similarity in them and in some respects they follow a pattern. The problem before Congress concerning the extent of court activity with regard to administrative action is essentially an *ad hoc* one as to each agency, and two extremes are to be avoided. Judicial review must not be too wide: it may involve nonjudicial functions beyond the power of constitutional courts. It must not be too narrow: it runs the risk of falling short of what the Constitution is thought to require.

METHODS OF ACCESS TO THE COURTS

Our principal concern is with statutory methods of access to the courts, for it is in this field that some of the most significant developments have taken place. There are three major groups of cases in which such access is provided with respect to administrative determinations: (1) application by an aggrieved party for relief from administrative action; (2) application by the agency itself, or by a party for whose benefit it has acted, for aid in the enforcement of its action; (3) criminal proceedings to enforce such action. But statutory methods are

[1] The discussion in this chapter is not concerned with the administrative or other nonjudicial functions which may be exercised by the so-called legislative courts. As to those courts and the variety of their functions, especially as exercised in the District of Columbia, see Katz, Federal Legislative Courts, 43 *Harv. L. Rev.* 894 (1930).

not always available; Congress has not provided a method for all agencies. In such situations, as Mr. Justice Brandeis suggested in *Crowell* v. *Benson*,[2] "the unwritten law supplied a remedy" at least to the extent necessary to keep the administrative officer within the limits of his authority. A brief account will be added later concerning some of these methods, for example, proceedings in equity and habeas corpus.

On Application by the Aggrieved Party

Developments under this head have been notable, and it is here that the statutory provisions are most numerous. They establish two different procedures, which nevertheless have much in common. The procedures have sometimes been characterized as (a) statutory bill in equity and (b) statutory appeal.[3] The former is a survival from an earlier administrative day; it has not been the subject of any considerable or detailed statutory development. The latter includes legislative efforts more recent and more explicit, and the continued and cumulative efforts in this direction have produced a distinctive statutory pattern.

STATUTORY BILL IN EQUITY

This procedure, the details of which are not set forth fully in the statutes, brings into play the general practices of equity. Suit is begun and for the most part carried on as an ordinary equity action for an injunction. In one respect, however, there is a substantial difference: it is not a *de novo* proceeding. While it is an original proceeding in the sense that it is begun in the court, yet it is concerned with the record made in the administrative agency and thus takes on an appellate character. Furthermore, there is no indication that the ordinary requirements for equitable jurisdiction will be insisted upon— for example, that there is no adequate remedy at law.

[2] 285 U.S. 22, 90 (1932).
[3] This is the terminology used in the unpublished MS of Frederic P. Lee, *Administration of Federal Agricultural Commodity Standards.*

The statutory bill in equity, as a method for court review of administrative action, originated in a proceeding prescribed for the review of orders of the Interstate Commerce Commission by the Hepburn Amendment in 1906. Prior to that date the orders of the Commission had no force of their own—that is to say, they were not given the force and effect of law and no penalty attached to their violation. To secure their enforcement it was necessary for the Commission or an interested party to apply to a federal court, jurisdiction being conferred for the purpose, for a decree compelling obedience. Under the original Act the report of the Commission was declared to be "prima facie evidence of the matters therein stated," and the courts felt free to admit new evidence, thereby granting a hearing *de novo.* An early case thus expressed the attitude of the Supreme Court: "We do not mean . . . that either party, in a trial in the court, is to be restricted to the evidence that was before the Commission. . . ."[4] It became a common practice for carriers to withhold evidence from the proceeding before the Commission and present it in the first instance in the court when the Commission sought to enforce its order. Reversals of the Commission's orders were rather frequent. The courts were wielding considerable influence on the Commission's activities and were gradually developing the relationships between it and the courts.

The Hepburn Amendment changed the legal set-up for the Commission's orders and accelerated the development above mentioned. It divided the orders of the Commission into two classes, reparation for the payment of money (as to which see *infra,* p. 188) and all others, and then provided that nonreparation orders should take effect within a reasonable time (not less than thirty days) and remain in force and be complied with unless set aside or suspended by the Commission or a court of competent jurisdiction. Severe penalties were provided for violations.

No explicit provision was made in the Hepburn Amendment for judicial review of the nonreparation orders of the Commission. But

[4] *Cincinnati, N. O. & Tex. Pac. Ry. Co.* v. *Interstate Commerce Commission,* 162 U.S. 184, 196 (1896).

there was an implied recognition of the right of an aggrieved party to bring an action "to enjoin, set aside, annul, or suspend in whole or in part any order of the Interstate Commerce Commission." The Judicial Code covers it now.[5] Venue is in the judicial district in which the party resides upon whose petition the order was made, with certain exceptions not here material. The final order and findings of the Commission are attached to the complaint and, where questions are involved concerning the sufficiency of evidence, a copy of the record, including a transcript of the evidence taken before the trial examiner, is usually brought into the court. Review is confined to the record made before the Commission. A noticeable feature is that in the district court the suit is heard by three judges, at least one of whom must be a judge of the circuit court of appeals. Appeal is directly to the Supreme Court. As will be seen later, the provisions for review by a statutory three-judge court followed by direct appeal to the Supreme Court make the statutory bill in equity similar to the "statutory appeal" to the circuit court of appeals with review by certiorari. The pendency of the suit does not of itself stay or suspend the operation of the order, but the court may stay or suspend it, in whole or in part, pending the determination of the suit.

Nowhere in the statutes are the grounds set forth upon which the courts may restrain the enforcement of the Commission's orders. Consequently, the relationship between the courts and the Commission has been shaped by the judiciary, and any conclusiveness which attaches to the findings or actions of the Commission is a product of self-imposed restraint. In an early case in which the question of the permissible scope of judicial review was raised, Mr. Justice White said:

Beyond controversy, in determining whether an order of the commission shall be suspended or set aside, we must consider, *a,* all relevant questions of

[5] 28 U.S.C. §41 (28). Under the Hepburn Amendment this jurisdiction existed in the circuit courts. It was made explicit and transferred to the Commerce Court by the Mann-Elkins Act of 1910. The Urgent Deficiency Appropriation Act of 1913 abolished the Commerce Court, and the jurisdiction was thereupon transferred to the several district courts of the United States.

constitutional power or right; *b,* all pertinent questions as to whether the administrative order is within the scope of the delegated authority under which it purports to have been made; and, *c,* a proposition which we state independently, although in its essence it may be contained in the previous one, viz., whether, even although the order be in form within the delegated power, nevertheless it must be treated as not embraced therein, because the exertion of authority which is questioned has been manifested in such an unreasonable manner as to cause it, in truth, to be within the elementary rule that the substance, and not the shadow, determines the validity of the exercise of the power.[6]

In *Interstate Commerce Commission* v. *Louisville & Nashville R. R. Co.,*[7] the Supreme Court rejected a contention that an order of the Commission based on a finding that existing charges are unreasonable is conclusive "even if the finding was wholly without substantial evidence to support it," and declared that the Court must "examine the record with a view of determining whether there was substantial evidence to support the order." If there is, the fact that there is a conflict in the evidence does not affect the situation, since, the Court said, it cannot settle the conflict or put its judgment against that of the Commission. The courts have repeatedly affirmed the doctrine that it is beyond their function to pass independent judgment upon

---

[6] *Interstate Commerce Commission* v. *Illinois Central R. R. Co.,* 215 U.S. 452, 470 (1910). Two years later, the following expanded version of the scope of judicial review was given: "it has been settled that the orders of the Commission are final unless (1) beyond the power which it could constitutionally exercise; or (2) beyond its statutory power; or (3) based upon a mistake of law. But questions of fact may be involved in the determination of questions of law, so that an order, regular on its face, may be set aside if it appears that (4) the rate is so low as to be confiscatory and in violation of the constitutional prohibition against taking property without due process of law; or (5) if the Commission acted so arbitrarily and unjustly as to fix rates contrary to evidence, or without evidence to support it; or (6) if the authority therein involved has been exercised in such an unreasonable manner as to cause it to be within the elementary rule that the substance, and not the shadow, determines the validity of the exercise of the power." *Interstate Commerce Commission* v. *Union Pacific R. R. Co.,* 222 U.S. 541, 547 (1912).

[7] 227 U.S. 88 (1913).

the weight of the evidence. They have adhered to their ruling that if the determination of the Commission finds substantial support in the evidence, they will not weigh the evidence. As a corollary to this ruling, they have held that an order unsupported by evidence is void.

Later acts, such as the Packers and Stockyards Act of 1921[8] and the Perishable Agricultural Commodities Act of 1930,[9] have incorporated by reference the procedure of the statutory bill in equity. Thus, a section of the Packers and Stockyards Act provides that "all laws relating to the suspending or restraining the enforcement, operation, or execution of, or the setting aside in whole or in part the orders of the Interstate Commerce Commission, are made applicable to the jurisdiction, powers, and duties of the Secretary [of Agriculture] in enforcing the provisions" of this Act.[10] No standards are established delimiting the scope of the review and, as in the case of the Interstate Commerce Commission, the restrictions upon the scope of the review are self-imposed. A suit attacking the order of the Secretary must be determined on the record made in the course of the administrative hearing.[11] An order will not be set aside by the court unless it clearly appears that it was based upon an erroneous rule of law or upon findings not supported by evidence.[12] The statutory bill in equity has produced little judicial interference with administrative action.

The review of orders of a deputy commissioner under the Longshoremen's and Harbor Workers' Compensation Act is similar to

[8] 7 U.S.C. §217.

[9] 7 U.S.C. §499k. Cf. another section of the Perishable Agricultural Commodities Act, 1930, 7 U.S.C. §499g (c), which is unusual in that it allows any party adversely affected by a reparation order to petition the district court to set it aside.

[10] Similar provisions, whether they incorporate the Interstate Commerce Act provision by reference or not, appear in the statutes of other agencies discussed in this study: Communications Act of 1934, 47 U.S.C. §402 (a); Longshoremen's and Harbor Workers' Compensation Act, 33 U.S.C. §921.

[11] *Denver Union Stock Yard Co.* v. *United States,* 57 F. 2d 735 (D. Colo., 1932).

[12] *Inghram* v. *Union Stock Yards Co.,* 5 F. Supp. 486 (D. Neb., 1933).

that in the statutory bill in equity proceedings, but it presents several unique characteristics. Deputy commissioners may make orders either awarding or rejecting claims for compensation, and the Act requires that on application a hearing must be granted at which both the claimant and the employer may present evidence. Hearings are public and must be reported stenographically, and the Commission must provide by regulation for the preparation of a record. Section 21 provides that if "not in accordance with law, a compensation order may be suspended or set aside, in whole or in part, through injunction proceedings, mandatory or otherwise, brought by any party in interest against the deputy commissioner making the order, and instituted in the Federal district court for the judicial district in which the injury occurred."[13]

Review is limited to the record, except in the matter of jurisdictional facts where it is *de novo,* and the administrative action is by implication made final if in accordance with law. In an action to set aside the award the deputy commissioner's findings of fact (jurisdictional facts excepted) are binding on the court if supported by substantial evidence.[14] The proceedings are brought in a one-judge district court. An appeal may be taken to the circuit court of appeals. In practice the commissioners appear to concern themselves only with questions of fact, not ruling upon legal issues except as such ruling is implicit in the making or refusing to make a compensation award. The district courts appear to confine themselves to questions of law, the findings of fact by the deputy commissioner being accepted as binding if they are supported by evidence.

STATUTORY APPEAL

One of the most fully developed statutory provisions for reviewing administrative action is contained in the Public Utility Holding Company Act of 1935 administered by the Securities and Exchange Commission.[15] Because of its typical character, it is printed in full in the

[13] 33 U.S.C. §921 (b). [14] *Crowell* v. *Benson,* 285 U.S. 22 (1932).
[15] "Court review of orders. (a) Any person or party aggrieved by an order

notes; its main features may be briefly summarized. Any person aggrieved by an order of the Commission may obtain a review of such order in a circuit court of appeals or in the Court of Appeals of the District of Columbia, by filing a petition within sixty days after the entry of such order. The Commission is thereupon required to file a transcript of the record upon which the order was entered. The court is forbidden to consider any objection to the order not urged before the Commission. The findings of the Commission as to the

issued by the Commission under this chapter may obtain a review of such order in the circuit court of appeals of the United States within any circuit wherein such person resides or has his principal place of business, or in the United States Court of Appeals for the District of Columbia, by filing in such court, within sixty days after the entry of such order, a written petition praying that the order of the Commission be modified or set aside in whole or in part. A copy of such petition shall be forthwith served upon any member of the Commission, or upon any officer thereof designated by the Commission for that purpose, and thereupon the Commission shall certify and file in the court a transcript of the record upon which the order complained of was entered. Upon the filing of such transcript such court shall have exclusive jurisdiction to affirm, modify, or set aside such order, in whole or in part. No objection to the order of the Commission shall be considered by the court unless such objection shall have been urged before the Commission or unless there were reasonable grounds for failure so to do. The findings of the Commission as to the facts, if supported by substantial evidence, shall be conclusive. If application is made to the court for leave to adduce additional evidence, and it is shown to the satisfaction of the court that such additional evidence is material and that there were reasonable grounds for failure to adduce such evidence in the proceeding before the Commission, the court may order such additional evidence to be taken before the Commission and to be adduced upon the hearing in such manner and upon such terms and conditions as to the court may seem proper. The Commission may modify its findings as to the facts by reason of the additional evidence so taken, and it shall file with the court such modified or new findings, which, if supported by substantial evidence, shall be conclusive, and its recommendation, if any, for the modification or setting aside of the original order. The judgment and decree of the court affirming, modifying, or setting aside, in whole or in part, any such order of the Commission shall be final, subject to review by the Supreme Court of the United States upon certiorari or certification as provided in sections 346 and 347 of Title 28.

"(b) The commencement of proceedings under subsection (a) shall not, unless specifically ordered by the court, operate as a stay of the Commission's order." 15 U.S.C. §79x.

facts, if supported by substantial evidence, are conclusive. However, the court may order, upon a showing of materiality and reasonable grounds for failure to adduce such evidence at the hearing, that additional evidence be taken before the Commission. The Commission may then modify its findings of fact and file recommendations for modifying or setting aside its order. The modified findings of fact, if supported by substantial evidence, are conclusive. The jurisdiction of the circuit court of appeals and the Court of Appeals of the District of Columbia is exclusive, and their judgments are final, subject to review by the Supreme Court upon certiorari or certification. Commencement of proceedings for review does not, unless specifically ordered by the court, operate as a stay of the Commission's order.[16]

This procedure made its first appearance in the original Federal Trade Commission Act in 1914.[17] Comparison of the provision there with the amplified form of the Public Utility Holding Company Act of 1935 will show that, aside from amplification, there are four respects in which the later procedure differs from the earlier: (a) venue includes the Court of Appeals of the District of Columbia, (b) time limit set for filing petitions, (c) objections restricted to those urged before the Commission, and (d) provision that commencement of review proceedings does not, unless specifically ordered by the court, operate as a stay of the Commission's order.

More explicit than even the Public Utility Holding Company Act of 1935 on the scope of review is the Communications Act of 1934, as amended. Under this interesting example of statutory development[18] it is provided that an "appeal" may be taken from the "decisions" of the Commission, that the appeal shall be determined "upon the record," that the court may "enter a judgment affirming or reversing the decision," that the review by the court "shall be limited

---

[16] Similar provisions are found in other statutes with which this study is concerned: Securities Act of 1933, 15 U.S.C. §77i; Securities Exchange Act of 1934, 15 U.S.C. §78y; Federal Trade Commission Act, 15 U.S.C. §45; Communications Act of 1934, 47 U.S.C. §402; National Labor Relations Act, 29 U.S.C. §160; Federal Power Act, 16 U.S.C. §825*l*.

[17] 15 U.S.C. §45.   [18] 47 U.S.C. §402.

to questions of law," and that findings of fact "if supported by substantial evidence" shall be conclusive unless it shall clearly appear that they are "arbitrary or capricious." In *Federal Radio Commission v. Nelson Bros. Bond & Mortgage Co.*[19] the Supreme Court discussed and approved the procedure and scope of the review thus authorized. In an earlier case it had been held that the statute, attempting to establish a general review of administrative action, went beyond judicial functions and that the matter was not within the jurisdiction of the constitutional courts. Thereupon the Act was amended to read as above indicated.

Questions of law, the Court observed in speaking of the amendment, form the appropriate subject of judicial determinations. "Whether the Commission applies the legislative standards validly set up, whether it acts within the authority conferred or goes beyond it, whether its proceedings satisfy the pertinent demands of due process, whether, in short, there is compliance with the legal requirements which fix the province of the Commission and govern its action . . ."—all these, said the Court, are appropriate questions for judicial decision. Moreover, as the Court continued, a finding without substantial evidence to support it is an arbitrary or capricious finding and does violence to the law. It is without the sanction of the authority conferred. And an inquiry into the facts before the Commission, in order to ascertain whether its findings are thus vitiated, belongs to the judicial province.

In view of these statutes and the Court's discussion of them it is possible to obtain a fairly comprehensive, but not necessarily exhaustive, estimate of the judicial review authorized by Congress. The outstanding feature is the *appellate* character of the procedure. The establishment of this appellate relationship between the courts and administrative agencies has been the result of a slow but steady growth of ideas in both Congress and the courts. After early doubts whether any case at all could be brought from such an agency into a constitutional court, there was developed the *de novo* original proceeding—

[19] 289 U.S. 266 (1933).

for example, the suit to enforce the orders of the Interstate Commerce Commission. This was followed by the statutory bill in equity development under which the courts gradually came to give weight to what the Commission had done and to look to the administrative record as the basis upon which to decide the case. Finally the statutes take on an appellate form, as exemplified in the amendment to the Communications Act where the term "appeal" is used, to which the Supreme Court has given its express approval.

The development of an appellate relationship seems to have overcome the difficulties thought to be involved in the doctrine of separation of powers. Court and agency, said Mr. Justice Stone,[20] are not to be regarded as wholly independent and unrelated instrumentalities of justice. Together they constitute the means adopted by Congress to attain the end prescribed in the statute, and the statute should be construed so as to attain that end through "coordinated action." And as if to emphasize the acceptance of the administrative agency as part of the governmental machinery for such coordinated action, he sounds a warning against repeating "in this day the mistake made by the courts of law when equity was struggling for recognition as an ameliorating system of justice." Neither court nor agency "can rightly be regarded by the other as an alien intruder, to be tolerated if must be, but never to be encouraged or aided by the other in the attainment of the common aim."

Pursuant to this appellate method, a petition is made by the aggrieved party directly to the court, a transcript of the record is sent up, objections are limited to those urged before the agency itself, and the findings of fact, if supported by evidence, are conclusive. Such are the express provisions. Not less significant are the implications: the requirement in respect of the transcript presupposes a hearing at which the parties have had an opportunity to present their objections and support them with evidence, as well as to combat the showing by the agency. All questions of law are open for determination by the courts. These include the following which, for convenience, are

[20] *United States* v. *Morgan,* 307 U.S. 183 (1939).

catalogued from the opinion in the *Nelson Bros.* case: (1) whether the agency acts within its statutory authority,[21] (2) whether it observes the legislative standards validly set up, (3) whether its proceedings satisfy the pertinent demands of due process, (4) whether its findings of fact are supported by substantial evidence. All these the Court gleans from the terms of the statute or discovers in the legislative purpose.

EQUITY AND HABEAS CORPUS

As previously indicated, proceedings in equity and habeas corpus have been the means by which the courts, without a specific statutory plan, have exercised a certain control over administrative action. It is not within present purposes to inquire generally into the possible common law or equitable remedies which might be available, but it has seemed desirable to give a brief account of the judicial development of methods in the diversified subjects of fraud orders in the Post Office Department, land grants in the General Land Office, and exclusion and deportation orders in the Immigration and Naturalization Service.

Post Office Department. An example of the utilization of injunction procedure is found in connection with fraud orders issued by the Post Office Department. Though the statute provides neither for an appeal within the Department nor for recourse to judicial proceedings, a method for review has been developed by the courts. And as far as findings of fact by the Postmaster General are concerned, the result has been much to the same effect as under the statutory methods. Thus, in *Leach* v. *Carlile*[22] the Supreme Court declared it to be a

---

[21] Of course, also, the question is open whether the statutory authority is one which Congress can constitutionally confer.

[22] 258 U.S. 138 (1922). In *National Conference on Legalizing Lotteries* v. *Farley*, 96 F. 2d 861 (App. D.C., 1938), the court, after reviewing the evidence on which the Post Office Department based its decision, said (p. 864): "In saying this we do not lose sight of the fact that a plausible argument may be made on the other side of the question, but the law commits the initial decision to the discretion of the Postmaster General, who is authorized to act 'upon evidence satisfactory to him,' and we are powerless unless his ruling is palpably wrong."

settled rule "that the conclusion of a head of an executive department on such a question [of fact], when committed to him by law,
will not be reviewed by the courts where it is fairly arrived at and
has substantial evidence to support it, so that it cannot justly be said
to be palpably wrong and therefore arbitrary."

Whether the judicial review must be made on the basis of the record is not clear. The early cases indicate that it need not be, whereas
the most recent indications are that the record itself is enough. *Public Clearing House* v. *Coyne*[23] is an example of the former. It was decided in 1904. An order had been issued on the theory that the complainant was conducting a fraudulent enterprise. A master appointed
by the district court found that while the scheme was not fraudulent
it was a lottery. Since lotteries were also forbidden, the order was sustained, the government meanwhile changing the theory of the case
to accord with the master's findings. The master's findings indicated
that evidence was before him which was not before the Department,
and the decision was affirmed by the circuit court "in view of all the
evidence introduced in the court below." Other cases exhibit a like
tendency. In *Hall* v. *Willcox*[24] the court spoke of the presumption of
correctness applicable to the Postmaster General's conclusion as placing a burden of proof on the complainant which he had not met by
the evidence. In *Sanden* v. *Morgan*[25] it was said that complainant
had the burden of overcoming by a preponderance of the evidence
the presumption of correctness which attached to the Postmaster
General's conclusions. Here, as further indicating that evidence in addition to the Department's record was received, the court mentioned
papers presented for its consideration among which were two affidavits verified after the issuance of the fraud order.

As against such a view, however, the language above quoted from
Leach v. *Carlile* has a familiar ring of decisions based on the record.
The Department's practice, followed consistently in the last fifteen
years or so, of issuing fraud orders only after a hearing, must be

---

[23] 194 U.S. 497 (1904).   [24] 225 Fed. 333 (C.C.N.Y., 1906).
[25] 225 Fed. 266 (D.N.Y., 1915).

counted as an important factor making for judicial acceptance of the record and findings. And a recent report of the operations of the Post Office Department says that "the judiciary has, by and large, steadfastly refused to interfere with the judgment of the Postmaster General in these cases."[26] So, while in practice the Department's findings appear to be tested against the record, the theoretical position of the findings may be that they are open to rebuttal by new evidence in what appear to be *de novo* proceedings.

General Land Office. Cases involving the General Land Office also illustrate the ways in which courts may review administrative action in the absence of specific statutory provisions on the subject.[27] As between private individuals it may be a bill in equity to decree that the defendant hold the land in trust for the plaintiff or it may be a suit in ejectment. No direct appeal from a decision by the Secretary of the Interior to a court is available.

In *Johnson* v. *Towsley*,[28] Towsley filed a bill in equity in a Nebraska state court to compel Johnson and others "to surrender their title to him, the existing evidence of which cast a cloud on his own." The trial court gave a decree as prayed for; this was affirmed by the supreme court of the State and this, in turn, by the Supreme Court of the United States. The contest arose out of rival claims to the right of preemption to the land in controversy. After hearing these claims the register and receiver decided in favor of Towsley and gave him a patent certificate. On appeal to the commissioner of the General Land Office that decision was affirmed, but on further appeal to the Secretary of the Interior it was reversed and the patent issued to Johnson. The basis of the reversal by the Secretary was that in his opinion the lower officers had misconstrued an act of Congress. The

[26] Monograph of the Attorney General's Committee on Administrative Procedure, Sen. Doc. No. 186, 76th Cong., 3rd Sess. (1940) pt. 12, p. 17.

[27] In general, on General Land Office proceedings and judicial review thereof, see Dickinson, *Administrative Justice and the Supremacy of Law in the United States*, pp. 277–289; McClintock, The Administrative Determination of Public Land Controversies, 9 *Minn. L. Rev.* 420, 542, 638 (1925).

[28] 13 Wall. 72 (U.S., 1871).

ultimate question for the Court was whether the decision by the Secretary was conclusive. In holding that it was not, the Court declared that in the absence of fraud or mistake the decision of the General Land Office is final on controverted questions of fact, except as they may be reversed on appeal in the Department itself, but when the members of the Department, "by misconstruction of the law, take from a party that to which he has acquired a legal right under the sanction of those laws," the courts have power to give relief.[29]

Concerning the function of the court in the General Land Office cases, the Court said that it had frequently and firmly refused to interfere with the officers in the discharge of their duties, either by mandamus or injunction, so long as the title remained in the United States and the matter was rightfully before those officers for decision. On the other hand, it had constantly asserted the "right of the proper courts to inquire, after the title had passed from the government, and the question became one of private right, whether, according to the established rules of equity and the acts of Congress concerning the public lands, the party holding that title should hold absolutely as his own, or as trustee for another."[30]

[29] In *Catholic Bishop of Nesqually* v. *Gibbon*, 158 U.S. 155 (1895), a suit was brought by one claimant to a certain tract of land praying for an injunction, a decree of title, and a surrender of possession. Defendants claimed under a decision by the Secretary of the Interior which limited the claim of the plaintiff to a small tract and denied it as to the remainder of the land in question. The circuit court dismissed plaintiff's bill, and on appeal to the Supreme Court of the United States the decree was affirmed. The Supreme Court declared (p. 166) that upon the facts as they appeared "it may well be doubted whether the decision of the Secretary of the Interior is not conclusive" and added that the rule in the administration of the public lands is that the "decision of the land department upon questions of fact is conclusive, and only questions of law are reviewable in the courts."

[30] The usual collateral attack upon General Land Office orders at law is by means of an action in ejectment. If ejectment is inadequate the recourse of the aggrieved party is to equity, and *Smelting Co.* v. *Kemp*, 104 U.S. 636, 647 (1882), indicates the nature of his remedy in shifting from law to equity: "If in issuing a patent its [the General Land Office's] officers took mistaken views of the law, or drew erroneous conclusions from the evidence, or acted from imperfect views of their duty, or even from corrupt motives, a court of law can afford no remedy

Immigration and Naturalization Service. As in the case of postal fraud orders and land patents, there is no specific statutory provision for judicial review in immigration cases. The only applicable provision is one which gives the federal district courts "full jurisdiction" of all cases arising under the immigration laws.[31] The courts have utilized the device of habeas corpus to assure protection of individual rights. In deportation cases the writ may be secured on the ground that due process was not accorded in the course of the administrative proceedings.[32] The same is true of exclusion proceedings.[33] The availability of habeas corpus has made it virtually impossible for the aggrieved parties to procure equitable relief.[34]

to a party alleging that he is thereby aggrieved. He must resort to a court of equity for relief, and even there his complaint cannot be heard unless he connect himself with the original source of title, so as to be able to aver that his rights are injuriously affected by the existence of the patent; and he must possess such equities as will control the legal title in the patentee's hands."

In *Lee* v. *Johnson,* 116 U.S. 48 (1885), the Court said it would not interfere with the title of the patentee when the alleged mistake related to a matter of fact concerning which the Land Office may have drawn wrong conclusions from the testimony; for such a "judicial inquiry as to the correctness of such conclusions would encroach upon a jurisdiction which Congress has devolved exclusively upon the Department." In *Guaranty Savings Bank* v. *Bladow,* 176 U.S. 448 (1900), the Court said that where the Office's proceedings were conducted in accordance with delegated authority, the resulting orders would be upheld if not made "arbitrarily and without evidence." In *Vance* v. *Burbank,* 101 U.S. 514 (1880), the Department's decision was held to be conclusive, in the absence of fraud, on all questions of fact. In *Marquez* v. *Frisbie,* 101 U.S. 473 (1879), the Court went further and declared "that where there is a mixed question of law and of fact, and the court cannot so separate it as to see clearly where the mistake of law is, the decision of the tribunal to which the law has confided the matter is conclusive." But to be accorded finality, the decisions must be "after a hearing in good faith, however summary in form." *Edwards* v. *Bodkin,* 249 Fed. 562 (C.C.A. 9th, 1918), 265 Fed. 621 (C.C.A. 9th, 1920), *aff'd,* 255 U.S. 221 (1921).

[31] 8 U.S.C. §164.

[32] *The Japanese Immigrant Case,* 189 U.S. 86 (1903).

[33] *Chin Yow* v. *United States,* 208 U.S. 8 (1908).

[34] In *Falfalios* v. *Doak,* 50 F. 2d 640 (App. D.C., 1931), *reh. denied* 1931, a bill in equity to cancel a deportation order was dismissed on the ground that habeas corpus was available; and in *Darabi* v. *Northrup,* 54 F. 2d 70 (C.C.A. 6th, 1931), a bill brought concurrently with the writ was dismissed.

The statutes provide that the decisions of the administrative officials shall be final in both exclusion and deportation cases.[35] So, if there is a hearing in good faith the order made within the authority of the statutes is final unless it be shown that the proceedings were "manifestly unfair, that the action of the executive officers was such as to prevent a fair investigation or that there was a manifest abuse" of discretion[36] or that the officers failed to act consistently "with the fundamental principles of justice embraced within the conception of due process of law."[37] The question before the court is not whether it would have decided differently on the same facts, but whether there was insufficient evidence to support the decision;[38] the weight of the evidence and credibility of the witnesses are questions for the administrative authorities.[39] Denial of a fair hearing is not shown by proving merely that the decision was wrong.[40] Questions of law are for the courts, including questions of procedure, of statutory interpretation, of whether the decision is supported by evidence. In *Gegiow* v. *Uhl*[41] the Supreme Court, in reversing the decision of the immigration commissioners because of an error in statutory construction, said that the conclusiveness mentioned in the statutes referred to matters of fact.

In *Lloyd Sabaudo Società Anonima per Azioni* v. *Elting*[42] the Court reviewed the action of the Secretary of Labor in a field where Congress has a wide range of choice between administrative and judicial methods, namely, in the exercise of its "plenary power to control the admission of aliens." The Secretary had imposed a fine on certain vessels for bringing diseased aliens into the United States, and the fine was challenged on the ground, among others, that if the law were construed to preclude a judicial trial of the issues before the

[35] 8 U.S.C. §§153, 155.

[36] *Low Wah Suey* v. *Backus*, 225 U.S. 460, 468 (1912).

[37] *Kwock Jan Fat* v. *White*, 253 U.S. 454, 459 (1920).

[38] *United States ex rel. Ng Kee Wong* v. *Corsi*, 65 F. 2d 564 (C.C.A. 2d, 1933).

[39] *Jung Yen Loy* v. *Cahill*, 81 F. 2d 809 (C.C.A. 9th, 1936).

[40] *Chin Yow* v. *United States*, 208 U.S. 8 (1908).

[41] 239 U.S. 3 (1915).　　　　　　　　　[42] 287 U.S. 329 (1932).

Secretary it would violate the due process clause of the Fifth Amendment. Denying that contention Mr. Justice Stone declared, for a unanimous Court, that the action of the Secretary is nevertheless subject to some judicial review. Thus the courts may determine "whether his action is within his statutory authority, . . . whether there was any evidence before him to support his determination, . . . and whether the procedure which he adopted in making it satisfies elementary standards of fairness and reasonableness, essential to the due administration of the summary proceeding which Congress has authorized."

This statement culminates a long development and represents, as declared in a recent report, "nothing less than a transformation in judicial doctrine" when compared with earlier views. That report thus sums the matter up:

Beginning with a conception of the immigration agencies as independent tribunals possessing substantially final authority with respect to all matters of construction and application of the immigration laws, the Court has swung around to a conception of them as, in effect, subordinate tribunals —entrusted, to be sure, with a wide range of discretion but subject to pervasive control by the courts. The powers attributed to executive officers in the early decisions were justified as resulting from the peculiarly absolute power of Congress over the admission and expulsion of aliens. Yet the powers attributed to them in Mr. Justice Stone's statement in the *Elting* case are not materially greater than the powers admittedly possessed by many administrative agencies over essential interests of citizens. And the restraints to which they are declared to be subject are not materially less.[43]

The question of what constitutes a jurisdictional fact, on which the petitioner is entitled to a trial *de novo* in the district court, has some-

---

[43] The Secretary of Labor's Committee on Administrative Procedure, *The Immigration and Naturalization Service*, 1940, p. 45. See *Whitfield* v. *Hanges*, 222 Fed. 745 (C.C.A. 8th, 1915), for a recital of the "indispensable requisites" of a fair hearing, and the following for discussions of the procedural elements of a fair hearing: Van Vleck, *The Administrative Control of Aliens*, pp. 157–185; Note, Due Process Restrictions on Procedure in Alien Exclusion and Deportation Cases, 31 *Col. L. Rev.* 1013 (1931).

times been raised. The statutes give the immigration officer authority over aliens, not over United States citizens. Is alienage a jurisdictional fact on which the person detained is entitled to a trial *de novo?* In *United States* v. *Ju Toy,*[44] a case of exclusion, it was decided that the statute made the decision of the officials final; in *Quon Quon Poy* v. *Johnson*[45] the Court said that a claim of citizenship by a petitioner *who had never resided in the United States* did not entitle him to a trial in court. But a different rule prevails in deportation cases. *Ng Fung Ho* v. *White*[46] held that when a resident who has been admitted after a hearing claims citizenship and supports his claim with evidence sufficient, if believed, to support a finding of citizenship, he is entitled to a judicial trial on that issue.

If the decision of the immigration officers is reversed, the Supreme Court can remand the case either to the immigration authorities (or discharge the petitioner unless he is given a fair hearing within a reasonable time) or to the district court for a trial on the merits. A trial on the merits in the district court was justified as the most convenient in *Chin Yow* v. *United States.*[47] The case was remanded to the immigration authorities in *Tod* v. *Waldman.*[48] It has been suggested that the court method might be used when it is felt that it would be an injustice to remand the case for retrial by the same administrative officers who have already failed to conduct the hearing fairly.[49]

On Application by the Administrative Agency or Benefited Party

TO ENFORCE A SUBPOENA

Sometimes at the instance of the agency itself the aid of a court may at the outset be invoked in support of administrative action. Thus, application may be made to a federal district court to compel, by use of its contempt power, obedience to the agency's subpoena for the attendance of witnesses or production of documents. Illustrative

[44] 198 U.S. 253 (1905).　　　　　　[45] 273 U.S. 352 (1927).
[46] 259 U.S. 276 (1922).　　　　　　[47] 208 U.S. 8 (1908).
[48] 266 U.S. 113 (1924).
[49] Van Vleck, *The Administrative Control of Aliens,* p. 208.

provisions will be found in the statutes administered by the Securities and Exchange Commission.[50] Such an application has possible disadvantages from the agency's point of view: it gives the court an opportunity to open up the scope of the statutory authorization and to interpose a check before the agency gets under way. Another means of enforcing compliance with a subpoena is the provision in many statutes making disobedience a criminal offense.[51]

TO ENFORCE A FINAL ORDER

Occasionally the statutes provide that the agency may apply to the courts for aid in enforcing obedience to its order. The earliest provision of this kind appeared in the Interstate Commerce Act to the effect that if any carrier "fails or neglects to obey" an order of the Commission other than for the payment of money, the Commission, or any party injured thereby, could apply to the appropriate federal

[50] The Commission, under the three statutes administered by it, has the power to subpoena witnesses, to administer oaths and affirmations, and to require the production of books, papers, and other records "which the Commission deems relevant or material to the inquiry." Attendance of witnesses and production of records may be required from "any place in the United States or any State" at any designated place of hearing. The Commission's subpoena is enforceable by an order of the district court issued upon the application of the Commission to the person who refuses to obey the subpoena. Failure to obey such a court order may be punished as a contempt. The Securities Exchange Act of 1934 and the Public Utility Holding Company Act of 1935 provide further that refusal to obey a subpoena shall be a misdemeanor punishable by fine or imprisonment.

The Securities Act of 1933, in a special provision for the subpoena of records in stop order proceedings, provides that the Commission or any officer designated by it shall have access to and may demand the production of any books and papers of the issuer, underwriter, or any other person. Also a special method is provided for the enforcement of this section in that, if the issuer or underwriter shall fail to cooperate or shall obstruct or refuse to permit the making of the examination, his conduct shall be "proper ground" for the issuance of a stop order. The power of the Commission was tested in a proceeding wherein the Commission applied to the district court for an order directing the respondent to appear and testify. On appeal the circuit court upheld the Commission's authority. *Jones* v. *Securities and Exchange Commission*, 79 F. 2d 617 (C.C.A. 2d, 1935), *rev'd on other grounds*, 298 U.S. 1 (1936).

[51] See, *e.g.*, Communications Act of 1934, 47 U.S.C. §409 (j).

district court for the enforcement of the order. If the court determined that the order was regularly made and duly served and that
the carriers were in disobedience of the same, it enforced obedience
by writ of injunction or other proper process to restrain such carrier
from further disobedience of such order and to enjoin upon it obedience to the same.[52]

Under this provision an order of the Commission took on a compulsory character only when the court had approved it. Whether or
not this was actually designed as a judicial check upon the newly
created administrative agency, it at least had that effect; for before a
decree could issue the court had to be satisfied that the order was
regularly made and served. Objections to the validity of the order
could be made in these proceedings. Indeed, the entire matter became, at least potentially, open for judicial examination when the aid
of a court was sought. This method put pressure on the Commission
to take the initiative in turning to the courts; and in its earlier days
the Commission did take that initiative. But the Hepburn Amendment, with its criminal penalty for violation of the order in the event
the order is adjudged valid, tended to put pressure on the carriers to
initiate the court proceedings. Rather than wait for the outcome in
that direction, the carriers now generally bring an action before the
effective date to enjoin the enforcement of an order whose validity
they desire to contest. As a consequence the Commission rarely finds
it necessary to resort to the courts, and that method of enforcement
has in the main become obsolete.

A somewhat similar evolution has come about under the Federal
Trade Commission Act. Prior to 1938 the statute provided that if
any person, partnership, or corporation "fails or neglects to obey" an
order the Commission could proceed in a circuit court of appeals for
enforcement. Thus it was necessary for the Commission to apply to
the court for affirmance of its order, a violation thereof then being
treated as contempt of court. The circuit courts of appeals differed

[52] 49 U.S.C. §16 (12).

as to the effect of that provision. One held that the Commission's application for an enforcement order involved the preliminary question whether the respondent had failed to obey the order, and this fact had to be proved before the validity of the order itself would be considered.[53] Another concluded that the question of the violation of the order was not presented until after it had been determined that a valid order had been issued.[54] Moreover, a respondent could, without incurring any liability, continue to use the unfair method until the Commission discovered the fact and secured an enforcement order. To remove the difficulties of enforcement produced by these conflicting interpretations the Act was amended in 1938. The amendment dispensed with the requirement for the judicial affirmance of the order of the Commission. It gave the aggrieved parties the right to petition the court for review of the order and made the order final unless, *inter alia,* such petition was filed within a prescribed time.

The procedure of the original Federal Trade Commission Act was substantially adopted in the Packers and Stockyards Act of 1921. Under this Act the Secretary of Agriculture is authorized to serve a complaint upon any packer who he has reason to believe is engaging in unfair trade practices. If after a hearing the charges are sustained the Secretary serves upon the packer an order requiring him to cease and desist from continuing such unfair practices. No enforcement order by the court is required; the order becomes "final and conclusive" unless within thirty days after service the packer appeals to a court praying that the order be set aside or modified. Violation of the order after the expiration of the period for court review or after it has been sustained by the courts is a criminal offense punishable by fine and imprisonment. On appeal the court has the power to affirm, modify, or set aside the order of the Secretary, and the decree of the court operates as an injunction to restrain the packer and his agents from violating the order. The findings of the Secretary are not made

[53] *Federal Trade Commission* v. *Standard Education Society,* 14 F. 2d 947 (C.C.A. 7th, 1926).

[54] *Federal Trade Commission* v. *Balme,* 23 F. 2d 615 (C.C.A. 2d, 1928).

conclusive by the Act; it provides simply that the Secretary shall file
in the court a full transcript of the record, including the complaint,
the evidence, and the report and order, and that the evidence admitted by the Secretary and certified and filed as part of the record
shall be considered by the court as evidence in the case. The courts
are therefore free to arrive at an independent determination of the
facts.

Application to the courts for enforcement of their orders is the
main procedure available to the National Labor Relations Board.
For this purpose the Board certifies and files in the court a transcript
of the entire record of its proceedings. This transcript must include
the pleadings and testimony upon which the order was entered and
the findings and order of the Board. Findings of fact, "if supported
by evidence," are conclusive. The court is empowered "to make and
enter upon the pleadings, testimony and proceedings set forth in
such transcript a decree enforcing, modifying, and enforcing as so
modified, or setting aside in whole or in part the order of the Board."
While the statute permits him to do so, there is no pressure on the
aggrieved party to take the initiative in petitioning the courts. Unlike
the amended Federal Trade Commission Act, this Act does not give
finality to the Board's order.

The procedural pattern in these statutes is of special interest on
the point of the relationship between the agencies and the courts.
Each of them marked an important advance in the effort of the National Government to reach and correct business practices deemed
contrary to the public interest. The first, the Interstate Commerce
Act, inaugurated the federal administrative activity for the regulation of railroads, and the last, the National Labor Relations Act,
brings that activity to a high state of development with respect to
unfair labor practices. But in none of them originally, except the
Packers and Stockyards Act, was the administrative order made final
and given the effect of law. Each agency had a broad mandate for
the protection of a public interest. Each was authorized to conduct
investigations and to issue orders. But if compulsion was needed to

obtain obedience to the order resort to the courts was necessary. The significant feature is that such a statute put the courts between the administrative agency and the parties against whom the agency's orders ran. Quite apart from technical limits upon the agency, the mere fact that it had to turn to the courts was calculated to produce a restraining influence upon it in the exercise of its powers. Judicial proceedings thus became the last, and necessary, stage in the administrative process for effective enforcement. And much may be said for that early plan, especially when governmental experimentation in new and controversial fields is being undertaken. As described above, however, recourse to the courts for enforcement has ceased to be a factor in either the Interstate Commerce Commission or the Federal Trade Commission. A significant evolutionary process has gone on with regard to them. Their orders, by the will of Congress, now have legal force of their own. The Labor Relations Board stands today where those Commissions stood in their first years.

TO ENFORCE A "PRIVATE RIGHT" AWARD

A distinction must be noted, in the character of cases decided by administrative agencies, between those of "public" and "private" right. The distinction was elaborated in *Crowell* v. *Benson*[55] and was deemed to be one of substantial constitutional import. In the "private right" category are included cases of liability of one individual to another. Such was the case of *Crowell* v. *Benson* itself, where the matter in issue was the right of a worker to secure an award against an employer under the Longshoremen's and Harbor Workers' Compensation Act. Even here, Mr. Chief Justice Hughes said, there is no requirement that all determinations of fact be made by constitutional courts.[56] Where they have to do with claims of employees within the purview of the Act, they may be determined by the agency. It is otherwise, he continued, where the determinations of fact are funda-

[55] 285 U.S. 22 (1932).
[56] No issue was raised as to questions of law. They were reserved by the terms of the statute itself to the courts.

mental or "jurisdictional" in the sense that their existence is a condition precedent to the operation of the statutory scheme. Upon demand of the aggrieved party (in this case the employer who denied that the injured worker was employed by him) the "jurisdictional fact" of employment must be tried in a constitutional court in *de novo* proceedings. In cases brought to enforce "constitutional rights," he added, the judicial power "necessarily extends to the independent determination of all questions, both of fact and law, necessary to the performance of that supreme function."

In addition to compensation awards, several other administrative determinations seem to belong in the private right category and are of sufficient importance to be noted here. Reparation orders by the Interstate Commerce Commission are especially in point. In many instances the administrative remedy would be incomplete unless damages were paid to a person aggrieved by another's actions in violation of the statute. If, for example, a common carrier overcharges a shipper or applies the wrong rate to a shipment, it is not enough to scold the carrier and order it in the future not to overcharge or apply improper rates. Or, again, if an employee is discharged in violation of the National Labor Relations Act, justice may require that the employer reimburse the employee for the damages suffered in consequence of such wrongful discharge. The reparation award and back-pay orders are designed to meet these requirements. They not only restore the injured person to the position he would be in but for the wrongful act of another, but they also constitute substantial sanctions inducing compliance with the orders of the agency or the provisions of the statute.

These awards are important, of course, only in situations where the agency seeks to resolve a controversy between private parties. They present difficulties peculiarly their own. If after a hearing the Interstate Commerce Commission determines that a party is entitled to a reparation award the Commission orders the carrier to pay him a specific sum. Such an order must be enforced through the courts; it does not become binding until the party in interest institutes proceedings for its enforcement. If a carrier fails to comply the party for whose benefit the order was made may file a petition setting forth the cause for which he claims damages and the order of the Commission in a federal district court or in a state court having jurisdiction over the parties. The suits proceed in the district court in all respects like other civil suits for damages, except that the order and findings of the Commission are prima facie evidence of the facts therein stated. Such methods do not violate the right of trial by jury.[57]

The National Labor Relations Act does not expressly authorize suit by a party, in whose favor a back-pay order has been issued, against the employer found guilty of unfair labor practices. Whether such a suit could be entertained is doubtful. Speaking in another connection the Court has said that the Board is entrusted "with the exclusive authority for the enforcement" of the Act.[58] Such orders have been enforced by the circuit court of appeals which acquired jurisdiction either by petition by the Board for enforcement of its order or by appeal by the respondent from an order of the Board. The ultimate sanction inducing compliance with that part of the order directing the payment of back wages is that failure to comply will constitute contempt of court.

An interesting means of enforcing reparation awards is contained in the Federal Power Act. Whenever a new schedule of rates is filed by a public utility, the Commission may upon its own motion or upon complaint initiate a hearing to determine the lawfulness of the rate. During the hearing the new schedule may be suspended for a period not exceeding five months beyond the period when it would

[57] It has been so held in respect to reparation awards, *Meeker* v. *Lehigh Valley R. R. Co.,* 236 U.S. 412 (1915), and back-pay orders, *National Labor Relations Board* v. *Jones & Laughlin Steel Corp.,* 301 U.S. 1 (1937).

[58] *Amalgamated Utility Workers* v. *Consolidated Edison Co.,* 309 U.S. 261 (1940). The Circuit Court of Appeals for the Second Circuit had ruled that a private party has no standing to press a charge of civil contempt for violation of an order of the Board as affirmed by the court; that the Board itself is the proper party not only to apply for an enforcement order but also to present charges of contempt. This was affirmed by the Supreme Court.

otherwise take effect. If the hearings are not concluded at the culmination of this five-month period the proposed change in rates goes into effect. However, the Commission may require the utility to keep an account of all amounts received by reason of any increase in rates, specifying by whom such amounts were paid. Upon completion of the hearing the Commission may order the refund with interest of such portion of the increased rates as the Commission shall find unjustifiable. Whenever a utility refuses to comply with a refund order the Commission may bring an action in court to enforce compliance.[59] The Act is silent concerning the right of the person for whose benefit a refund order is issued to bring an action upon the order.

On Prosecution for a Criminal Offense

It is sometimes provided that an administrative order has the effect of law, violation of which subjects the offender to criminal prosecution. The form of the statute may vary: in some instances violation of the order itself constitutes the offense; in others, as where a license is required to do a particular act or engage in certain conduct and such license has been denied or not secured, the doing of the act or engaging in the conduct is said to constitute a violation of the statute. Illustrations of the latter appear in the statutes administered by the Securities and Exchange Commission. It has already been noted that the sanctions available to that Commission are largely in the nature of a denial of a right which the party otherwise would have. But under the structure of the statute such denial takes on a new character if it is ignored. For example, under the Securities Act of 1933, in the absence of a stop order, a registrant after filing a registration has the right to deal in the securities, but the Commission's stop order makes dealing in such securities in interstate commerce a violation of the statute.[60] Again, under the Public Utility Holding Company Act of 1935 the Commission has power to classify companies as holding companies, subsidiaries, or affiliates, with the re-

[59] 16 U.S.C. §§824d (e), 825m.   [60] 15 U.S.C. §§77e, 77h (d).

sult that these companies become subject to certain provisions of the statute and on noncompliance are subject to certain penalties.[61]

Statutes which give finality to orders normally provide a method, available within a limited time, for testing their validity.[62] If the method so provided gives a fair opportunity for a full test of the order it may be made the exclusive method;[63] and it would seem permissible to throw around such method a reasonable time limit for its invocation. A plan of this character was incorporated in the New York Labor Law in 1915.[64] There it is provided that an order of the industrial board shall be final unless within thirty days a party in interest shall begin an action in a specified court, as an appeal from the board, to determine the validity of the order. Furthermore, in an action to impose a penalty for violation of the order, the order shall "be deemed valid unless prior thereto" it has been revoked or modified by the board or annulled by a court in accordance with the above-mentioned procedure. It is also provided that no court shall have jurisdiction to review or annul any order or to restrain or interfere with its enforcement except as provided in the statute. Congress adopted a similar plan in the Packers and Stockyards Act authorizing the Secretary of Agriculture to issue cease and desist orders against packers

[61] 15 U.S.C. §79b (a).

[62] There are exceptions. In immigration cases, for example, the statute provides that the administrative order shall be final and there is no provision for appeal. 8 U.S.C. §§153, 155.

[63] See *Central Union Tel. Co.* v. *Edwardsville,* 269 U.S. 190 (1925), and the dissenting opinion by Mr. Justice Brandeis in *Ohio Valley Water Co.* v. *Ben Avon Borough,* 253 U.S. 287, 292 (1920). In *American Bond & Mortgage Co.* v. *United States,* 52 F. 2d 318 (C.C.A. 7th, 1931), *cert. denied* 285 U.S. 538 (1932), defendant's application for renewal of his license had been denied but he continued to operate despite the fact that the Radio Act of 1927 prohibited operation without a license, and the Attorney General of the United States sued for an injunction. Defendant's contention that the order was void was dismissed, the court saying that he was in no position to attack the order without first exhausting his statutory remedies, to wit, by appealing to the Court of Appeals of the District of Columbia. The time limit for appeal was only twenty days.

[64] New York State Labor Law, §§110–112.

engaged in unfair trade practices. Such an order becomes final and conclusive unless within thirty days the packer files an appeal.[65] If he violates the order after the time for appeal has expired or after it has been sustained by the courts he is guilty of a criminal offense punishable by fine or imprisonment or both.

A striking example of an administrative procedure which depends upon a criminal penalty for its enforcement is provided by the Federal Food, Drug, and Cosmetic Act. Evidence is collected by the agents of the Food and Drug Administration and if it appears to point to a breach of law the person against whom a proceeding is contemplated is "given appropriate notice and an opportunity to present his views, either orally or in writing."[66] The hearing is private and informal. If it appears after the hearing that there is a violation the Secretary of Agriculture recommends the case for prosecution to the Department of Justice. The administrative hearing, it should be noted, does not culminate in an order or any other mandatory decree. The facts as found by the officers of the Department of Agriculture have no probative value, and there are no findings based on the evidence. The result of the hearing is the recommendation made to the Attorney General, though the latter appears to have discretion whether or not to institute the criminal proceedings.

Criminal proceedings as a means of securing obedience to administrative orders may involve several potential checks. The fact that the case goes over to the Department of Justice brings a new arm of government between the administrative agency and the individual with whom it is in controversy. Also, a check may be encountered in the jury room or at the bench. Thus the jury may refuse to convict or they may bring in a verdict entailing only light punishment; or the trial judge may be lenient in imposing sentence. In any event there is considerable opportunity in criminal proceedings for the play of public opinion for or against the administrative action involved. It has been said that "the jury system operates to retain an important

[65] 7 U.S.C. §194 (a).   [66] 21 U.S.C. §335.

element of popular veto against governmental attempts to enforce the law tyrannically."[67]

CONSTITUTIONAL BACKGROUND FOR STATUTORY DEVELOPMENT

In accepting administrative agencies as instrumentalities of justice for working out and effectuating legislative policy the courts, especially the Supreme Court, appear to be striving for at least four objectives: (1) that the procedures in the agencies shall preserve the elements of fair play; (2) that the judicial tradition of responsibility, independence, and impartiality shall be observed within the agencies; (3) that an appellate relationship shall be established between agencies and courts broad enough to enable the latter to see to it that the former stay within the bounds of law; and, over all, (4) that the public, and more particularly the increasing number of individuals who come into contact with government through these agencies, may have assurance of recourse against arbitrary and capricious action.

Some of these matters, the procedural steps for example, are such as to enable the courts to lay hands upon them and apply a corrective. On the other hand the observance of the judicial tradition is largely beyond the reach of the courts, though much may be done by example to keep the tradition alive and constantly within view of the agencies. To the extent that the first and second objectives are more nearly approached, the courts will have less occasion to be concerned about the third and the public will be more confident of the fourth.

Meanwhile the courts, always in a stand-by position, are called into action from time to time. They are amply equipped, under the basic and elastic doctrines of due process of law and separation of powers, to make their presence felt. It is abundantly clear, if not from specific decisions at least from many a dictum and other pronouncement, that the judicial estimate of fairness tends to produce a constitutional minimum below which administrative procedure will not be permitted to fall. In the main, however, the technique for accomplishing

[67] Evatt, *Rum Rebellion,* p. 169.

this result is to ascribe those requirements to the legislative intent and read them into the statutes. Thus there is a tendency on the part of the courts to find an identity between statutory and due process requirements.[68] Manifestly there is a constitutional motivation in the interpretation of statutes,[69] the fountainhead of which is the "fundamental requirements of fairness which are of the essence of due process."

The interpretation of the statutory term "full hearing" in the widely discussed *Morgan* cases provides an excellent illustration of the matter.[70] Those cases were concerned with the power of the Secretary of Agriculture under the Packers and Stockyards Act to fix maximum rates to be charged by stockyard dealers. The controversy has been twice before the Supreme Court on points involving internal procedure, and on both occasions the judgments were reversed and the cases remanded because of the procedural inadequacies under the statute; in neither case was a decision rendered on the merits.[71]

---

[68] "The conception of identity is supported by state court holdings that unless the statute specifies notice and a hearing it is unconstitutional." Note, Judicial Control of Administrative Procedure: The Morgan Cases, 52 *Harv. L. Rev.* 509, 510 (1939).

[69] It is, of course, not peculiar to this group of statutes alone. It finds frequent and familiar expression—as, for example, that if an interpretation is fairly possible which will save the constitutionality of the statute such must be adopted, or that interpretations should be avoided which raise serious constitutional doubts. See *Crowell* v. *Benson*, 285 U.S. 22, 62 (1932).

[70] *Morgan* v. *United States*, 298 U.S. 468 (1936); *Morgan* v. *United States*, 304 U.S. 1 (1938).

[71] Another phase of the controversy was before the Supreme Court in 1939, *United States* v. *Morgan*, 307 U.S. 183 (1939). In this case the Court directed the district court to retain possession of the funds paid into the district court pending the final determination of the validity of the rate order.

A fourth case in this series was recently determined by the Supreme Court, *United States* v. *Morgan*, 313 U.S. 409, 421, 422 (1941). After concluding that the order of the Secretary furnished an "appropriate basis for action in the district court in making distribution of the fund in its custody," the Court considered the propriety of the action of the district court in authorizing, over the government's objection, the market agencies to take the deposition of the Secretary. The Secretary appeared in person at the trial and was questioned at length

The case was this: A rate order issued in 1933 was attacked by the market agencies as illegal and arbitrary and in violation of the due process clause of the Fifth Amendment. A suit was brought to enjoin the enforcement of the order. In the trial court an allegation that the "full hearing" required by the statute had not been given was stricken out, the bill of complaint dismissed, and the order sustained. More particularly, the allegation which the trial court struck out was that the Secretary made the order without having heard or read any of the evidence and without having heard the oral arguments or having read or considered the briefs which the plaintiffs submitted. The Supreme Court reversed: plaintiffs were entitled to have the allegation answered and a determination made whether or not they had had the required hearing.

In considering this allegation the Court, through Mr. Chief Justice Hughes, discussed the essential quality of the proceeding under review and the nature of the hearing which the statute requires. The Secretary's duty carries with it "fundamental procedural requirements." There must be a full hearing. There must be evidence adequate to support pertinent and necessary findings of fact. Nothing can be treated as evidence which is not introduced as such. Facts and circumstances must not be considered which should not legally influence the conclusion. Findings based on the evidence must embrace the basic facts which are needed to sustain the order. Even though it looks to legislative action, a proceeding of this sort which requires

on the process by which he reached the conclusions of his order, including the manner and extent of his study of the record and his consultation with subordinates. Mr. Justice Frankfurter, speaking for the Court's majority, said that the Secretary "should never have been subjected to this examination" since the proceeding before the Secretary "has a quality resembling that of a judicial proceeding." A similar examination of a judge "would be destructive of judicial responsibility" and the "integrity of the administrative process must be equally respected." In conclusion, Mr. Justice Frankfurter stated: "It will bear repeating that although the administrative process has had a different development and pursues somewhat different ways from those of courts, they are to be deemed collaborative instrumentalities of justice and the appropriate independence of each should be respected by the other."

the taking and weighing of evidence, determinations of fact based upon the consideration of the evidence, and the making of an order supported by such findings, has a quality resembling that of a judicial proceeding.

The statutory requirement of a "full hearing" in such a situation, the Chief Justice continued, has obvious reference to the tradition of judicial proceedings in which evidence is received and weighed by the trier of the facts. The "hearing" is designed to afford the safeguard that the one who decides shall be bound in good conscience to consider the evidence, to be guided by that alone, and to reach his conclusion uninfluenced by extraneous considerations which in other fields might have play in determining purely executive action. The "hearing" is the hearing of evidence and argument. If the one who determines the facts which underlie the order has not considered evidence or argument, it is manifest that the hearing has not been given.

Nor is it a sufficient answer to say that the question for the courts is whether the evidence supports the findings and the findings support the order. The Chief Justice pointed out that the weight ascribed by the law to the findings—their conclusiveness when made within the sphere of the authority conferred—rests upon the assumption that the officer who makes the findings has addressed himself to the evidence and upon that evidence has conscientiously reached the conclusion which he deems it to justify. "That duty cannot be performed by one who has not considered evidence or argument. It is not an impersonal obligation. It is a duty akin to that of a judge. The one who decides must hear." So the "full hearing" prescribed by Congress means, for one thing, that he who decides must hear. More than that, he is bound in good conscience to consider the evidence and to be guided by that alone. This is what Congress intended. Such being the case it became unnecessary for the Court to go beyond the terms of the statute in order to consider the constitutional requirement of due process as to notice and hearing. The first *Morgan* case may be left there for the moment and attention given to the second, where the Court further defines the statutory term.

After the remand of the first case, further proceedings were had which included a consideration of the part taken by the Secretary himself in the departmental proceedings. It was held that the hearing before the Secretary was adequate. Thereupon the case came back to the Supreme Court[72] on a renewed contention, in addition to objections on the merits, that the "full hearing" required by the statute still had not been accorded to the plaintiffs. This contention was sustained: the hearing was held "fatally defective." In reaching that conclusion the Court put to one side any further discussion of the extent to which the Secretary examined the evidence. He had read the summary presented by the briefs and had conferred with his subordinates who had sifted and analyzed the evidence. He, it would be assumed, sufficiently understood its purport. That met the specific objection of the first case.

But, in the Court's estimate, a "full hearing" requires substantially more than that. The contention that such a hearing had not been accorded to the complainants "goes to the very foundation of the action of administrative agencies entrusted by the Congress with broad control over activities which in their detail cannot be dealt with directly by the legislature." The right to such a hearing "embraces not only the right to present evidence but also a reasonable opportunity to know the claims of the opposing party and to meet them. The right to submit argument implies that opportunity; otherwise the right may be but a barren one." And the Court was emphatic in asserting that those "who are brought into contest with the Government in a quasi-judicial proceeding aimed at the control of their activities are entitled to be fairly advised of what the Government proposes and to be heard upon its proposals before it issues its final command." But no such reasonable opportunity was accorded appellants, nor did the oral argument reveal these claims in any appropriate manner.

In making the statutory requirement of a full hearing Congress

[72] *Morgan* v. *United States,* 304 U.S. 1 (1938). A petition by the Solicitor General for rehearing was denied. 304 U.S. 23 (1938).

It is now in order to bring together the several items mentioned in the foregoing extracts and to add such others as may be discoverable bearing upon the question of the constitutional protection with regard to notice and hearing in administrative agencies. It is assumed by the courts, even if not actually established by specific decisions, that certain features are comprehended within the concept of due process of law. First, as to notice: there must be "due notice" having regard to (a) actual notification or methods reasonably calculated to reach the party concerned, (b) its sufficiency to inform him of the nature of the proceedings and the matters on which he may desire to be heard, and (c) the time allowed to prepare for the hearing.

Second, as to hearing: a fair and open hearing is the right of every litigant. The tribunal must be an impartial one.[78] The procedure must be consistent with the essentials of a fair trial. The litigant is entitled to introduce evidence in support of his own case or in opposition to that of the government and may cross-examine witnesses. He is entitled to be informed of what the government proposes to do. The person who decides must hear and consider the evidence and argument. The hearing must be conducted in such a way that a court may determine whether the applicable rules of law were observed. The place of hearing must be fixed with fair regard for the convenience of the parties and their witnesses and records.[79]

be allowed to weaken the control of the Courts, and that no obstacle should be placed by Parliament in the way of the subject's unimpeded access to them." *Report of the Committee on Ministers' Powers,* p. 114.

[78] *Johnson* v. *Michigan Milk Marketing Board,* 295 Mich. 644, 295 N.W. 346 (1940), discussed in 89 *U. of Pa. L. Rev.* 977 (1941), is "apparently the first to require disinterestedness in a state administrative board regulating a competitive industry." The board consisted of five members of whom a majority (two producers and one distributor as required by the statute) were deemed to be disqualified for interest in the business regulated.

[79] *National Labor Relations Board* v. *Prettyman,* 117 F. 2d 786 (C.C.A. 6th, 1941). In this case the Circuit Court of Appeals denied the petition of the Board for a decree to enforce an order of the Board. The respondent was engaged in business in Michigan and the hearings were held in Washington. This was held not to constitute proper regard for the convenience of the respondent. The case

Whether and to what extent judicial notice may be taken and whether the facts so noticed must be entered on the record, whether the agencies may avail themselves of the technical knowledge of the administrative personnel, whether findings of fact must be made, and whether the agency must state and make public the reasons for its decision—these are questions to which no full answers have been found. One of them, the keeping of a record, seems indispensable if judicial review is to have a real and substantial significance.

Though the due process clause constitutes the foundation for the foregoing features, it must be remembered that due process is not a fixed and constant requirement. What is due process in one situation may not be in another. Due regard, as the Court has often said, must be had "to the nature of the proceedings and the character of the rights which may be affected by it." The same procedure may not be

probably goes down as one of statutory construction though the Court spoke in some detail of the due process rights of the employer. Thus, "An employer is entitled to a hearing of and decision on the charges against him according to the fundamental principles that inhere in due process of law, and indispensable requisites of such hearings are that the course of proceedings shall be appropriate to the case and just to the employer; that he shall be notified of the charges against him in time to meet them and shall have an opportunity to be heard and cross-examine the witnesses against him and shall have time and opportunity at a convenient place, after the evidence against him is produced and known to him, to produce evidence and witnesses to refute the charges, and that the decision of the Board shall be governed by and based upon the evidence produced at the hearing. . . .

"The petitioner urges on us that . . . it [the Board] has the uncontrolled discretion to hold hearings at whatever point it deems proper within the United States and its territories. To this we cannot agree. . . .

"The power conferred on the Board by the Act to hold hearings anywhere within the territorial limits of the United States, was not conferred for its sole benefit, but for the benefit also of those subject to the provisions of the Act. It was not intended that those affected by the Act should be penalized by being required to travel and transport witnesses unreasonable distances to attend hearings pursuant to complaint, nor was it intended that the Act should be used as an instrument of intimidation or oppression on those affected by it. One of the purposes to be accomplished in the administration of every law is the maintenance of public confidence in the value of the measure."

terstate Commerce Act under which "all orders of the commission, except orders for the payment of money, shall take effect within such reasonable time, not less than thirty days, and shall continue in force for such period of time not exceeding two years, as shall be prescribed in the order of the commission, unless the same shall be suspended or set aside by a court of competent jurisdiction." This provision, it will be noted, disclosed no grounds upon which a court should or could suspend or set aside an order. As far as Congress was concerned it left the Court free to develop the judicial power as it saw fit; and it was in this situation that Mr. Justice White wrote the well-known paragraph previously quoted. After enumerating the powers of the courts he added that they are of the "essence of judicial authority." As such, neither may they be "curtailed" nor may the discharge of them be "avoided" in proper cases. These are strong and measured words.

Reservations of questions of law for the courts, as found in the statutes or judicially implied, are themselves proof of the pervasive conviction that they are desirable, if not indispensable, in the public interest. "When dealing with constitutional rights (as distinguished from privileges accorded by the Government, *United States* v. *Babcock,* 250 U.S. 328, 331) there must be the opportunity of presenting in an appropriate proceeding, at some time, to some court, every question of law raised, whatever the nature of the right invoked or the status of him who claims it."[81]

One aspect of the matter, particularly as to jurisdiction, is illus-

[81] Brandeis, J., concurring, in *St. Joseph Stock Yards Co.* v. *United States,* 298 U.S. 38, 77 (1936). "In our opinion the maintenance of the rule of law demands that a party aggrieved by the judicial decision of a Minister or Ministerial Tribunal should have a right of appeal from that decision to the High Court on any point of law. In matters which really pertain to administration, jurisdiction is often appropriately assigned to Ministers or Ministerial Tribunals rather than to the ordinary Courts of Law, but we see no justification for sheltering them from the Courts of Law in so far as the exercise of their jurisdiction involves a judicial decision; and we are of opinion that to confer such immunity upon them is contrary to the constitutional principle underlying the rule of law." *Report of the Committee on Ministers' Powers,* p. 108.

trated by *Crowell* v. *Benson*.[82] This case bears evidence of a titanic
struggle within the Court on constitutional as well as statutory issues,
and it called forth elaborate opinions by Mr. Chief Justice Hughes,
concurred in by Justices Van Devanter, McReynolds, Sutherland, and
Butler, for the majority, and by Mr. Justice Brandeis, concurred in by
Justices Stone and Roberts, for the minority.

The case itself presented a simple issue, but the opinions deserve
careful attention, for the constitutional discussion has a certain bearing on the relationship between these agencies and the courts. An injured worker brought a claim against Benson for compensation under the Longshoremen's and Harbor Workers' Compensation Act
and secured an award from the deputy commissioner, Crowell. Benson then instituted a suit pursuant to the Act to enjoin the enforcement of the award. He alleged that the award was contrary to law
for the reason that the worker was not an employee of his at the time
the injury occurred, and he contended that any attempt by Congress
to authorize an administrative officer to determine the fact of employment would violate the due process clause of the Fifth Amendment and the provisions of Article III with respect to the judicial
power of the United States. The district judge granted a hearing *de
novo* upon the facts and the law to determine the issue of employment, expressing the view that the Act would be invalid unless construed to permit such a hearing, and upon the trial of that issue the
district court decided that there was no employer-employee relationship. Thereupon a decree issued restraining the enforcement of the
award. The decree was affirmed by the circuit court of appeals and,
on certiorari to review the question of principle, by the Supreme
Court. In so doing, the Supreme Court appears to have approved the
district judge's view that the Act would be unconstitutional unless
construed to permit *de novo* proceedings on the issue of employment.[83]

[82] 285 U.S. 22 (1932).

[83] Employment was treated as a "jurisdictional fact." More than that, the relationship of employer-employee was treated as a "constitutional fact" in the sense

CHAPTER V. CONCLUSIONS

THE making of policy and the changing of policy to conform with experience, with new points of view, or with a new trend of public opinion, are major tasks of administrative agencies as instruments of government. They enter in a greater or less degree into the work of each agency, so that no study of the judicial function of administrative agencies can leave out of consideration the importance of the agencies' policy-determining function. The broad policy of an agency and certain ends which it seeks to accomplish may not even be put into official form, but they will be the background for the policies which find expression in an agency's judicial action, its regulations for the public, and its instructions for the guidance of the members of its staff.

The agencies have the help of expert assistants to investigate the conditions with which they have to deal and to advise them on policy. These experts are trained in their subjects and by long experience in the service of an agency they become familiar with the problems which present themselves in its work and with the practical as well as the technical aspects under which they may be presented. Furthermore the experts during their long experience build up a great mass of information to which they can turn in advising on policy. The large staff of the Interstate Commerce Commission, the engineering staff of the Federal Communications Commission, the accounting staff of the Securities and Exchange Commission are a necessary part of the machinery of these agencies if they are to carry out the task confided to them by Congress of developing policy as well as the duty of doing justice in particular cases. Sometimes a specialized bureau, such as the Bureau of Chemistry in the Department of Agriculture, is used by independent agencies, the Federal Trade Commission, for instance, and in such case its scientific findings have the advantage of being prepared by a specialized organ outside the staff of the agency.

Competent as their experts may be and experienced as the heads of an agency may become in the subjects over which they have jurisdiction, the heads of the agency should not depend wholly upon their own judgment in the process of policy forming. The findings of technical experts of equal ability are often widely at variance. They tend to be less so in the more strictly scientific and engineering fields, as in the analyses by the Bureau of Chemistry and the conclusions of the engineering division of the Federal Communications Commission, and become more so in the economic and social fields, where the opinions of economists and sociologists vary greatly. If the agency is fixing policy in other ways than in the course of judicial procedure, it should check the findings of its experts and its own judgment with the experience and opinions of the persons in the business or social activity under regulation.

The ways of applying the check of consultation with the interested public should not be standardized. Private conferences are frequently effective, especially where technical questions are being discussed, but in acting on a policy which affects a considerable number of persons there are advantages in public conferences at which records are made that may not only inform the policy-making agency but also form the basis for criticism and for defense of the policy finally adopted. These methods are not the subject of this study, although in many agencies they are more important than judicial procedure in determining policy. They should, however, be kept in mind as a means other than judicial procedure of carrying out the conception of these agencies as governmental bodies regulating business or social activities and in most cases not being set up only to determine the rights of individuals.

In judicial procedure, however, the rights of individuals are involved, and it is in this aspect of its functions that the dual activities of an agency—making policy and deciding cases—play a part in the combination of function of prosecutor and judge to which such strong objection is made. The agency receives or initiates the complaint, investigates the circumstances, frames the charges, acts as

example of a separation of functions. There is a separate force of trial examiners who deal with a case only when it is brought before them for hearing. The case is prepared by the division of the agency which is concerned with the particular subject in controversy. The division makes the original examination upon which the action is based and is responsible for recommending the initiation of action, but the trial examiner comes from a different division of the agency.

In both the Securities and Exchange Commission and the Department of Agriculture the trial examiners are members of the agency or the Department. They are concerned with its policies and are subject to control by the heads of the agency or Department. They are not, however, part of the particular bureau or division which has prepared the case. They will therefore be at least partly removed from the risk of bias attending the preparation and advocacy of the government's case, and the division or bureau which is presenting the case and its counsel can argue their own side of the case and depend on the private parties to present their side, with the trial examiner under a duty of protecting the right to a fair hearing both of the agency and of the private party.

Separation through internal organization, however, is only a partial answer to the objection. No matter how complete may be the separation between the trial examiner and the prosecuting counsel, the final decision is with the head of the agency, who frequently authorizes the issuance of the original complaint and is concerned in carrying out its policy.

To meet this objection it has been proposed that a tribunal wholly separate from the administrative agencies be created to which cases would come, either originally or for review on both the facts and the law.[2] This tribunal would have no administrative, investigatory, or prosecutory function. The agency would appear before it as a complainant, and the tribunal would conduct the hearings uninfluenced by an interest in maintaining the position taken in the complaint.

[2] Report of the Special Committee on Administrative Law, *Reports of Amer. Bar Assoc.,* vol. 59, p. 539 *et seq.* (1934); vol. 61, p. 720 *et seq.* (1936).

There would thus be put between the investigatory and prosecutory agency and the courts a sort of special court which would make the record upon which the findings and order would have to be based.[3]

The great variation in the types of situations treated by the different agencies would stand in the way of setting up an effective single administrative tribunal to pass on their decisions. Each agency in formulating its policy is in contact with the private persons concerned and has its staffs of experts and its accumulated experience to call upon for aid in formulating a policy or in making an order. An appeal from such a body as the Interstate Commerce Commission to another administrative tribunal could only mean a reexamination of the facts and of the policies of the Commission as expressed in the case under review. It is unlikely that Congress would empower the review tribunal to pass finally on questions of law, even if that were permissible. The same objection though in a different degree would hold to appeals from other agencies, and there is the further consideration of the resulting delay and consequent inconvenience to the parties and to the government itself. A tribunal without the power to pass finally on questions of law would be in effect a new policy-formulating organization without close contact with the interested parties and without specialized technical staffs to counsel it.

This proposal involves many difficulties, especially in agencies whose principal task is the making of policies. The procedure leading to the making of an order cannot be easily divided between the functions of a prosecutor and a judge. If the power to make orders

[3] A step in this direction was taken when Senator Logan, assisted by the Special Committee of the American Bar Association, but without the official approval of that Committee or the Bar Association, introduced S. 3787, 74th Cong., 2d Sess. (1936). The bill created an administrative court in whose original jurisdiction would be included power over revocations and suspensions of "licenses, permits, registrations, or other grants for regulatory purposes. . . ." Neither the Senate bill nor the identical House bill, H.R. 12297, 74th Cong., 2d Sess. (1936), ever came out of committee. *Reports of Amer. Bar Assoc.,* vol. 61, p. 759 (1936). The important provisions of the bill are reprinted in The Proposed United States Administrative Court, by Colonel O. R. McGuire, 22 *A.B.A.J.* 197, 199, n. 1 (1936).

self. Such a hearing would present difficulties where the stockyard was distant from Washington and the testimony would have to be taken in the locality in which the stockyard was situated. This added wheel in the machinery might delay final decisions, which are frequently too long deferred under the present system. It would not seem necessary to set up such an appeal board in the Perishable Agricultural Commodities Act, and whether a board would be an advantage is a matter which would require careful study of the situation in each Department. Probably in some Departments more than one board would be required. For example, the present Board of Immigration Appeals in the Department of Justice is fully occupied and should not be asked to take on appeals from other divisions of the Department with whose work it is unfamiliar.

No single solution can be found to meet the very real problem of prosecutor and judge. In some situations separation within the agency to a greater or less degree may be effective. In others boards independent of the agency are practicable. The determination whether either method should be adopted must rest in an analysis of the nature of the problems dealt with by each agency. No matter where the application of law to facts is being performed, whether in courts or administrative agencies, policy is being shaped and applied. The distinction between an agency acting judicially and a court is largely in the extent to which policy is determined by decision or previously defined by statute or common law. When an agency's policy has been sufficiently formulated either by the agency through its rules or by the statute under which it operates so that the development of policy by decision becomes subordinate, the agency in deciding a case is doing practically the same thing that the courts ordinarily do. In fields such as this the judicial function may be vested in a special body within the agency, as was done in the Immigration and Naturalization Service by the creation of the Board of Immigration Appeals. With this separation of function within the agency the general policy of strict or liberal interpretation of the law is decided by the administrative officer. Policies having to do with the interpretation of doubtful provisions of law, the use of evidence in formal hearings, and the treatment of the alien during the progress of the proceedings are also determined by the administrative officers but may be reviewed by the judicial. All policies, however, are subject to the final decision of the Attorney General as the head of the Department, so that policy forming remains a function of the agency. In some fields a tribunal wholly independent of any administrative agency may be created as a court with jurisdiction limited to a special class of cases, as has been done, for example, in customs, patents, and taxes.

A possibility that has received too little consideration is the division of the problems which are dealt with within a single agency. Where certain aspects of an agency's field of operation become standardized, and the lines of policy with respect to these aspects are clarified, subordinate independent boards within the agency could be set up to deal with them. At present there is a tendency to treat matters of this type either by an extremely simplified procedure, as in reparation cases before the Interstate Commerce Commission, or by routine action by the agency with the actual decision at some other point in the procedure, as in many phases of the duties of the Secretary of Agriculture. However, such matters continue to occupy attention which might better be given by the agency itself to more important aspects of the formulation of policy in the fields where standards are still in a developing state. Moreover, the practice involves a failure to put responsibility, and perhaps to feel responsibility, where responsibility belongs. It leads to the complaint that the final decision, at least formally, rests with a judge to whom there is no opportunity of direct approach by the litigants. This complaint would be met if special boards were set up with power of making decisions.

No special competence, for example, is required for the determination of the charges of violations of the Communications Act of 1934 by amateur operators. Nor will the decision of the case ordinarily have any appreciable effect in shaping or determining the general policy of the Federal Communications Commission. The setting up

The head of the agency has not the time to hold many public hearings. The hearing must usually be held before a subordinate officer, and the duty of the control of the hearing and of preparing a record should be vested in a responsible officer of the agency. These proceedings deal with the rights of individuals, who are entitled to fair play and a judicial attitude on the part of the trier of the facts. The dual role of being both an administrative and a judicial officer makes his position difficult. He is not a judge hearing a contest between two parties and controlling the evidence which is to go to a jury and deciding points of law. He passes upon both the law and the facts. This gives him a wide range in admitting evidence and makes unnecessary at a hearing many of the rules of evidence evolved for the protection of the jury. On the administrative side he must give due attention to the policy of the agency, he must take care that the record contains the facts which the agency needs to take action, and he must be mindful that the administrative body is set up primarily not to determine individual rights but to effectuate the policy of the statute. The judicial side of his office, however, must condition his procedure and the powers which he exercises.

The trial examiner, as the only officer who has heard the evidence, should make findings of fact to submit to the official or body which makes the order. He has the advantage of having been present at the hearing and listened to the witnesses, so he is able to estimate the weight of evidence on one side or the other. Further, he acts on his individual responsibility and the results of his work are subject to public criticism. The parties, if his findings are served on them, will have an opportunity to compare with them the findings of the head of the agency and note differences. This is a spur to more careful preparation by the office staff and by the head of the agency and a check on arbitrariness in making the order.

The trial examiner exercises a vital function in the judicial procedure of an agency. He should be subordinate only to a chief trial examiner appointed directly by the head of the independent agency or by the Secretary, and in a hearing he should be free from direct interference by any person in the agency. The case for the government, especially in a disciplinary matter, should be brought out publicly at the hearings, as well as the case of the private parties, so that there will be no doubt as to the evidence on which the decision is made and so that the test of cross-examination may be applied to all of it. The trial examiner should not be subjected to pressure by the head of the agency during the progress of the hearing.

Independence from interference, however, is not enough. The officer who exercises this function should have a position in the government service commensurate with the importance of his duties. The salary should be sufficient to attract persons of capacity and judicial temperament. The position should have the protection of the civil service, and the special examination should take into account a candidate's experience and qualifications. However, the agency should be free in cases of special difficulty to appoint non-civil-service examiners but should use this power sparingly.

It is not necessary that the trial examiner be a lawyer; but for the handling of cross-examination, the decision as to the admissibility of the testimony, and the interpretation of the law and of the regulations of the agency, and subsequently in the weighing of evidence and the preparation of findings of fact and report, a lawyer's training would seem to be the best preparation. A person not a lawyer who has had experience in the labor field and who has good judgment might well make a better compensation commissioner than a lawyer, but if such a person had also legal training, he should be better equipped to find the facts upon which the judges could depend if a case were appealed.

It is the head of the agency, however, and not the trial examiner, who decides the case. The head of the agency may modify or set aside the recommendation of the trial examiner and may modify his findings of fact if not satisfied with them. It is the agency, therefore, that finally determines on the policy which is to be applied in the case and makes the final determination as to what the facts show. The agency may decide that it will apply to a particular case a policy

termined with a view to the whole background and the place in that picture of the matter under consideration.

Limitations on the imposition by administrative agencies of sanctions which are traditionally imposed by the criminal courts are few and of little practical importance. Economic penalties, far more cogent than those imposed by courts, are frequently within the powers exercised by the administrative agencies. Withdrawal of license, for example, is comparable in an intricately organized economic society to the penalties entrusted by a simpler society to administration by the courts. To the extent that administrative agencies employ judicial procedure in the imposition of penalties, they tend to become courts with other names. The importance of policy development, the general atmosphere of administration, and other factors may impede the assumption of a truly judicial attitude, but the review of procedure by the courts is a defense against arbitrariness. On the other hand, most of the actual power of administrative agencies lies in sanctions which do not involve judicial procedure. The power to prosecute and the power of publicity are instruments of control for which the restraint of judicial procedure is not available and in most cases may not in fact be appropriate. Yet an agency may be able to effectuate its purposes in full by the use of or even by threatening to use these powers alone.

The growth of administrative power has been characterized also by the use of other types of informal sanctions less directly coercive in nature. The use of that cluster of controls which is designated supervision and which includes inspection, investigation, consultation, education, advice, cooperation, and the like is becoming increasingly the method of government regulation as against the policing and judicial procedure.

The problem of administrative sanctions is not primarily that of their efficacy. Because efficiency in regulation cannot be the only purpose of government, the effectiveness of a sanction in shaping conduct toward the end conceived by administration to be the desirable end is not the sole test of the desirability of the sanctions. Those elements of fair play and individual justice which are called liberty are equally a purpose of government whatever may be their effect on regulatory efficiency. Achieving a balance of interests in the administrative agencies requires a reexamination of procedure in terms of sanctions and in terms of the ends other than the mere dispatch of business which procedure is designed to serve.

A feature of great significance in respect to administrative agencies and the courts is the appellate character of the relationship which has come to exist between them. The development which has led to this result has been one of gradual and steady growth through the combined efforts of the courts and Congress.

Its significance is twofold, constitutional and procedural. From a constitutional point of view this appellate relationship substantially overcomes the difficulties thought to be involved in the doctrine of separation of powers, for it recognizes both courts and administrative agencies as "instrumentalities of justice" engaged in effectuating the policy of Congress through "coordinated action."[8] In a very real sense, then, proceedings in the agencies and in the courts may be considered as separate parts of the whole process of the enforcement of law. Procedurally the appellate relationship presupposes notice and opportunity to be heard in the agency, a point often covered by express statutes, and it ascribes to the record of the case, as made in the agency and as constituting the basis of review in the courts, a position of prime importance. The fullness and accuracy of the record will in large part determine the adequacy of judicial review; at the same time they will have a persuasive influence on the courts to accept the appellate relationship and treat the matter as one on appeal rather than *de novo*. All this in turn emphasizes the responsible task involved in the making of the record.

Such appellate relationship is particularly noticeable where Congress has dealt with the matter by specific statutory provisions. Also noticeable is the fact that methods of access to the courts and the

[8] The quoted terms are Mr. Justice Stone's in *United States* v. *Morgan*, 307 U.S. 183, 191 (1939).

a limited reach and control. To be sure, policies must be embodied in definite standards in the statute and the agency must stay within the standards. Both of these phases come within range of the courts in their power of statutory interpretation and thus enable the courts, just as in determining questions of law generally, to exert a considerable control in fixing the scope of the agencies' activities. The Federal Trade Commission, for example, has recently had its sphere of operations restricted by the Supreme Court, not on the ground of lack of power in Congress to expand such sphere but rather on the want of statutory purpose so to do.[9]

Where the national policy is effectuated by means of benefits granted or withheld or contracts made or denied through administrative agencies the courts so far have done least for the protection of individuals. It is usually said that the individual has no "right" for the vindication of which he can come to court. But with the vast expansion in the activities of the National Government, the power which it wields is of immense concern and may be as potent as any regulation enforced in disciplinary proceedings. No less than in those proceedings the individual ought to be entitled to protection against arbitrary or capricious action. An alien has no "right" to enter the country, but the courts have shown themselves capable of throwing a protecting arm around him. A citizen may have no "right" to a benefit from his government but, where such benefits have been authorized on conditions prescribed by statute, may he not have a right to a fair chance to secure it—at least a chance freed from arbitrary or capricious action on the part of the agency administering it?[10]

The responsibility of Congress in setting up new administrative agencies is increased by the tendency of the courts to withdraw from

[9] *Federal Trade Commission* v. *Bunte Bros.*, 312 U.S. 349 (1941).

[10] Public administrative judicial procedure with court review has been introduced into the Food, Drug, and Cosmetic Act to provide this chance in the making of certain orders (21 U.S.C. §371), into the Agricultural Adjustment Act of 1938 applying to crop allotments to individual farmers (7 U.S.C. §1365), and into the Sugar Act of 1937 applying to the allocation among individual concerns of the sugar to be marketed or imported in the year (7 U.S.C. §1115).

interference with the policy laid down in the statute, or with the policy of the agency except to keep that policy within the limits of the standard set in the statute. Control over formal procedure, when the agency is exercising the judicial function of deciding cases involving individuals, Congress has entrusted to the courts, to assure a fair hearing from which a record may be made upon which the court may act on appeal; but there may be details in regard to the treatment of evidence, the control of attorneys, the right to intervene or to appeal, which should vary widely in different agencies and which Congress may provide for expressly in the statute or by authorizing the agencies to make their own rules. Congress therefore has a wide field in which it is free to act and must assume full responsibility for a careful consideration of the situation which is to be controlled and the procedure suited for a new agency if any should be set up and for the reconsideration of the procedures of the agencies already in existence. There is great variety in the situations which must be regulated and variety in the purposes which may lead to their regulation. No general rules can be laid down, but each situation must be studied and the advantages and disadvantages of different devices of administration carefully weighed. The experience of existing agencies will of course throw light on the problems before Congress, but it must be regarded only as throwing light on those problems rather than freeing the congressional committee from the duty of the careful consideration which the importance of even the details of the problem may assume.

It is not a "task for a summer's day" to determine whether an agency should exercise the great power of the judicial function studied in this volume. In some instances it will be found better to require an action to be brought in the district courts by an agency to enforce its orders and, where policy forming plays a minor role, it may be appropriate to vest the power to judge the cases of individuals in a tribunal with a specialized jurisdiction apart from the agency, such as the Court of Customs and Patent Appeals or the Board of Tax Appeals. If the judicial function is left in the agency it will be a question each time a new act is being considered or an existing act amended whether it is better to provide for a body inside the agency, separated from the other duties of the agency, as in the Immigration and Naturalization Service, or to vest the powers of policy making, of administrative control, and of decision on the rights of individuals in a single body, as in the Federal Trade Commission.

Many reasons have been advanced to justify the growth of administrative jurisdiction, which emphasize the importance of policy making and enforcement in what an agency considers the public interest, even where it is deciding individual cases. It is claimed by the enthusiasts for the administrative method of meting out justice that it is aggressive[11] in contrast with "the legal approach" which "is necessarily static, unprogressive, *laissez faire.*"[12] Also it is said that in "administrative decisions, more significance is likely to be given to imponderables," such as the public interest, and that administrators are partisan and zealous in behalf of this public interest.[13] Indeed, it is suggested that the enforcement of the public interest or policy justifies dispensing with judicial safeguards, the public interest taking the place of the due process of the courts.[14]

The ideal of administrative justice is simply the enforcement of policy; the scrutiny of that policy in the light of a traditional law—the duty which necessitates judicial independence of government—is no part of the administrative function. . . .

Of course, a recognition that judicial justice is not a perfect model for administrative justice does not preclude use by the latter of some of the

[11] Hyneman, Administrative Adjudication: An Analysis II, 51 *Pol. Sci. Q.* 516, 530 (1936).

[12] Haines, Effects of the Growth of Administrative Law upon Traditional Anglo-American Legal Theories and Practices, 26 *Am. Pol. Sci. Rev.* 875, 882 (1932).

[13] "Partisanship or zeal on the part of administrative tribunals in behalf of the rights they are created to protect is as much expected of them as zeal on the part of judges in the defense of that body of rights we are pleased to call our liberties." Landis, *in* Symposium on Administrative Law, 9 *Am. L. School Rev.* 139, 181 (1939).

[14] Herring, *Public Administration and the Public Interest,* p. 23.

safeguards developed in connection with the former. . . . [But] the culti-
vation of professional judicial attitudes on the part of administrative tribunals should be discouraged rather than the reverse.[15]

These opinions represent an extreme position in respect to the
duties of the agencies. They make evident the place of policy in the
work of the agency and the importance of checks on policy as well
as on procedure. Partisanship and zeal in what is conceived as the
public interest are less appropriate in the judicial than in the other
functions of an agency, as, for example, prosecution or rule making.

The officials who formulate and administer the policies of an
agency are doing so under an Act of Congress, and their policies
may be reversed or modified by Congress if that body does not agree
with the view of the public interest which is held by the agency.
Congress is the policy-originating body in the American system of
government, and Congress may exercise control over the policies developed by the agencies in furtherance of the statutory standard. Its
members are directly responsible to the voters, and it is to them that
complaints will be brought against specific action of officials or
against policies. Proposals will be made to them that they amend the
law to make it easier for the agency to carry out its policies or to prevent or limit the enforcement of certain of those policies. Congress
should not act on such proposals without consideration of the effect
of their adoption on the whole scheme of regulation set up for the
agency to enforce, and such consideration must be by the appropriate
standing committee or one of its subcommittees.

A subcommittee might well be charged with observing the operation of a particular agency, not acting in any formal way to modify
its policies but to serve as an official means of keeping the committee
informed of the agency's policies and purposes. It would serve as a
body to which the members of the agency itself could turn to explain what they were doing and the reasons for their action, and to
which individuals, or more likely organized groups like trade unions

[15] Cole, Some Recent Proposals in the Sphere of Administrative Justice, 32
Am. Pol. Sci. Rev. 926, 927–928 (1938).

or business or social organizations, might come with their attacks on or defenses of the agency. Individual members of Congress might go to the subcommittee with complaints from their constituents, instead of going to the agencies themselves. Where a number of members of Congress have complaints in respect to a particular policy or practice of an agency, the accumulation of these protests in the subcommittee would give it a ground for considering possible change in the law or for bringing the matter before the agency for a reconsideration of its practice. Whenever a question arose in the committee or in Congress concerning the agency or its activities, there would be a group of members, informed by experience and by attention to the activities of the agency, who could come to its defense or propose amendments to the law if such were required.

The relations between the Treasury and Congress in the preparation of tax bills furnish an example of the cooperation between a Department and Congress. The congressional committee must call on the experts in the Department for information upon which to base estimates of revenue, both from the existing taxes and from the proposals for new taxation. The administrative and legal officials who have been dealing with the problems of taxation, who have learned those methods of administration which work most smoothly, who have become acquainted with the complicated legal questions involved in many tax statutes, must be consulted by the committee and its experts. The opinions of the policy-making officers must be given great weight by the committee when it is passing upon their proposals or developing proposals of its own. The experienced officers of the Treasury, who are administering the statute, come to the committee for amendments to prevent evasions or to make smoother its administration, as well as for minor changes in the law, which they recommend either to meet the consequences of a court decision or as a result of their practical experience.

The procedure suggested here would be less the adoption of a new principle than the putting of machinery into effect which would carry out the principle of consultation between the administrative agencies and Congress and enable Congress to act with greater confidence on proposals for changes in the law in respect to the application of its policy through an agency. There would be greater concentration of the duties of Congress as a policy-forming body, and the relations of an agency to Congress would probably result in the designation by the agency of one of its officials to keep constantly in touch with the subcommittee. The result of improving the channels of communication between the two branches of government should secure a steadier and better-rounded judgment in the law-making branch and a better appreciation in the agency itself of the criticism coming from the public through members of Congress.

The important agencies for the control of business and social activities which have been considered in this study combine in themselves, within the area which they are created to regulate, a substantial merger of the powers of government. Within the limits of the statutes which set them up they establish their policies, which they may carry out by informal administrative methods enforced by very persuasive sanctions, by legislative action through regulations, or by judicial action. The orders resulting from judicial action usually are subject to only appellate review by the courts. The problem stated by Mr. Root, of the regulation of "these agencies of regulation" and of the making plain of the rights of the citizens against them, can be dealt with by the courts only within a narrow scope. By interpretation of the statutes the courts can restrict the powers of the agencies to those which in the opinion of the judges were granted by Congress, and they can regulate procedure in the formal cases which reach them and so assure a fair hearing. They can have little influence on the policies which the agencies adopt. These are subject to control in different ways by the constitutional policy-making branches of the government—Congress and the President—and indirectly by public opinion through pressure upon the agencies themselves and upon Congress and the President. We have gone far from what Mr. Root termed "the old methods of regulation by specific statutes enforced by the courts."

Government regulation in the wide area to which it is now applied is carried out by these agencies. In each of these agencies Congress has vested powers which it might have exercised directly "by specific statutes enforced by the courts" but which it was not practical for it so to exercise. For example, Congress has given a wide control over the national means of transportation to the Interstate Commerce Commission under general directions as to policy and with some specific instructions. By vesting power in the Commission it has removed to some degree from the area of politics the difficult task of finding solutions for the conflicting interests in transportation matters of localities, of industries, of employees, and of carriers— rail and road and water. Political control over the Commission is lessened by the staggered terms of its members, which gives a certain independence to the body and assures a certain continuity in its policy. Its attention is concentrated on the important functions entrusted to it. It is aided in the task of policy fixing by its long experience as a continuing body in a special field and by its permanent staff. The judicial method used in its procedure is designed to ensure a fair hearing under the scrutiny of the courts, and the publicity of its findings, opinions, and orders gives to Congress and to the public a chance to know the trend of its policy and to modify that trend by statute or by protest.

Other agencies dealing with other activities differ in organization and in procedure from the Interstate Commerce Commission, but, whether they are independent or under the Secretary at the head of a Department, they exercise similar wide powers and form a part of the machinery which has evolved as a means of carrying on the extensive regulatory function of government. The reasonable protection of the rights of individuals must be reconciled with the public purposes for which the agency is constituted and must be sought in all the procedures of the agency, not alone in the judicial.

BIBLIOGRAPHY

Administrative Law: Stare Decisis in NLRB and SEC. New York University Law Quarterly Review, 16:618–630, 1939.

Administrative Sanctions: Power of Federal Commissions to Compel Testimony and the Production of Evidence. Harvard Law Review, 51:312–320, 1937.

American Bar Association, Special Committee on Administrative Law. Report. In Annual Report of American Bar Association, 59:539–564 (1934); 61:720–794 (1936); 62:789–850 (1937). Chicago.

Back Pay Orders under the National Labor Relations Act. Yale Law Journal, 48:1265–1273, 1939.

Black, Forrest R. Does Due Process of Law Require an Advance Notice and Hearing before a License Is Issued under the Agricultural Adjustment Act? University of Chicago Law Review, 2:270–290, 1935.

Borchard, Edwin. Declaratory Judgments. Cleveland, Banks-Baldwin Law Publishing Co., 1934.

Borchard, Edwin M. Governmental Responsibility in Tort—A Proposed Statutory Reform. American Bar Association Journal, 11:495–500, 1925.

Brown, Ray A. Administrative Commissions and the Judicial Power. Minnesota Law Review, 19:261–307, 1935.

Brown, Ray A. The Excise Tax as a Regulatory Device. Cornell Law Quarterly, 23:45–71, 1937.

Caldwell, Louis G. Comments on the Procedure of Federal Administrative Tribunals, with Particular Reference to the Federal Communications Commission. George Washington Law Review, 7:740–776, 1939.

Cavers, David F. The Food, Drug, and Cosmetic Act of 1938: Its Legislative History and Its Substantive Provisions. Law and Contemporary Problems (Duke University School of Law), 6:2–42, 1939.

Clark, Jane Perry. Deportation of Aliens from the United States to Europe. New York, Columbia University Press, 1931.

Cole, Kenneth C. Some Recent Proposals in the Sphere of Administrative Justice. American Political Science Review, 32:926–931, 1938.

Comer, John Preston. Legislative Functions of National Administrative Authorities. New York, Columbia University Press, 1927.

The Corporation as a Federal Administrative Device. University of Pennsylvania Law Review, 83:346–357, 1935.

Cushman, Robert E. Social and Economic Control through Federal Taxation. Minnesota Law Review, 18:759–783, 1934.

Dickinson, John. Administrative Justice and the Supremacy of Law in the United States. Cambridge, Harvard University Press, 1927.

Dimock, Marshall E. Modern Politics and Administration. New York, American Book Company, 1937.

Dodd, Walter F. Administration of Workmen's Compensation. New York, The Commonwealth Fund, 1936.

Due Process Restrictions on Procedure in Alien Exclusion and Deportation Cases. Columbia Law Review, 31:1013–1024, 1931.

Evatt, Herbert Vere. Rum Rebellion. Sydney, The University of Queensland Press, 1937.

The Federal Trade Commission Act of 1938. Columbia Law Review, 39:259–273, 1939.

Fletcher, Robert V. Power of the Interstate Commerce Commission to Award Damages. Yale Law Journal, 25:489–496, 1916.

Freund, Ernst. Administrative Powers over Persons and Property. Chicago, The University of Chicago Press, 1928.

Fuchs, Ralph F. Procedure in Administrative Rule-Making. Harvard Law Review, 52:259–280, 1938.

Gaguine, Benito. The Federal Alcohol Administration. George Washington Law Review, 7:844–866, 949–982, 1939.

Garrison, Lloyd K. The National Railroad Adjustment Board: A Unique Administrative Agency. Yale Law Journal, 46:567–598, 1937.

Gellhorn, Walter, and Seymour L. Linfield. Administrative Adjudication of Contract Disputes: The Walsh-Healey Act. Michigan Law Review, 37:841–873, 1939.

Gellhorn, Walter, and Seymour L. Linfield. Politics and Labor Relations: An Appraisal of Criticisms of NLRB Procedure. Columbia Law Review, 39:339–395, 1939.

Grant, J. A. C. Commerce, Production, and the Fiscal Powers of Congress. Yale Law Journal, 45:751–778, 991–1021, 1936.

Great Britain. Committee on Ministers' Powers. Report. Presented by the

Lord High Chancellor to Parliament by Command of His Majesty, April, 1932. London, H. M. Stationery Office, 1936.

Haines, Charles G. Effects of the Growth of Administrative Law upon Traditional Anglo-American Legal Theories and Practices. American Political Science Review, 26:875–894, 1932.

Hale, Robert L. Force and the State: A Comparison of "Political" and "Economic" Compulsion. Columbia Law Review, 35:149–201, 1935.

Hale, Robert L. Our Equivocal Constitutional Guaranties. Columbia Law Review, 39:563–594, 1939.

Handler, Milton. The Constitutionality of Investigations by the Federal Trade Commission. Columbia Law Review, 28:708–733, 905–937, 1928.

Handler, Milton. The Control of False Advertising under the Wheeler-Lea Act. Law and Contemporary Problems (Duke University School of Law), 6:91–110, 1939.

Handler, Milton. Unfair Competition. Iowa Law Review, 21:175–262, 1936.

Hayes, Lauffer T., and Frank J. Ruff. The Administration of the Federal Food and Drugs Act. Law and Contemporary Problems (Duke University School of Law), 1:16–35, 1933.

Henderson, Gerard C. The Federal Trade Commission. New Haven, Yale University Press, 1925.

Herring, E. Pendleton. The Federal Power Commission and the Power of Politics. Public Utilities Fortnightly, 15:223–231, 1935.

Herring, E. Pendleton. Public Administration and the Public Interest. New York, McGraw-Hill Book Co., Inc., 1936.

Holmes, Oliver Wendell. Collected Legal Papers. New York, Harcourt, Brace and Company, 1921.

Holmes, Oliver Wendell. The Path of the Law. Harvard Law Review, 10:457–478, 1897.

Hyneman, Charles S. Administrative Adjudication: An Analysis. Political Science Quarterly (Columbia University), 51:383–417, 516–537, 1936.

Judicial Control of Administrative Procedure: The Morgan Cases. Harvard Law Review, 52:509–515, 1939.

Katz, Wilber Griffith. Federal Legislative Courts. Harvard Law Review, 43:894–924, 1930.

Kittelle, Sumner S., and Elmer Mostow. A Review of the Trade Practice Conferences of the Federal Trade Commission. George Washington Law Review, 8:427–451, 1940.

Labor Law—National Labor Relations Act—Power to Order Employer to Post Notices that It Will Cease and Desist from Unfair Practices. Harvard Law Review, 52:1016, 1939.

Landis, James M. The Administrative Process. New Haven, Yale University Press, 1938.

Landis, James M. The Study of Legislation in Law Schools. Harvard Graduates' Magazine, 39:433–442, 1931.

Langeluttig, Albert. Constitutional Limitations on Administrative Power of Investigation. Illinois Law Review, 28:508–524, 1933.

Lee, Frederic P. The Enforcement Provisions of the Food, Drug, and Cosmetic Act. Law and Contemporary Problems (Duke University School of Law), 6:70–90, 1939.

Lee, Frederic P. Legislative and Interpretive Regulations. Georgetown Law Journal, 29:1–35, 1940.

Lindahl, Martin L. The Federal Trade Commission Act as Amended in 1938. Journal of Political Economy (University of Chicago Press), 47:497–525, 1939.

McClintock, Henry L. The Administrative Determination of Public Land Controversies. Minnesota Law Review, 9:638–656, 420–441, 542–554, 1925.

McGuire, O. R. Matters of Procedure under Government Contracts. Rev. ed. Baltimore, Fidelity and Deposit Press, 1935.

McGuire, O. R. The Proposed United States Administrative Court. American Bar Association Journal, 22:197–202, 1936.

McIntire, John A. Government Corporations as Administrative Agencies: An Approach. George Washington Law Review, 4:161–210, 1936.

McLaughlin, James A. Legal Control of Competitive Methods. Iowa Law Review, 21:274–304, 1936.

National Labor Relations Act: Employer Domination of or Interference with a Labor Organization. California Law Review, 26:611–622, 1938.

Oppenheimer, Reuben. Recent Developments in the Deportation Process. Michigan Law Review, 36:355–384, 1938.

Pittman, William H. The Doctrine of Precedents and the Interstate Commerce Commission.   George Washington Law Review, 5:543–579, 1937.

The Power of Administrative Agencies to Commit for Contempt.   Columbia Law Review, 35:578–591, 1935.

The Power of Dispensation in Administrative Law: A Critical Survey. University of Pennsylvania Law Review, 87:201–219, 1938.

Radio Censorship and the Federal Communications Commission.   Columbia Law Review, 39:447–459, 1939.

Reeder, Benjamin G.   Some Problems of the Bituminous Coal Industry. West Virginia Law Quarterly, 45:109–133, 1939.

Reuschlein, Harold G., and Albert B. Spector.   Taxing and Spending: The Loaded Dice of a Federal Economy.   Cornell Law Quarterly, 23:1–38, 1937.

Root, Elihu.   Public Service by the Bar.   In Reports of American Bar Association, 41:368–369, 1916.

Sharfman, I. L.   The Interstate Commerce Commission.   New York, The Commonwealth Fund, 1931–1937.   5 vols.

Sigler, Lewis A.   The Problem of Apparently Unguided Administrative Discretion.   St. Louis Law Review, 19:261–321, 1934.

Subpoenas and Due Process in Administrative Hearings.   Harvard Law Review, 53:842–851, 1940.

Symposium on Administrative Law.   The American Law School Review (West Publishing Co.), 9:139–184, 1939.

Thayer, James Bradley.   A Preliminary Treatise on Evidence at the Common Law.   Boston, Little, Brown and Co., 1896.

United States.   Administrative Procedure in Government Agencies.   Monograph of the Attorney General's Committee on Administrative Procedure.   Sen. Doc. No. 186, 76th Cong., 3d Sess. (1940) in 13 parts.   Sen. Doc. No. 10, 77th Cong., 1st Sess. (1941) in 14 parts.   Washington, Government Printing Office.

United States.   Administrative Procedure in Government Agencies.   Report of the Committee on Administrative Procedure, Appointed by the Attorney General, at the Request of the President, to Investigate the Need for Procedural Reform in Various Administrative Tribunals and to Suggest Improvements therein.   Sen. Doc. No. 8, 77th Cong., 1st Sess.   Washington, Government Printing Office, 1941.

United States. Department of Agriculture. Administrative Procedure and Practice in the Department of Agriculture under the Perishable Agricultural Commodities Act, 1930. Mimeographed, Washington, 1939.

United States. Department of Agriculture, Bureau of Animal Industry. Annual Report, 1936. Washington, Government Printing Office.

United States. Department of Labor. Annual Reports of the Secretary, 1937, 1940. Washington, Government Printing Office.

United States. Department of Labor. National Labor Relations Board. Annual Report, 1939. Washington, Government Printing Office.

United States. Department of Labor. The Secretary of Labor's Committee on Administrative Procedure. The Immigration and Naturalization Service. Mimeographed, Washington, 1940.

United States. Federal Communications Commission. Annual Report, 1940. Washington, Government Printing Office.

United States. Federal Deposit Insurance Corporation. Annual Reports, 1934-1938. Washington, Government Printing Office.

United States. Federal Trade Commission. Annual Reports, 1927, 1938, 1939, 1940. Washington, Government Printing Office.

United States. Hearings before the Committee on Agriculture, House of Representatives, on Packer Act Amendments, 68th Cong., 1st Sess. Washington, Government Printing Office, 1924.

United States. Hearings before Committee on Interstate Commerce on S. 1629, 74th Cong., 1st Sess. Washington, Government Printing Office, 1935.

United States. Hearings before the Subcommittee of the Committee on Appropriations, House of Representatives, on Independent Offices Appropriation Bill for 1940, 76th Cong., 1st Sess. Washington, Government Printing Office, 1940.

United States. Interstate Commerce Commission. Annual Reports, 1901, 1916, 1940. Washington, Government Printing Office.

United States. National Commission on Law Observance and Enforcement. Report No. 5, The Enforcement of the Deportation Laws of the United States. Washington, Government Printing Office, 1931.

United States. President's Committee on Administrative Management. Report. Washington, Government Printing Office, 1937.

Vanderbilt, Arthur T. Functions and Procedure of Administrative Tribunals. University of Cincinnati Law Review, 12:117-147, 1938.

Van Vleck, William C. The Administrative Control of Aliens. New York, The Commonwealth Fund, 1932.

Wigmore, John Henry. A Treatise on the Anglo-American System of Evidence in Trials at Common Law. 3d ed. Boston, Little, Brown and Co., 1940. Vol. 5.

Withdrawal of Registration Statements: The Jones Case. Illinois Law Review, 31:369–379, 1936.

TABLE OF CASES

TABLE OF STATUTES

INDEX